Fundamentals
of Information
Systems
Interoperability

Stefanie Rinderle-Ma • Jürgen Mangler •
Daniel Ritter

Fundamentals of Information Systems Interoperability

Data, Services, and Processes

 Springer

Stefanie Rinderle-Ma
Technische Universität München
Garching, Germany

Jürgen Mangler
Technische Universität München
Garching, Germany

Daniel Ritter
SAP SE
Walldorf, Germany

ISBN 978-3-031-48321-9   ISBN 978-3-031-48322-6   (eBook)
https://doi.org/10.1007/978-3-031-48322-6

This Springer imprint is published by the registered company Springer Nature Switzerland AG
The registered company address is: Gewerbestrasse 11, 6330 Cham, Switzerland

Paper in this product is recyclable.

Preface

The interoperability of their information systems in terms of data, services, and processes remains an ongoing challenge for companies due to the heterogeneity and complexity of their IT landscapes. Although areas such as data and (enterprise) application integration have been researched and tackled for many years, developments such as streaming and event-based data require an ongoing understanding and new approaches. Moreover, interoperability challenges regarding data, services, and processes cannot be treated in isolation but must be tackled in interplay, in order to avoid, for example, undesired side effects.

This book presents fundamental concepts and technologies to tackle interoperability between information systems. It brings together interoperability at different levels, i.e., the data, service, and process level, and combines the theoretical foundations with hands-on presentation of technologies in order to enable the development of sound and practical interoperability solutions.

Chapter 1 sets out the scope of this book based on discussing interoperability foundations from three perspectives, i.e., from the perspectives of (i) interoperability levels and tasks, (ii) integration scenarios and methods, and (iii) interoperability concerns. Regarding perspective (i), interoperability levels comprise syntactical, semantic, and organizational interoperability and combine these levels with the three interoperability tasks of exchange, integration, and orchestration. Regarding perspective (ii), integration scenarios comprise user-interface-oriented, message-oriented, and query-based scenarios, and the integration methods comprise the application domains, the realization, and the specification method. Finally, regarding perspective (iii), the interoperability concerns in information systems comprise their data, services, and processes. The three perspectives, (i)–(iii) are means to explain which aspects are covered by this book and what is outside its scope, i.e., mainly technical interoperability at the protocol level as well as the business aspect of interoperability. With the covered perspectives, the book aims at a comprehensive treatment of foundations and technologies in the context of information systems interoperability.

Besides the scope of the book, Chap. 1 provides interoperability challenges and describes the structure of the book. The structure develops along the interoperability concerns, levels, and tasks, i.e., starts with data exchange and integration of data between information systems, over the exchange between services, to the orchestration, integration, and choreography of processes.

Along this line, Chap. 2 presents technologies for the exchange of data between two selected and highly relevant data formats, i.e., relational databases and XML. Note that a thorough introduction to XML and related technologies is provided throughout the book such that the book can also be used as an introduction to Web technologies. Different concepts and the SQL/XML standard build a basis for tackling the publication of relational data as XML documents and the storage and querying of XML data in relational databases. The presentation of XML technologies is rounded off by a discussion of more specialized exchange formats, i.e., JSON, YAML, BSON, and MSGPACK. In this context, further considerations such as readability by users and performance issues are discussed.

The publication of relational data in exchange formats such as XML lays the foundation for the exchange and integration of this data via XML technology as presented in Chap. 3. The main challenge is that the information systems that aim at interoperating might use different schemas and data models, resulting in conflicts between the data to be exchanged. Chapter 3 presents concepts for resolving such conflicts via schema matching and mapping and data integration. Moreover, it provides the technological basis for implementing these concepts based on querying and transformation languages, i.e., XPath and XSLT.

After laying the conceptual and technological foundation for extracting, exchanging, and integrating data between information systems, the next level is service interoperability as tackled in Chap. 4. First of all, the main goals of service orientation are explained, including loose coupling, scalability, reusability, flexibility, and efficient monitoring. The chapter explains two technologies for service interoperability in details, i.e., REST and GraphQL. The explanations of both technologies are illustrated by a variety of examples such that, again, this chapter can be also used for entering the world of service orientation in general. At the end, Chap. 4 features a case study from the higher-education domain that illustrates the concepts and technologies presented in Chaps. 2–4 in a combined fashion. The interoperability challenges and requirements are defined, and the system architecture is outlined. Finally, it is shown how the service orientation goals as mentioned above, e.g., loose coupling, can be achieved by the system design.

After presenting concepts and technologies for data and service interoperability in Chaps. 2–4, the book turns toward the concept of processes and, by doing so, to the organizational interoperability level and orchestration task.

In Chap. 5, fundamentals for designing process orchestrations at the conceptual level are presented, focusing on how to model process orchestrations and how to verify their correctness/soundness. The verification is essential as process orchestrations build interoperability approaches, i.e., process orchestration models, and realizes the integration and interoperation of various services, application programs, machines, and human work. If this integration is not defined in a correct/sound way, i.e., the process orchestrations contain errors, then the interoperability project can run into undesired effects and problems. For modeling process orchestrations,

Chap. 5 illustrates Business Process Modeling and Notation (BPMN) as de facto standard. For the verification of the process orchestrations, Chap. 5 shows how to transform BPMN models into Petri Nets and how they can then be formally checked for properties such as being deadlock-free.

Chapter 6 picks up the conceptual design concepts presented in Chap. 5 by presenting the concepts and languages for the implementation design of process orchestrations. This includes the presentation of execution languages for process orchestrations that are equipped with a formal semantics, for example, Workflow Nets, the Refined Process Structure Tree, and CPEE Trees. Moreover, concepts for task design and implementation including endpoint definition and worklist design are presented, which realize the integration of services and application programs as well as human work into the process orchestration and, in the sequel, the integration with other services, application programs, and human participants. In this context, data flow concepts play an important role as they handle the transfer of data from one task (and the invoked service or human participant) to other tasks, realizing data exchange between these tasks. As such, process orchestration provides a powerful interoperability approach: several services, application program, and human work can be integrated and interoperate along a well-defined process logic. The realization of service invocation, from a technological point of view, is based on correlation, i.e., the rule-based exchange of messages between the services, application programs, and worklists invoked by the process orchestration. Both the concepts of Chaps. 5 and 6 are illustrated by means of a case study from manufacturing.

While Chaps. 5 and 6 focus on the orchestration of applications, services, and processes through interoperable or tightly integrated systems, Chap. 7 aims at dealing with the growing number of distributed, loosely coupled, and often non-interoperable applications through the concepts of enterprise application integration. This specifically enables the orchestration across non-interoperable components. To achieve this goal, Chap. 7 provides the formal foundation based on integration patterns and processes. The formalization is grounded in Colored Petri Nets (CPN) and illustrated by means of BPMN. On top of the conceptualization, the realization of enterprise application integration patterns is explained based on selected patterns, e.g., the content-based router. The patterns can then be composed into pattern flows using timed DB-nets with boundaries. Chapter 7 concludes with an implementation of the presented concepts in CPN Tools and case studies from customer relationship management and predictive maintenance.

Chapter 8 lifts the process orchestration and integration concepts and technologies presented in Chaps. 5–7 to the choreography level, i.e., dealing with the interoperability between different process orchestrations. Such scenarios can occur within organizations, e.g., between different departments or between different organizations (inter-organizational choreographies). A process choreography consists of two or more process orchestrations that interoperate via message exchanges. Each partner can have a public process orchestration that reflects the interactions with the other partners and a private one that might contain business secrets and process details to be hidden from the other partners. Overall, process choreographies comprise a model stack from the choreography model reflecting the contract between the partners over the public process orchestrations, down to the private ones. Chapter 8 presents two possibilities to set up this model stack, i.e., in a (i) top-down and (ii) bottom-up way. For (i), Chap. 8 presents choreography and collaboration models in BPMN. Moreover, as correctness/soundness of the models along the entire model stack is vital, several correctness/soundness criteria for choreographies are explained, and their verification is shown based on Workflow Nets as formal language. For the bottom-up development of process choreographies, Chap. 8 sketches methods for process matching and process mining. The latter is connected with the execution concepts for process choreographies, i.e., correlation, logging, and monitoring, as particularly logging provides the basis for mining (private) process orchestration behavior from the partners that can build input for setting up choreographies in a bottom-up manner. The concepts and languages presented in Chap. 8 are illustrated based on a supply chain case study.

Chapter 9 concludes the book. First of all, open interoperability aspects and perspectives are discussed, including ontologies and standards. Moreover, Chap. 9 discusses different interoperability approaches, i.e., structured ways of running interoperability projects. Prominently, the orchestration-based interoperability approach is followed throughout the book. Finally, the conclusion features success factors for interoperability projects and provides a range of open and future research directions for interoperability such as compliability, sensor fusion, and blockchain technologies.

The book at hand is timely and necessary for the following reasons: Particularly, the process perspective—although reflecting the business logic of companies—has not been considered in related areas yet. Moreover, depending on the company size, interoperability demands for tailored solutions. Hence, this books aims at providing a comprehensive overview on interoperability challenges in the light of recent developments with concrete solutions to different practical cases.

The book is accompanied by a website containing supplementary material:
https://is-interop.info

Garching, Germany   Stefanie Rinderle-Ma
Garching, Germany   Jürgen Mangler
Walldorf, Germany   Daniel Ritter

Acknowledgments

We would like to thank our colleagues, Matthias Ehrendorfer and Janik-Vasily Benzin, for their input and critical views, Ralf Gerstner for his patience, and our families for their continuous support.

Contents

About the Authors

Jürgen Mangler holds a PhD in Business Informatics from the University of Vienna and is working as senior postdoc at the Technical University of Munich, Germany. He is chief developer of the open-source process execution engine CPEE (cpee.org). Jürgen has gained deep insights into interoperability concepts and their realizations during several research projects such as the EU FP7 project ADVENTURE and the Austrian Center of Digital Production (acdp.at). The latter raises challenges in vertical and horizontal integration of data, machines, systems, and humans. Jürgen has taught various software engineering related topics since 2004.

Stefanie Rinderle-Ma is a full professor at the Technical University of Munich, Germany, and head of the Chair of Information Systems and Business Process Management. Stefanie's research focuses on distributed and flexible process technology, Enterprise Application Integration, and business intelligence. Stefanie has more than 300 publications with 11,000 citations and an h-index of 51 (according to scholar.google.com, accessed 04-09-2023). Moreover, Stefanie has led several industry projects with strong interoperability challenges, e.g., in the manufacturing and healthcare domain. Stefanie co-authored the Springer book Fundamentals of Business Intelligence (with W. Grossmann), which was published in 2015 and has currently 59K downloads (according to https://link.springer.com/book/10.1007/978-3-662-46531-8). Stefanie has developed and taught the master's course on interoperability and its contents at different universities since 2010.

Daniel Ritter is a database architect at SAP SE for SAP HANA Cloud and OrientDB and a postdoctoral researcher in the SAP HANA Research Campus. In 2021 and 2022, he was a postdoctoral research fellow, leading the Autonomous Database Group at the Chair of Prof. Hasso Plattner at the University of Potsdam. He completed his PhD in Computer Science at the University of Vienna in 2019, where he was advised by Prof. Stefanie Rinderle-Ma. He has 20+ years of experience in software development, engineering, and architecture, application integration, data wrangling, and analysis.

Chapter 1
Introduction

1.1 Motivation and Outline

The idea for this book solidified in 2019, after designing and reading the master's course "Interoperability" at the Faculty of Computer Science, University of Vienna, Austria, for the 10th time in a row since 2010. The course has offered a mix of fundamental concepts of interoperability conveyed in a theoretical and hands-on manner in the exercises, complemented by the industry view. Still, the course exists, and its concepts continue to be taught at several universities nowadays. Interoperability has also always been at the core of our research work. Examples comprise the fundamentals on enterprise application integration, e.g., [188–190, 192]; our work on process automation and orchestration, e.g., [136, 138, 178, 179]; as well as the Internet of Processes and Things (IOPT)[1] initiative, where an international network of researchers investigates interoperability between (business) processes and IoT data by, for example, suggesting stream extensions for process event logs [137]. Last but not least, we have encountered a multitude of challenges and questions in our industry projects where the horizontal and vertical integration of data, systems, and machines is paramount, e.g., [161, 208], in order to avoid data lakes and silos. Another example is healthcare where the power of analytical insights can only unfold on integrated, high-quality data, e.g., [37].

What Does Interoperability Mean? The United Nations in their Trade Facilitation Implementation Guide [215] define interoperability as *"the ability of two or more systems or components to exchange information and to use the information that has been exchanged,"* *"the technical capability of different programs to exchange data via a common set of exchange formats, to read and write the same*

---

[1] https://zenodo.org/communities/iopt/?page=1&size=20.

© Springer Nature Switzerland AG 2024
S. Rinderle-Ma et al., *Fundamentals of Information Systems Interoperability*,
https://doi.org/10.1007/978-3-031-48322-6_1

file formats, and to use the same protocols," and "the capability to run processes seamlessly across organisational boundaries without losing context or meaning."

Gartner has a focused view on interoperability as "ability for a device from one manufacturer to work with one from another" [89, interoperability]. Techtarget sees interoperability as "the ability of different systems, devices, applications or products to connect and communicate in a coordinated way, without effort from the end user," which "helps organizations achieve higher efficiency and a more holistic view of information" [130]. Forrester regards interoperability as key to success for social media [166], healthcare [201], and artificial intelligence operations [46].

Interoperability also constitutes the main pillar for *hyperautomation* as current mega trend. "Hyperautomation involves the orchestrated use of multiple technologies, tools or platforms, including: artificial intelligence (AI), machine learning, event-driven software architecture, robotic process automation (RPA), business process management (BPM) and intelligent business process management suites (iBPMS), integration platform as a service (iPaaS), low-code/no-code tools, packaged software, and other types of decision, process and task automation tools" according to the Gartner glossary, entry hyperautomation [89, hyperautomation]. "Interoperability reduces or eliminates the problems of islands of automation. It enables business processes to flow from one application to another. Interoperability enables one system to work with another, in near real-time fashion, to share critical business information. Interoperability options become the glue between systems and applications" [211].

These definitions and goals of interoperability show that interoperability is not confined to data exchange but has to cover the triangle of data, services, and processes. To the best of our knowledge, there is no book addressing interoperability in a way that connects all three aspects of data, services, and processes. However, according to our experience, only the integrated treatment of these three aspects contributes to the full understanding and mastering the challenges of interoperability.

In the following, we present three interoperability perspectives that define interoperability and its scope in the context of this book.

At first, this book is not targeting *technical interoperability* in the sense of communication protocols but the other three interoperability levels as defined in [217], i.e., *syntactical, semantic,* and *organizational* interoperability. Syntactical interoperability is concerned with the format and semantic interoperability with the meaning of the data be exchanged, transformed, and integrated. Both form the precondition for organizational interoperability, where data is exchanged across the border of (information) systems and organizations.

From the definitions provided above, key interoperability tasks can be derived, i.e., *exchange, integrate,* and *orchestrate.* Exchange of data and information is crucial to establish interoperability between different services, organizations, and business partners. Integration of data and information is another key task in order to create exchange structures between different partners. Orchestrate refers to the (cross-) organizational definition and execution of integration scenarios and processes.

For understanding the challenges of interoperability in the context of this book and subsequently its contributions and structure, in the following, we investigate three perspectives on interoperability.

1.1.1   Interoperability Perspectives I: Levels and Tasks

The first perspective on interoperability is based on the cross-product between the three levels of interoperability, i.e., syntactical, semantic, and organizational, as described in [217], in combination with its three main tasks, i.e., exchange, integrate, and orchestrate (cf. Table 1.1).

For addressing syntactical interoperability in **exchange** scenarios, an understanding of exchange formats is indispensable. Prevalent exchange formats are XML and relational databases, complemented with more specialized formats such as JSON, BSON, YAML, and MessagePack. Moreover, in order to extract specific information from one source or partner to be exchanged, query languages are required, depending on the underlying exchange format. For XML, query languages comprise XPath and XQuery. For relational databases, SQL is the query language of choice. Finally, transformation languages such as XSLT are required in order to transform the data of one source into data of another source. For realizing semantic interoperability in an exchange scenario, concepts for mapping the information of

Table 1.1 Interoperability perspectives I: levels and tasks

Levels ⤳/tasks ⟲	Syntactical	Semantic	Organizational
Exchange	Exchange formats, e.g., XML, relational databases, JSON, BSON, YAML, MessagePack; query languages: XPath, XQuery, SQL; transformation languages, e.g., XSLT	Schema matching and mapping; ontologies	Message exchange; correlation
Integrate	SQL/XML standard; native XML databases; REST and GraphQL	Edge table, shredding; XML schema and RNG; schema and data integration; service integration	Correlation and choreography
Orchestrate	BPMN, Petri Nets, Workflow Nets, RPST, CPEE Trees, Colored Petri Nets	Verification; task and worklist design; service invocation; correlation; integration patterns and processes	Choreography

one source onto the information of another source are required. This includes a matching concept in order to prepare the mapping. Ontologies and domain models can support the understanding of the meaning of concepts in the one or the other data source. Finally, from an organizational perspective, the exchange of information is realized via message exchanges. The message exchanges, in turn, are realized based on correlation mechanisms, i.e., based on rules in order to "understand" message content and to assign message to the right partner and partner process.

Integration scenarios at the syntactic level require the integration of data in different formats such as XML or relational databases. Here, the SQL/XML standard has been proposed and implemented in commercial database systems. Moreover, native XML databases bridge the gap between the XML and relational world. Moreover, when going from data to service integration, technologies such as Representational State Transfer (REST) play an important role. From a semantic point of view, generic as well as user-defined schema and data integration approaches have been proposed. From an organizational perspective, integration scenarios demand for correlation concepts in order to enable message exchange between services and processes. The integration of processes also demands for concepts in process matching and choreography.

Orchestration scenarios, from a syntactical perspective, require orchestration languages at different levels and with different goals, including Business Process Modeling and Notation (BPMN) and Petri Nets. Note that orchestration might refer to the orchestration of tasks within one organizational context or span across several parties/partners within one or several organizations. Examples include a network of production processes for one manufacturer and the supply chain process where the manufacturer interoperates with suppliers. Moreover, different notations and languages are needed for the conceptual design and the execution design of process orchestrations. At the semantic level, concepts for the verification of process orchestration models and the design of process tasks, especially with respect to the inclusion of human users and the invocation of services, are required. In addition, at the semantic as well as the organizational level, concepts for correlation and choreography of are required.

1.1.2   Interoperability Perspectives II: Integration Scenarios and Methods

The technologies and concepts summarized in Table 1.1 are mostly *query-based* using, e.g., XML, SQL, or *message-oriented*. The term *message-oriented* or *messaging* denotes a data exchange via messages and is thus different from other common integration styles such as *remote procedure call*, *shared database*, and *file transfer* (e.g., see classification by Hohpe and Woolf [107]). What has not been mentioned yet are interoperability approaches that are based on integration of user interfaces.

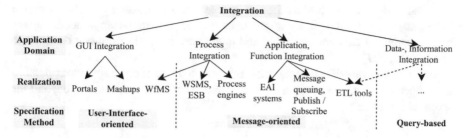

Fig. 1.1 Interoperability perspectives II: integration scenarios and methods

Similar to [40], Fig. 1.1 takes a classification perspective, distinguishing the three interoperability approaches along their application domain and realization. Regarding the *application domain* in the context of the *specification method*, we differentiate the user-interface-oriented *GUI integration*, from message-oriented or application-tier *process integration* (e.g., [72, 119]) and *application integration* (cf. EAI), and the more database-tier, query-based *data integration* (e.g., [69, 127]) and *information integration* (e.g., [15]). The *realization* provides a concrete system aspect that represents the different integration approaches (incl. EAI).

GUI integration denotes the integrated visualization of or access to heterogeneous and distributed data sources (e.g., in the form of *portals* [66, 84]). In contrast, *mashups* (e.g., [17]) are dynamically composed Web content for small applications that focus more on content integration. Both approaches use a virtual, hierarchical network topology.

The categories *application integration* and *process integration* refer to a loosely coupled integration type, where messaging is used to decouple sender and receiver endpoints. While both approaches physically propagate and store—and thus materialize—data, application integration refers to the integration of heterogeneous, non-compliant system or applications, and process integration refers to a more business process-oriented integration of homogeneous services (e.g., Web services [14]). In other words, application integration is more data-centric in terms of the efficient message routing and transformation, and process integration is more focused on procedural aspects in the sense of controlling the overall business process. In this context, there exist manifold realizations like ETL tools, *Message-oriented Middleware* (e.g., message queuing, *Publish-Subscribe*) [26, 38, 56, 74], and EAI systems for application integration and *Business Process Execution Language* engines (BPEL [53]), *Web Service Management Systems* (WSMS [207]), and *Workflow Management Systems* (WfMS [90, 216]), for process integration. Despite working on materialized data, the latter has a strong focus on user-centric tasks and interaction and is thus categorized as user-interface-oriented. Note that there were attempts to converge these system categories in the past [99, 210], in the form of overlapping functionalities [210]. For example, process integration standards such as BPEL are also partly used to specify application integration tasks (e.g., experimental evaluation by Scheibler et al. [200]). However, that never gained practical relevance, due to the different concepts and processing models. *Data and Information Integration* refers to database-centric integration approaches, where huge amounts of data are replicated and integrated, typically from one database to another [15, 127].

In this book, we will elaborate message-oriented and query-based interoperability concepts, i.e., approaches on user-interface-oriented approaches are beyond the scope of this book.

1.1.3   *Interoperability Perspectives III: Interoperability Concerns*

Table 1.1 summarizes levels and tasks of interoperability (interoperability perspectives I), and Fig. 1.1 depicts a classification of scenarios and methods (interoperability perspectives II). Figure 1.2 displays interoperability concerns data, services, and processes as stated in [226] where we deliberately exclude the fourth interoperability concern business as we take an information systems view in this book.

Firstly, interoperability is to be established between information systems with respect to the data stored, managed, and processes by them, e.g., database systems. Secondly, interoperability is to be established between services invoked and employed by or accessing information systems. Finally, interoperability is to be established in and between processes. For all three artefacts, i.e., data, services, and processes, two questions arise: what is to be exchanged and how is it exchanged. The "what" mainly refers to the exchange formats with respect to data and messages with respect to services and processes. The "how" includes technologies such as REST and GraphQL. At the organizational, i.e., process, level, the processes itself as well

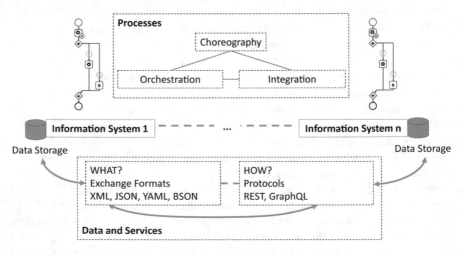

Fig. 1.2 Interoperability perspectives III: interoperability concerns

as their choreographies establish the orchestration of different tasks, their data, and invoked services.

For the organizational or process level, Fig. 1.2 elaborates the three tasks that have been included as orchestration so far, i.e., orchestration referring to integration of tasks along a well-defined process logic, integration referring to enterprise application integration, and choreography referring to the message-oriented networks of process orchestrations.

Interoperability perspectives I–III (Table 1.1 and Figs. 1.1 and 1.2) show the broad understanding of interoperability and its vast coverage of technologies, applications, and methods. In the following section, we will derive several interoperability challenges that will be addressed in the course of this book.

1.2   Interoperability Challenges

While interoperability might be regarded as being around for a long time, which is actually true, it is still relevant till this date. Several interoperability challenges are still unsolved, practical interoperability projects are still (partly) failing, and with the advent of new technologies and hypes such as artificial intelligence, machine learning, and automation, existing and new interoperability challenges arise, e.g., communicating with a multitude of systems and heterogeneous data sources for improved accuracy of AI/ML results [114]. As for business intelligence projects, often, only the shiny side of the medal is presented, i.e., the analysis part, but the thorny way bringing together several partners, data sources, services, and applications to interoperate often remains invisible. In the following, we present interoperability challenges from different domains.

A major share of interoperability literature and studies has been conducted in **healthcare**, elaborating on a variety of challenges. One of the scenarios is to introduce the electronic health record (EHR) in order to share patient-related information among healthcare providers. If a patient is transferred to a specialist or a clinic by the family doctor, all required information should be available electronically. This sharing of patient information poses many challenges, in particular with respect to security and privacy, and requires interoperability between the related information systems. According to a study conducted by Forrester [141], the majority of the consulted 145 senior-level interoperability leaders in healthcare see valuable *"opportunities that improved interoperability unearths"* but suffer from a lack of a comprehensive interoperability strategy, internal expertise, and sufficient resources. In an article from 2017 [173], interoperability for EHR is predicted to take until 2024 to be achieved with the ultimate goal *"to break down health data silos and allow patient health information to be available across all settings of care."*

In **cloud computing**, avoiding vendor lock-in and overcoming lack of integration are of utmost importance [163]. A selection of challenges, hence, comprises enabling the migration between cloud vendors (programming perspective), data exchange and workflow management (application perspective), service and system monitoring (monitoring perspective), service discovery and service behavior prediction (deployment perspective), auditing, authentication, and authorization (security perspective), as well as cost-effective mapping of services to resources (market perspective). Petcu [163] also mentions the obstacles in *standardization* efforts. Standardization, in general, constitutes an instrument for facilitating interoperability. For interoperability between **Web services**, challenges arise due to heterogeneity at different message levels, i.e., domain, entity definition, and abstraction, causing conflicts in naming, data and schema representation, generalization, and aggregation [158].

The Internet of Things (IoT) *"is a network of interrelated devices that connect and exchange data with other IoT devices and the cloud"* [91] and hence, at its core, demands for interoperability. One example for an IoT scenario is a smart weather station for which different sensors measure, for example, the temperature and precipitation to predict weather forecasts [168]. Another example is smart manufacturing where sensors are used to measure parameters on the product quality, which are then aggregated in a process-oriented manner [71]. For IoT applications, different interoperability levels are to be addressed, including the devices (e.g., sensors), the network, syntactic and semantic interoperability (cf. Table 1.1), as well as cross-platform and cross-domain interoperability [160]. For smart cities, [13] states the following interoperability challenges (selection), i.e., lack of definitions, common terminology, and standards, privacy and security issues, scalability, data and service quality, and shared services.

The domains and challenges summarized above only reflect a part of the domains and applications where interoperability plays an important role. Other domains include, for example, financial services [22]. Also, additional challenges as mentioned above might arise. In the subsequent section, we will introduce the applications and case studies used in this book that help to illustrate interoperability challenges and solutions.

1.3   Introduction to Case Studies

In the previous section, interoperability challenges along different domains such as healthcare, cloud computing, and IoT are outlined. In this book, we will use the following case studies and applications in order to illustrate interoperability challenges and solutions.

1.3.1   Higher Education

In higher education, typically, a variety of data is stored, processed, and exchanged in and through information systems, e.g., on courses, students, and instructors.

Moreover, learning is often supported by blended learning platforms such as Moodle[2] or CEWebS [65]. A learning platform facilitates interoperability in the communication and collaboration between students and teachers. CEWebS is a learning platform that is based on Web services technology, realizing learning services such as a forum service, a registration service for the students, and a submission service for uploading exercises [133]. The different services exchange information and hence also have interoperability requirements. In order to make the teaching offer of a higher education institution available to interested persons such as (prospective) students, the course information is in most cases presented through the Web. For this, a search system is used. Moreover, information might have to be exchanged between different parties, in particular, in the context of e-learning. e-Learning has experienced a tremendous push during the COVID pandemic as, for example, 1.2 billion children were affected by school closures worldwide according to [131]. However, as stated in [23], *"[t]he interoperability of e-learning systems and the absence of coherent content and data standards has been a problem for many years."* Aside from free learning offers, there is significant market for learning and e-learning offers, for example, valued at USD 214.26 billion in 2021 [165].

1.3.2 Manufacturing and Supply Chains

As already shortly elaborated in Sect. 1.2, the manufacturing domain faces several interoperability challenges. One challenge is the need for integration, more precisely for vertical and horizontal integration. Vertical integration has been traditionally realized across the different levels of the automation pyramid that ranges from the field level to the management level. Only the functions between two "neighboring" layers can communicate with each other. As proposed by Bettenhausen and Kowalewski, [36], the next step is the CPS-based automation architecture (CPS: cyber-physical system). This architecture dissolves the layers of the automation pyramid and connects the functions through a network. In [161], finally, the network idea is carried forward toward the process-oriented integration of the functions. By using a process-oriented integration approach, the horizontal and vertical integration goals of manufacturing applications are satisfied, i.e., systems are integrated across the layers of the pyramid layers (vertical), and several systems, services, machines, and human workers are integrated (horizontal). Horizontal integration can also mean the intra- and interorganizational cooperation of different partners and their processes such as supply chains, mostly realized via message exchange. Similar requirements for integration of processes hold in the context of **predictive maintenance and services** in smart manufacturing and IoT applications.

---

[2] moodle.org.

1.3.3   Hybrid Integration by Example of Customer Relationship Management

For traditional application systems and packaged applications, e.g., Enterprise Resource Planning and Customer Relationship Management (CRM), integration shall allow for cases like a secure and flexible extension and adaptation to changing requirements such as legal regulations, e.g., for business trends like postmodern ERP [88]. Consequently, many organizations have started to connect their on-premise applications such as CRM systems with cloud applications to extend and adapt their business processes using integration capabilities [188, 190].

This is complemented by the trend of building cloud applications or moving existing applications to cloud environments, leading to a growing need for communication with on-premise applications [190]. For instance, SAP ERP/CRM on Demand and SAP S/4 HANA applications require status changes of on-premise applications as well as data replication, while existing on-premise applications tend to delegate integration with governmental organizations and institutions for legal aspects, to cloud environments. In addition to standardized data exchange formats like XML, the schema-flexible JSON format gains importance for those scenarios that reach peak throughput of up to several hundreds of thousands of messages per second, depending on the integration style, and the patterns used in these scenarios mostly require transformation and routing capabilities [190].

The case studies cover a range of domains and illustrate different interoperability requirements. The goal of this book is not to present interoperability solutions at an abstract level but to showcase how concepts and technologies actually work.

1.4   Outline

In Sects. 1.1.1–1.1.3, we have introduced three perspectives on interoperability, i.e., regarding levels and tasks, regarding integration scenarios and methods, and regarding interoperability concerns. The perspectives build on top of each other, culminating in interoperability perspective III on data, services, and processes reflecting the overall scope of this book. For relating the content of the different chapters to the interoperability perspectives, we will use the interoperability perspectives I as provided in Table 1.1 and give pointer to interoperability concepts as depicted in Fig. 1.2.

The book is structured into 9 chapters including the introduction, i.e., the chapter at hand, and conclusion and outlook in Chap. 9. This leaves seven content chapters, i.e., Chaps. 2–8, which will be shortly introduced and put into the overall context of the book in the following.

Chapter 2 (**From Databases to Exchange Formats**) starts off by tackling the question "how to prepare data from the databases of the information system for exchange?", i.e., transforming relational data into exchange formats such as XML,

Levels ↗ / Tasks ↙	Syntactical	Semantic	Organizational
Exchange	Exchange formats, e.g., XML, relational databases, JSON, BSON, YAML, MessagePack; query languages: XPath, XQuery, SQL; transformation languages, e.g., XSLT	Schema matching and mapping; ontologies;	Message exchange; correlation
Integrate	SQL/XML standard; native XML databases; REST and GraphQL	Edge table, shredding; XML schema and RNG; schema and data integration; service integration	Correlation and choreography
Orchestrate	BPMN, Petri Nets, Workflow Nets, RPST, CPEE Trees, Colored Petri Nets	Verification, task and worklist design; service invocation; correlation; integration patterns and processes	Choreography

Fig. 1.3 Interoperability perspectives I: Chap. 2

JSON, YAML, or BSON and vice versa. This primary goal of Chap. 2 can be classified into the interoperability perspectives I as shown in Fig. 1.3, as mainly tackling the syntactical interoperability level and interoperability tasks exchange and integrate. For task integrate, also solutions for semantic interoperability will be explained, i.e., the edge table and shredding. For interoperability perspectives III, Chap. 2 provides formats and concepts for exchanging data between different information systems (cf. Fig. 1.2). The technologies and concepts presented in Chap. 2 are illustrated based on the higher-education case study as presented in Sect. 1.3.1. Note that the higher-education case study will illustrate the concepts and technologies for Chaps. 2–4 in a combined way in Sect. 4.4.

Chapter 3 (**Transformation of Exchange Formats**) then shows "how to transform data in different exchange formats in order to enable interoperability". From a technology point of view, Chap. 3 introduces XML schema and RelaxNG (RNG) as XML schema definition languages and XPath and XQuery as XML query languages. Moreover, XSLT is introduced in detail as XML transformation languages (cf. Fig. 1.2). From a conceptual point of view, Chap. 3 explains the different steps of schema mapping, including schema matching methods. Regarding the interoperability perspectives I, Chap. 3 presents several technologies at the syntactical interoperability level, addressing interoperability tasks exchange and integrate (cf. Fig. 1.4). Regarding interoperability perspectives III, Chap. 3 focuses on the transformation and integration between data (formats) of different information systems. In this sense, Chaps. 2 and 3 are strongly related, while Chap. 2 focuses more on the exchange of two concrete formats, i.e., relational and XML data. Chapter 3 is rounded off by illustration of the presented technologies and concepts based on the higher-education case study as presented in Sect. 1.3.1. Note

Levels ... / Tasks ↓	Syntactical	Semantic	Organizational
Exchange	Exchange formats, e.g., XML, relational databases, JSON, BSON, YAML, MessagePack; query languages: XPath, XQuery, SQL; transformation languages, e.g., XSLT	Schema matching and mapping; ontologies;	Message exchange; correlation
Integrate	SQL/XML standard; native XML databases; REST and GraphQL	Edge table, shredding; XML schema and RNG; schema and data integration; service integration	Correlation and choreography
Orchestrate	BPMN, Petri Nets, Workflow Nets, RPST, CPEE Trees, Colored Petri Nets	Verification, task and worklist design; service invocation; correlation; integration patterns and processes	Choreography

Fig. 1.4 Interoperability perspectives I: Chap. 3

that the higher-education case study will illustrate the concepts and technologies for Chaps. 2–4 in a combined way in Sect. 4.4.

Chapter 4 (**Service Interoperability**) moves from the question "what to exchange" to the question "how to exchange and integrate" (cf. Fig. 1.2). This starts with services and technologies such as REST and GraphQL and follows up with concepts for service integration and transformation. Regarding interoperability perspectives I, Chap. 4 focuses on the syntactic interoperability level by introducing REST and GraphQL (cf. Fig. 1.5). From a conceptual point of view, techniques for the integration and transformation of services are provided. The higher-education case study motivated in Sect. 1.3.1 will illustrate the concepts and technologies for Chaps. 2–4 in a combined way in Sect. 4.4.

Chapter 5 (**Process Orchestration: Conceptual Design**) tackles the question "how to orchestrate services, systems, and human work in a process-oriented way", i.e., following a well-defined process logic. As depicted in Fig. 1.2, Chap. 5 starts off the triangle of process-based interoperability consisting of process orchestration (cf. Chaps. 5 and 6), integration (cf. Chap. 7), and choreography (cf. Chap. 8). Regarding the interoperability levels, Chap. 5 provides process notations at the syntactical level, i.e., BPMN and Petri Nets (cf. Fig. 1.6), and verification techniques for the process orchestrations at the semantic level. As mentioned before, the main interoperability task is orchestration. Chapter 5 is rounded off by an illustration of process orchestration design and verification based on the manufacturing case study described in Sect. 1.3.2.

Chapter 6 (**Process Orchestration: Execution Design**) addresses the question on "how to orchestrate and execute services, systems, and human work in a process-oriented way", i.e., is complementary to Chap. 5 where the conceptual design is

Levels .../ Tasks ↓	Syntactical	Semantic	Organizational
Exchange	Exchange formats, e.g., XML, relational databases, JSON, BSON, YAML, MessagePack; query languages: XPath, XQuery, SQL; transformation languages, e.g., XSLT	Schema matching and mapping; ontologies;	Message exchange; correlation
Integrate	SQL/XML standard; native XML databases; REST and GraphQL	Edge table, shredding; XML schema and RNG; schema and data integration; service integration	Correlation and choreography
Orchestrate	BPMN, Petri Nets, Workflow Nets, RPST, CPEE Trees, Colored Petri Nets	Verification, task and worklist design; service invocation; correlation; integration patterns and processes	Choreography

Fig. 1.5 Interoperability perspectives I: Chap. 4

Levels .../ Tasks ↓	Syntactical	Semantic	Organizational
Exchange	Exchange formats, e.g., XML, relational databases, JSON, BSON, YAML, MessagePack; query languages: XPath, XQuery, SQL; transformation languages, e.g., XSLT	Schema matching and mapping; ontologies;	Message exchange; correlation
Integrate	SQL/XML standard; native XML databases; REST and GraphQL	Edge table, shredding; XML schema and RNG; schema and data integration; service integration	Correlation and choreography
Orchestrate	BPMN, Petri Nets, Workflow Nets, RPST, CPEE Trees, Colored Petri Nets	Verification, task and worklist design; service invocation; correlation; integration patterns and processes	Choreography

Fig. 1.6 Interoperability perspectives I: Chap. 5

presented (cf. Fig. 1.2). Chapter 6 takes the conceptual design and equips it with formal execution semantics based on notations such as Workflow Nets, Refined Process Structure Tree (RPST), and CPEE Trees. This part on notations can be classified at the syntactical interoperability level in Fig. 1.7, addressing interoperability task orchestrate. The syntactical part is complemented with concepts on

Levels ... / Tasks ↘	Syntactical	Semantic	Organizational
Exchange	Exchange formats, e.g., XML, relational databases, JSON, BSON, YAML, MessagePack; query languages: XPath, XQuery, SQL; transformation languages, e.g., XSLT	Schema matching and mapping; ontologies;	Message exchange; correlation
Integrate	SQL/XML standard; native XML databases; REST and GraphQL	Edge table, shredding; XML schema and RNG; schema and data integration; service integration	Correlation and choreography
Orchestrate	BPMN, Petri Nets, Workflow Nets, RPST, CPEE Trees, Colored Petri Nets	Verification, task and worklist design; service invocation; correlation; integration patterns and processes	Choreography

Fig. 1.7 Interoperability perspectives I: Chap. 6

task and worklist design (semantic level). The task design realizes the invocation of services (cf. Chap. 4). The worklist design realizes the integration and inclusion of human work into the process orchestration. The integration of data is realized by the concepts for data flow in process orchestrations. The notations and concepts presented in Chap. 5 are illustrated based on the manufacturing case study described in Sect. 1.3.2.

Chapter 7 (**Integration Patterns and Processes**) tackles the question on "how to integrate enterprise applications", i.e., aims at lifting up the integration of single services to the level of processes, starting with integration patterns and scenarios. Chapter 7 forms the second pillar in the triangle of process-based interoperability as depicted in Fig. 1.2. Regarding interoperability perspectives I, Chap. 7 utilizes an extension of Colored Petri Nets as notation (syntactical level) and presents integration patterns and processes at the semantic level (cf. Fig. 1.8). From an interoperability task point of view, Chap. 7 sits at the orchestration level. Chapter 7 illustrates the presented notation, i.e., Colored Petri Nets and the concepts for integration patterns and processes based on two case studies, one from manufacturing (cf. Sect. 1.3.2) and one from customer relationship management in SAP (cf. Sect. 1.3.3).

Chapter 8 (**Process Choreography**) addresses the question on "how to establish interoperability between different partners across enterprises" based on process choreographies. Chapter 8 builds the third pillar in the triangle or process-based interoperability as depicted in Fig. 1.2. Regarding the levels of interoperability perspectives I (cf. Fig. 1.9), Chap. 8 refers to the syntactical level by BPMN-based choreography modeling and to the syntactical and semantic level for verification of choreography and collaboration models based on Workflow Nets. Chapter 8 also

Levels .../ Tasks ꜜ	Syntactical	Semantic	Organizational
Exchange	Exchange formats, e.g., XML, relational databases, JSON, BSON, YAML, MessagePack; query languages: XPath, XQuery, SQL; transformation languages, e.g., XSLT	Schema matching and mapping; ontologies;	Message exchange; correlation
Integrate	SQL/XML standard; native XML databases; REST and GraphQL	Edge table, shredding; XML schema and RNG; schema and data integration; service integration	Correlation and choreography
Orchestrate	BPMN, Petri Nets, Workflow Nets, RPST, CPEE Trees, Colored Petri Nets	Verification, task and worklist design; service invocation; correlation; integration patterns and processes	Choreography

Fig. 1.8 Interoperability perspectives I: Chap. 7

Levels .../ Tasks ꜜ	Syntactical	Semantic	Organizational
Exchange	Exchange formats, e.g., XML, relational databases, JSON, BSON, YAML, MessagePack; query languages: XPath, XQuery, SQL; transformation languages, e.g., XSLT	Schema matching and mapping; ontologies;	Message exchange; correlation
Integrate	SQL/XML standard; native XML databases; REST and GraphQL	Edge table, shredding; XML schema and RNG; schema and data integration; service integration	Correlation and choreography
Orchestrate	BPMN, Petri Nets, Workflow Nets, RPST, CPEE Trees, Colored Petri Nets	Verification, task and worklist design; service invocation; correlation; integration patterns and processes	Choreography

Fig. 1.9 Interoperability perspectives I: Chap. 8

refers to the organizational level and spans across all three interoperability tasks, i.e., exchange via message exchanges between the partners in the choreography, integrate based on process-based partner integration and correlation, and choreography, presenting the basic strategies for setting up choreographies, i.e., top-down versus bottom-up. The technologies and concepts provided in Chap. 8 are illustrated based on a supply chain scenario (cf. Sect. 1.3.2).

The book is concluded by Chap. 9 (**Conclusion and Outlook**). Chapter 9 discusses strategies and success factors for interoperability projects and rounds the book off with a summary.

Chapter 2
From Databases to Exchange Formats

2.1 Motivation and Goals

This chapter addresses the extraction and exchange of data from information systems (cf. Fig. 2.1).

As a first popular format, we choose XML and discuss approaches on how to create XML documents from relational databases (e.g., using SQL/XML functions) and, in turn, to store XML content in relational databases. In detail, this chapter explains approaches such as the edge table to store arbitrary XML data in a relational database, shows how to use SQL/XML functions to create XML documents from relational data, and explains how to manage transformation of XML data for exchange. For understanding purposes, we provide an introduction into XML foundations. XML is then compared to specialized exchange formats such as JSON, YAML, BSON, and MSGPACK that focus on factors such as understandability or performance. The choice of relational data and XML illustrates the question on how to manage the transformation of table-oriented and hierarchically structured data. This question will be picked up and elaborated in Chap. 3 on schema matching, mapping, and data integration. The presented concepts are illustrated based on a case study from higher education in Sect. 4.4. Conclusions and lessons learned complete this chapter.

In general, XML (Extensible Markup Language) is an important standard for the exchange of structured data. The extraction of XML documents from (relational) databases and vice versa and the transformation and storage of XML-based content in (relational) databases arose as "hot topics" around 2002/2003, resulting in a number of books, e.g., [143, 202, 219]. The high interest was also underpinned by the introduction of the SQL/XML standard that was adopted by major database systems and vendors, e.g., DB2 [156]. Techniques for exchanging database information via XML documents thus are well-known and established. Hence, we focus on the exchange of XML and relational databases in Sects. 2.3 and 2.4, relying on existing literature [143, 202, 219]. Working with these techniques

© Springer Nature Switzerland AG 2024
S. Rinderle-Ma et al., *Fundamentals of Information Systems Interoperability*,
https://doi.org/10.1007/978-3-031-48322-6_2

Levels ... / Tasks ↓	Syntactical	Semantic	Organizational
Exchange	Exchange formats, e.g., XML, relational databases, JSON, BSON, YAML, MessagePack; query languages: XPath, XQuery, SQL; transformation languages, e.g., XSLT	Schema matching and mapping; ontologies;	Message exchange; correlation
Integrate	SQL/XML standard; native XML databases; REST and GraphQL	Edge table, shredding; XML schema and RNG; schema and data integration; service integration	Correlation and choreography
Orchestrate	BPMN, Petri Nets, Workflow Nets, RPST, CPEE Trees, Colored Petri Nets	Verification, task and worklist design; service invocation; correlation; integration patterns and processes	Choreography

Fig. 2.1 Interoperability perspectives I: Chap. 2

raises an understanding for interoperability as a challenge and can quickly lead to solutions that have a broad practical applicability. Nonetheless, we also aim at a more current and more general point of view and hence provide techniques for data exchange through further, more specialized formats, i.e., JSON, YAML, BSON, and MSGPACK.

In order to provide a foundation for further understanding of the presented concepts, Sect. 2.2 starts off with an introduction into the foundations of XML.

2.2   XML Foundations

XML (Extensible Markup Language) is an important standard for the exchange of structured data especially between Web-based applications. XML structures data in simple trees consisting of elements containing arbitrary text, with each element (and its children) being furthermore described by optional attributes as can be seen from the small example in Listing 1, which will be elaborated in the course of this section.

Listing 1 Simple example

```
1    <book name="InterOp">
2      <chapter number="1">Intro</chapter>
3      <chapter number="2">XML</chapter>
4    </book>
```

A wide variety of XML generators, parsers, and APIs for all common programming languages and operating systems exists. The simple XML core is furthermore extended by a wide range of additional standards covered in this book, to further improve the utility for a wide range of interoperability scenarios:

- **Namespaces:** Names of elements/attributes might not be unique when, e.g., XML files from two different organizations are merged. Namespaces provide a means to prefix elements/attributes for unique identification.
- **Describing contained structures, data, dependencies between them:** A variety of schema standards such as DTD (Document Type definition), XML Schema, and Relax NG deal with describing allowed nestings of elements, which attributes can occur for each element, as well as which datatypes are allowed inside elements/attributes. Some of these standards furthermore delve into the topic of data dependencies. If, for example, one part of an XML file defines a list of concepts each identified by an id, these ids can be used to reference these concepts in another part of the XML file. In this case, the schema can be used to ensure that only existing concepts are referenced.
- **Querying:** Besides APIs to explore XML trees, there exists also a set of standardized query languages. Like SQL, they allow to query, filter, and extract parts of XML documents, independent of XML library APIs and programming languages. This is useful to increase modularity and portability of code.
- **Transformation:** While any programming languages with an XML API could be used to transform or merge XML files, specialized languages such as XSLT (Extensible Stylesheet Language Transformation) provide a dedicated independent means of transformation, which can again be utilized in arbitrary programming languages. XSLT is based on functional ideas, although it lacks the ability to treat functions as a first class data types. Again, the usage of XSLT improves modularity and facilitates portability through separation of concerns.
- **Referral and referencing:** In order to allow an XML document to refer to/include other documents, parts of other documents, or parts of itself, standards such as XLink/XPointer allow to refer to XML artefacts.

Another common scenario is the creation of standards to describe **domain specific applications** utilizing XML files. By defining a fixed (but extensible) set of elements and attributes, it is possible to specify a common data structure for a domain. Examples include:

- the Atom and RSS (Rich Site Summary) standards describe the data format of subscribable information feeds.
- the RDF (Resource Description Format) standard describes how triplets of semantic information can be stored.
- the XHTML (Extensible Hypertext Markup Language) standard defines how websites can be structured.
- the ebXML (electronic business XML) family of standards defines data formats for everything from business processes to secure transactions between business partners.

- the BPEL (Business Process Execution Language) standard defines a file format for describing executable business processes.
- the BPMN (Business Process Modeling Notation) standard includes a file format for storing graphical business process models.
- SOAP (Service-Oriented Access Protocol) and WSDL (Web Service Description Language) describe a protocol and file format how Web services can be defined and data exchange between client and server has to be conducted.

2.2.1   XML Properties

XML is a meta-language. It describes a framework for writing documents for domain-specific applications. As such, it consists of a set of rules for writing XML conformant documents. Its main properties are:

- machine read- and writeable
- hierarchical document structure
- platform independent (hardware, programming language, OS)
- language and region independent (can deal with any language, character set, and encoding)
- vendor independent (W3C standard[1])
- based on XML processors—software modules that allow to read, write, and modify XML trees. XML processors work on behalf of the application that utilizes them.

Since its inception ca. 1998, it became ubiquitous, being a staple for defining configuration, exchanging and storing data, as well as defining complex ontologies. As such, it is part of all of our interactions with technology, ranging from phones to high-performance computing clusters driving today's cloud-based infrastructure.

2.2.2   Anatomy of XML Documents

As depicted in Fig. 2.2, the anatomy of XML documents is defined by a small number of distinctive concepts.

Processing Instructions have the following form `<?name data?>`, with a name possibly consisting of unicode characters (expect whitespace and some others) and data. While in the given example `version="1.0"` and `encoding="utf-8"` look like XML attributes, they are just generic data, interpreted by XML parsers.

---

[1] https://www.w3.org/XML.

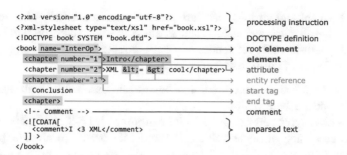

Fig. 2.2 XML document anatomy

The second line shows a **DOCTYPE definition**. This allows to give the parser hints about the structure of the documents, i.e., which elements/attributes/entities can be used. DOCTYPE definitions (DTD) come in two forms:

- with internal data: `<!DOCTYPE name [...]>`
- with external data: `<!DOCTYPE name [SYSTEM|PUBLIC] data>`

Internal definitions have a name and then contain the definition inline between two square brackets. External definitions contain one of the keywords `SYSTEM` or `PUBLIC` after the name. `SYSTEM` denotes that the following data denotes a url where to find the definition, whereas `PUBLIC` denotes that the following data is a symbolic identifier, which allows the parser to identify and include the potentially standardized DTD from a source of its choosing (i.e., many public DTDs are provided as part of the parser).

DTD, which are discussed in more detail in the next chapter, can contain *entity* definitions in the form `<!ENTITY [[SYSTEM|PUBLIC] "..." [data]>`. Entities are text blocks that can be included in documents through references. % defines that these entities can be used as macros inside other entities or DTD elements. Entities furthermore have a name, employ the `PUBLIC/SYSTEM` concept explained above, and contain arbitrary data.

As depicted in Fig. 2.2 the document needs to have one root **element**. An element has always the form `<name>...</name>`. Naming an element has to follow a set of rules: names (1) are case-sensitive, (2) must start with a letter or underscore, (3) cannot start with xml (case insensitive), and (4) can contain letters, digits, hyphens, underscores, and periods but (5) cannot contain whitespace.

Elements can be arbitrarily nested and can contain a set of **attributes** (there is no defined order in which they are connected to an element). Attributes follow the form `name="value"`.

Each Element and attribute can furthermore contain arbitrary **character data**, except the five characters <, >, ", ′, and &. These five characters have to be escaped through the built-in entity references < > " ' and &.

Multiple types of **entity references** exist:

- **Built in** to substitute characters that have to be escaped in both element text content and attribute values.
- **UTF-8 character references** to include arbitrary UTF-8 characters in element text content and attribute values. If the XML parser receives a processing instruction to parse utf-8 characters, all characters can be inserted directly, but for all other cases, this allows to include other characters.
- self-defined references can be used to insert common text phrases, either in the document or in other entities (see Listing 2).

Listing 2 Nested entities and use in document

```
 1 <?xml version="1.0" encoding="utf-8"?>
 2 <!DOCTYPE SYSTEM [
 3    <!ENTITY p "Good_Goods_Inc." >
 4    <!ENTITY m "orders@gg.com" >
 5    <!ENTITY cm "&p;,_&m;" >
 6 ]>
 7 <email>
 8    Dear Customer,
 9    please order the newest products from our partner &pm;.
10 </email>
```

In order to simplify arbitrary data, without having to resort on conversions to substitute special characters, XML also supports **unparsed text**. This is realized through CDATA sections in the form of `<![CDATA[data]]>`. CDATA section can only appear inside elements (but not inside attributes).

Finally, *comments* can be used to annotate your document. Comments can appear in more places than CDATA sections, e.g., outside the root element. However, comments (1) cannot appear before the XML process instruction, (2) cannot appear within attributes, and (3) cannot be nested inside other comments.

2.2.3 Well-Formed XML and Valid XML

XML well-formedness deals with nesting. Two general rules apply:

- Each element has a start and an end tag.
- One root element exists, which contains all other XML elements,
- Every start tag has a parent, i.e., a start tag that occurs before it, which is not yet closed through an end tag.
- For each element, the end tag must occur before the end tag of its parent element.

The XML document thus forms a tree with a single root, branches, and leaves. An XML document can be well-formed and still invalid. As mentioned, a variety of standards such as DTD, XML Schema, and Relax NG exist (cf. Sect. 3.4), which deal with the correct nesting of elements, i.e., which (named) elements are allowed to occur in which order or nesting.

2.2.4   Text and White Space in XML Elements

As discussed above, an XML element can be empty, contain text, contain other elements, or can be both text and elements.

Listing 3   White space

```
1 <?xml version="1.0" encoding="utf-8"?>
2 <book name="InterOp">
3    <chapter number="1">Intro</chapter>
4    <chapter number="2">
5        XML
6    </chapter>
7    <chapter number="3">
8      <subchapter/>
9      <subchapter/>
10   </chapter>
11   <chapter number="4"><strong>Important</strong> Conclusion</chapter>
12 </book>
```

Whitespace (spaces, tabs, newlines, returns) inside a tag, like the space between name (`<book`) and attribute (`name="interop"`), is part of the syntax. Attributes have to be separated with arbitrary whitespace. Whitespace inside elements is typically treated by XML parsers as follows:

- If an element only contains other elements and whitespace, the whitespace is ignored (it is insignificant). For example, in Listing 3, `<chapter number="3">` contains two subchapters that are indented and thus also whitespace (spaces and newlines). Any other indentation or even zero whitespace is deemed identical. XML parsers are allowed to re-format potential output.
- If an element contains text or combinations of text and children (mixed content), whitespace is significant. For example, in Listing 3, `<chapter number="2">` contains the text XML; all spaces and newlines before and after XML are part of this text. Listing 3 `<chapter number="4">` shows mixed content. Here, the space after the strong element is significant as well. An XML parser is expected to no reformat such contents.
- Whitespace in attributes is always deemed significant.

Some applications of XML such as XHTML of course can employ a specific way of dealing with whitespace. XHTML, for example, zips significant whitespace: all subsequent spaces, enters, newlines, and tabs are combined into one space for output as part of the rendering of a website.

2.2.5   XML Namespaces

The purpose of namespaces is to remove ambiguity for XML elements with the same name. For example, Listing 4 shows a collection of products for a goods vendor. Different suppliers provide details about their goods in a similar form but unveil some key differences. While attribute id exists for both products, it is in a different format and represents supplier internal information. Thus, it is perceivable that the same id is utilized by different suppliers.

Listing 4 XML namespaces required

```
1  <?xml version="1.0" encoding="utf-8"?>
2  <products>
3     <product id="17">
4        <type>Book</type>
5        <name>Interoperability Stories</name>
6        <authors>
7           <first>Juergen Mangler</first>
8           <second>Martin Luther</second>
9        </authors>
10    </product>
11    <product id="550e8400-e29b-11d4-a716-000000000042" category="food">
12       <name>Relaxation Tea</name>
13       <ingredient amount="40%">chamomile</ingredient>
14       <ingredient amount="59%">fennel</ingredient>
15    </product>
16 </products>
```

Additionally, for the first product, the type is stored in an element named *type*, whereas for the second product, the type is stored in an attribute *category*. Thus, each product contains the same information but is structured differently. While the *name* is stored in the same form, things further deviate for *ingredients* vs. *authors*. Even if all suppliers, like for the first product, were to supply books, the authors might be represented very differently, e.g., the information about first and second authors might not be contained, and all individual authors might be represented as <author>.

Listing 5 XML namespaces

```
 1 i<?xml version="1.0" encoding="utf-8"?>
 2 <products xmlns="https://best-vendor-ever.int" xmlns:vendor="https://best-
       ↪ vendor-ever.int" xmlns:b="urn:teashop:tea" xmlns:a="tel:
       ↪ +1-212-555-2368">
 3   <a:product a:id="17" quantity="3">
 4     <a:type>Book</a:type>
 5     <name>Interoperability Stories</name>
 6     <a:authors>
 7       <a:first>Juergen Mangler</a:first>
 8       <a:second>Martin Luther</a:second>
 9     </a:authors>
10   </a:product>
11   <b:product b:id="550e8400-e29b-11d4-a716-000000000042" b:category="food"
       ↪ a:id="17" quantity="12">
12     <name>Relaxation Tea</name>
13     <b:ingredient b:amount="40%">chamomile</b:ingredient>
14     <b:ingredient b:amount="59%">fennel</b:ingredient>
15   </b:product>
16   <product xmlns="email:john.bag@tea.com" xmlns:c="email:john.bag@tea.com"
       ↪ c:id="12" vendor:quantity="3">
17     <vendor:name>Healthy Tea</vendor:name>
18     <ingredient c:amount="59">rosehip</ingredient>
19   </product>
20 </products>
```

Listing 5 demonstrates the introduction of namespaces to make the differences between in the data structures between the two different vendors explicit:[2]

- Namespaces can be declared in any element in the XML document with `xmlns` and are then available for usage.
- A **default namespace** has the form `xmlns="[uri]"`. If applied to an element, it is valid for the element and all its children.
- Namespaces can be defined with a shorthand identifier in the form `xmlns:[id]="[uri]"`. As shown in Listing 5, each element and attribute being associated with a certain namespace can be simply prefixed with `[id]:`.
- Namespace by default do not apply to any attributes, only when they are explicitly decorated.[3]

In the example given in Listing 5, some elements such as name and some attributes such as quantity still are assumed to belong to the default namespace. This denotes that they are either (1) semantically identical for all products or were (2) inserted by the vendor into the individual products.

The product from the supplier `email:john.bag@tea.com` contains a default namespace. All child elements by default belong to the same namespace. In this case, the name is exempted from this rule by adding the `vendor` namespace. In comparison, for the other two products, each element (i.e., also certain child elements of product) had to be decorated separately with the namespace.

---

[2] The inferior alternative would be to hard-code the semantic differences into the application logic that reads the data.

[3] Application logic might assume that all attributes belong to the same namespace as the element they are associated with. The XML standard and thus related standards such as XPath are unambiguous in this regard.

2.2.6 XLink, XPointer, & XInclude

Although not part of the core XML standard, these separate standards/recommendations are considered essential, as they allow to reference and include parts of XML. The goal of each standard is slightly different:

- **XLink** allows to reference (like an HTML `<a/>`) element, the same or other XML documents.
- **XPointer** allows to point to parts of the content of an XML document by utilizing the XPath standard. In addition to XPath expressions, which allow to select parts of a document it introduces functions such as `start-point`, `end-point`, and `*range*`.
- **XLink & XPointer** are typically combined for creating references to parts of other (seldom the same) documents.
- The purpose of **XInclude** is to combine multiple documents/fragments into one.

So while XLink & XPointer are used to provide links to other resources to a document, which may or may not be used by an application logic, XIncludes are typically resolved in preprocessing, i.e., if a document with XIncludes is opened, the XIncludes are replaced by the documents they point to, and the application logic has only access to the compound document.

Listing 6 XLink & XPointer

```
1 <link  xmlns:xlink="http://www.w3.org/2000/xlink"
2        xlink:href="products.xml#xpointer(/products/product[@id=12])">
3 </link>
```

XLinks typically can be specified as attributes of arbitrary XML elements. In the example shown in Listing 6, the link element points to `products.xml` (see Listing 7) and inside `products.xml` to the product with the attribute `id=17`.

As mentioned above, the XPointer function used as part of the XLink provides a number of possibilities to specify points in the document:

Listing 7 products.xml with XLink targets

```
 1 <?xml version="1.0" encoding="utf-8"?>
 2 <products>▼¹
 3   <product id="17">
 4     <type>Book</type>
 5     <name>Interoperability Stories</name>
 6     <authors>
 7       <first>Juergen ▼²Mangler</first>
 8       <second>Martin Luther</second>
 9     </authors>
10   </product>▼³
11   <product id="12">
12     <type>Food</type>
13     <name>Relaxation Tea</name>
14     ▼⁴ˢ<ingredient amount="40%">chamomile</ingredient>▼⁴ᵉ
15     <ingredient amount="59%">▼⁵ˢfennel▼⁵ᵉ</ingredient>
16   </product>
17 </products>
```

Different XLink functions can specify different points or ranges in documents. In Listing 7, a series of points are marked with triangles:

- ▼¹ can referenced by:

  - xpointer(start-point(/products))
  - xpointer(start-point(range(//products/product[1])))
  - 17

The start-point of a particular selected element, in this case the root element named products, is always at the very beginning inside the element. The start-point of a range of selected elements, in this case the first selected product, is always before the element starts. In this case, also xlink:href="products.xml#17" leads to the same point, as the default version of XPointer leads to the start-point of an element with a particular id attribute, thus working similar to an HTML anchor.

- ▼² can referenced by:

  - xpointer(start-point(string-range(//*,'Mangler')))

With the string-function it is possible to point before or after a certain text.

- ▼³ can referenced by:

  - xpointer(end-point(range(//products/product[@id=17])))
  - xpointer(start-point(range(//products/product[@id=12])))
  - 12

  This example demonstrates that before and after, a range can be the same point. In this case, also xlink:href="products.xml#12" leads to the same point.

- Everything between ▼⁴ˢ and ▼⁴ᵉ, i.e., the element itself, attributes, and text, can be referenced by:

  - xpointer(range(//product[@id=12]/ingredient[1]))

- Everything between ▼⁵ˢ and ▼⁵ᵉ, i.e., inside the selected element, can be referenced by:

  - xpointer(range(//product[@id=12]/ingredient[1]))

XInclude in comparison serves as much simpler purpose, i.e., the transparent inclusion of documents in documents. XInclude typically work recursively.

Listing 8 products.xml with XLink targets

```
1 <?xml version="1.0" encoding="utf-8"?>
2 <products xmlns:xi="http://www.w3.org/2001/XInclude">
3   <xi:include
4     href="http://supplier-a.int/product.xml">
5     <xi:fallback>
6       <product id="0">
7         <type>Error</type>
8       </product>
9     </xi:fallback>
10   </xi:include>
11   <xi:include href="http://supplier-b.int/product.xml" xpointer="17"/>
12   <xi:include href="http://supplier-c.int/product.xml" xpointer="xpointer
        ↪ (...)"/>
13 </products>
```

As depicted in Listing 8, in their simplest form, XInclude includes a whole document, but through the XPointer attribute, they gain the full power of XPointers, thus allowing to include either individual elements through their id attribute or more complex fragments.

2.3   Extracting XML Documents from Relational Databases

After introducing XML foundations in the previous section, this section aims at extracting XML documents from information stored in relational database(s) of one information system in order to exchange this information with another information system (cf. Fig. 1.2). In this context, the following questions arise:

1. *Which database is used for extraction?* Aside from relational databases, other types of databases have gained interest during the last years such as NoSQL or object-oriented/object-relational databases. Storing and managing XML documents in, for example, an XML database (see Sect. 2.4) already implies a NoSQL databases, i.e., the XML database itself. Object-relational databases are basically well suited for storing XML-like types (e.g., lists) [203]. Chapter 2 focuses on relational databases due to their practical importance. As a preview to Sect. 2.4, the choice of the database to store XML documents might be influenced by the type of XML document: *data-centric documents are regular in structure and homogeneous in content* [35] and are typically mapped onto relational databases. Document-centric XML documents resemble documents with typically a few XML tags for some structure. Obviously, the mapping to a relational database seems less straightforward, and another type of database that is more suited for storing documents (e.g., an XML database) might be chosen. Note that there might be also hybrid XML documents that contain data-centric and document-centric parts [35].

2. *What is the main challenge when extracting XML documents from relational databases?* The challenge in extracting XML documents from relational databases (and vice versa; see Sect. 2.4) results from the different meta models of XML and relational databases. XML follows a hierarchical structure, and relational databases are based on sets of tuples, i.e., can be seen as "flat" structure. Hence, we have to deal with building up hierarchical structures from flat ones and vice versa, in particular, without any loss of information. Hence, as depicted in Fig. 2.3, the extraction of XML documents comprises two steps, i.e., the transformation of relational content and the publishing of this content as an XML document. As we will illustrate later on, these two steps are resembled by the SQL/XML standard, providing, for example, publishing functions.

3. *What to extract from the database?* This can be (a) the complete database content and (b) the results of queries.

Let us start with an example database that stores information about courses that are offered to participants (cf. Fig. 2.3). The database name is `CourseDB`. In Fig. 2.3, the left side depicts relation `Participants` with the attributes `PNR` (i.e., participant number), `Name`, and `Location`. As motivated in the second question above, from the "flat" content of relation `Participants`, a hierarchically structured XML document has to be constructed to be published in the sequel. If we think about a possible hierarchy in the relation `Participants`, one can come up with the three levels shown in Fig. 2.3, i.e., the database name as Level 1, the relation name as Level 2, and the attribute names as Level 3 (cf. the three-level method as proposed in [143] or as *"table-based method"* in [43]. These levels can be mapped to a hierarchically structured XML documents with corresponding elements as depicted in Fig. 2.3 on the right side.

These basic considerations can be applied in general and will produce data-centric XML documents. If the database contains more than one relation, the corresponding XML document can be generated as depicted in Fig. 2.4. However, does this mapping from the relational tables on the left side to the XML document on the right side preserve all information? The answer is that the information on primary and foreign keys are lost (actually the primary key information is already lost in the mapping depicted in Fig. 2.3). Moreover, the information on the attribute types (e.g., PNr as INTEGER) should be preserved during the mapping. The information on attribute types, keys, references, and integrity constraints are not expressed at the XML document level but at the XML schema level.

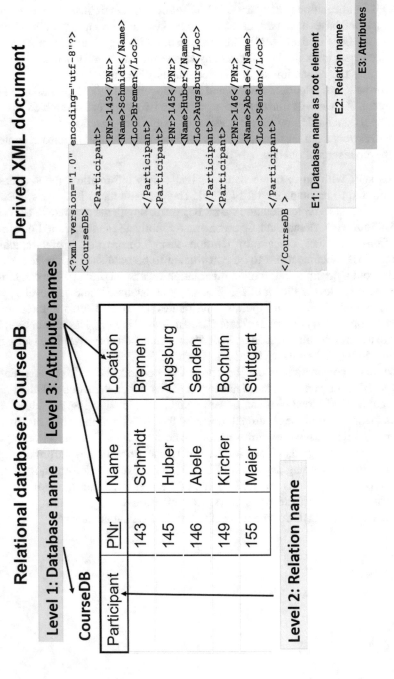

Fig. 2.3 Example: Course database and mapping to XML document

```xml
<?xml version="1.0" encoding="utf-8"?>
<CourseDB>
  <Participant>
    <PNr>143</PNr>
    <Name>Schmidt</Name>
    <Loc>Bremen</Loc>
  </Participant>
  <Participant>
    <PNr>145</PNr>
    <Name>Huber</Name>
    <Loc>Augsburg</Loc>
  </Participant>
  <Participant>
    <PNr>146</PNr>
    <Name>Abele</Name>
    <Loc>Senden</Loc>
  </Participant>
  <Course>
    <CNr>C11</CNr>
    <Label>Databases</Label>
    <Desc>XXX</Desc>
  </Course>
  <Course>
    <CNr>C12</CNr>
    <Label>Interoperability</Label>
    <Desc>YYY</Desc>
  </Course>
  <Enrolled>
    <PNr>143</PNr>
    <CNr>C11</CNr>
  </Enrolled>
  ...
</CourseDB >
```

Participant	PNr	Name	Location
	143	Schmidt	Bremen
	145	Huber	Augsburg
	146	Abele	Senden

Course	CNr	Label	Description
	C11	Databases	XXX
	C12	Interoperability	YYY

Enrolled	PNr	CNr
	143	C11
	143	C12
	145	C11
	146	C12

Fig. 2.4 Example (ctd.): Course database and mapping to XML document

Assume the following SQL statement 1① for creating table Participants. The corresponding type definition at the XML schema (XSD) level can be seen in Statement 1② with corresponding XSD data types, for example, XML element PNr being defined as of type xs:integer.

Statement 1 (Table/XSD Participants)

```
① create table Participant(
      PNr Integer Not Null Primary Key,
      Name VARCHAR(20),
      Location VARCHAR(30))


② <xs:element minOccurs="0" maxOccurs="unbounded" name="Participant">
    <xs:complexType>
      <xs:sequence>
        <xs:element minOccurs="0" name="PNr" type="xs:integer"/>
        <xs:element minOccurs="0" name="Name" type="xs:string" />
        <xs:element minOccurs="0" name="Location" type="xs:string" />
      </xs:sequence>
    </xs:complexType>
  </xs:element>
```

Statement 2 contains the definitions of xs:keys and xs:keyref in XML schema reflecting the primary keys PNr and CNr as well as the foreign key of table Enrolled referencing PNr and CNr. Figure 2.5 depicts a visualization of the usage of xs:key and xs:keyref in the XML schema of the Course example.

Statement 2 (XML Schema with References)

```
<xs:key name="PNr_key">
    <xs:selector xpath="Participant"/>
    <xs:field xpath="PNr"/>
</xs:key>
<xs:key name="CNr_key">
    <xs:selector xpath="Course"/>
    <xs:field xpath="CNr"/>
</xs:key>
<xs:keyref name="is_enrolled_PNr" refer="PNr_key">
    <xs:selector xpath="Participant"/>
    <xs:field xpath="PNr"/>
</xs:keyref>
<xs:keyref name="is_enrolled_CNr" refer="CNr_key">
    <xs:selector xpath="Course"/>
    <xs:field xpath="CNr"/>
</xs:keyref>
```

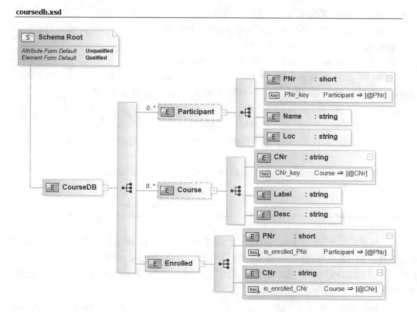

Fig. 2.5 Example (ctd.): Course XML Schema visualization using LiquidStudio©

We can see that it is beneficial to create XML documents with accompanying XML schema. Hence, in accordance with literature, a claim is to create XML documents with accompanying XML schema whenever possible.

In the following, we will discuss how to construct XML documents from the database—recall that this means to create a hierarchical structure based on a flat one—using the *SQL/XML* standard [1].

In general, *publication functions* of SQL/XML standard generate XML documents from relational data. In a first step, the relational data is transformed into a database-internal XML value. Then the internal XML value can be converted into external formal. This step is called *serialization*. Note that publication functions are also called *constructor functions*. In this book, we use the SQL/XML functions of PostgreSQL[4] However, publication functions are also part of, for example, Oracle or DB2 (for details on SQL/XML usage in DB2, we refer to [156]).

The first XML extension in the standard is a new SQL data type, i.e., XML. It can be used for defining columns, variables, and parameters. The following SQL snippet 3 shows the definitions of two tables. In table `Course2`, attribute `Description2` is of type `TEXT` (cf. `CLOB`). In Table `Course`, attribute `Description` is of type `XML`. The difference is that attribute `Description` can be queried using *XQuery* as part of a `SQL` statement as shown below.

Statement 3 (Attribute of Type XML)

```
① create table Course2(CNr2 VARCHAR(3) Not Null Primary Key, Label2
VARCHAR(20), Description2 TEXT);
insert into Course2 values ('C13', 'Databases2',
   '<desc><lit>book1</lit><struct><ch>Ch1</ch><ch>Ch2</ch></struct></desc>');
create table Course(CNr VARCHAR(3) Not Null Primary Key, Label
VARCHAR(20), Description XML );
insert into Course values ('C11', 'Databases',
   '<desc><lit>book1</lit><struct><ch>Ch1</ch><ch>Ch2</ch></struct></desc>');


② SELECT xpath('.//struct/ch', Description) FROM COURSE
```

The possibility to define attributes of type XML is an option to store XML documents in relational databases (cf. Sect. 2.4). The option of using XPath also enables the extraction of the entire XML documents or its parts from the relational database.

After introducing the SQL type of XML, we want to introduce the publishing or constructor functions provided by the SQL/XML standard that can be used to construct XML documents from relational data and publish it in the sequel.

---

[4] postgresql.org and https://www.postgresql.org/docs/current/functions-xml.html.

The direct realization of the "table-based method" as proposed by Boureet [43] and depicted in Fig. 2.3 is the usage of predicate `table_to_xml` as shown in Statement 4①.

Statement 4 (Table-based method)

```
① SELECT table_to_xml('Course', true, false, ");

② <course xmlns:xsi="http://www.w3.org/2001/XMLSchema-instance">
    <row>
      <cnr>C11</cnr>
      <label>Databases</label>
      <description><desc>...</desc></description>
    </row>
    <row>
      <cnr>C12</cnr>
      <label>Interoperability</label>
      <description><content>YYY</content></description>
    </row>
  </course>
```

The basic element in an XML document is the *XML element* (cf. Sect. 2.2). The SQL/XML standard provides a publishing function `xmlelement` that creates an XML element of a given `Name`. The XML element can be created without accessing any content from the databases but also—and this is the goal of this chapter—using the database content. Assume that we want to create XML element `Location` based on the participants' location from the CourseDB. The following snippet depicts how the XML function is used within the select statement. The XML element is given a name, i.e., `Location`, and the values are selected from Table `Participant`. If a number of XML elements is to be created at once, this can be done by a sequence of `xmlelement` statements or by using `xmlforest` as the second statement in Statement 5 shows. Note that the usage of `xmlforest` in this example resembles the usage of three `xmlelement` functions. Note also that we have already made some design decision with respect to the resulting XML document, i.e., its structuring. We could alternatively decide to work with function `xmlattributes` as in the third statement of the following snippet. Already in this simple example, several choices can be made. Thinking of interoperability the constructed XML documents can be designed, for example, in such a way that they match an expected format of the partner we aim at exchanging information with.

Statement 5 (XML forest)

```
①  select xmlelement(name "Location", P.Location) from Participant as P

②  select xmlelement(name "Participant",
     xmlforest(P.PNr as "PNr", P.Name as "Name", P.Location as "Location"))
       from Participant as P

③  select xmlelement(name "Participant", xmlattributes(PNr, Name),

     xmlelement(name "Location", Location)) from Participant
```

Further design choices include to concatenate (function xmlconcat) or aggregate (function xmlagg) relational content for the resulting XML document. xmlconcat concatenates two or more columns of one or several tables. Statement 6① concatenates two columns Description and Description2 from two tables Course and Course2 (note function xmlparse that casts type TEXT of attribute Description2 to type XML as the arguments of xmlconcat have to be of type XML). The result will be a the set of XML elements desc_con containing the info of all combinations of entries in columns Description and Description2. xmlagg, by contrast, aggregates rows of a column, for example, the entries attribute Description of table Course as in Statement 6②.

Statement 6 (XML functions for concatenation and aggregation)

```
①  select xmlelement(name "desc_con",

     xmlconcat(Description, xmlparse(content Description2)))
       from Course, Course2;

②  select xmlelement(name "desc_list", xmlagg(Description)) from Course;
```

For an overview on XML functions in PostgreSQL, we refer to https://www.postgresql.org/docs/current/functions-xml.html.

What about the corresponding XML schema information? As discussed in [43], the generation of XML documents is a design time task, i.e., when publishing database contents as XML, schema information should be already available. PostgreSQL offers the option to create XML schema based on SQL tables as in Statement 7①, resulting in the XML schema excerpt in Statement 7②. This excerpt shows that the function aims at covering the SQL types, e.g., VARCHAR, as close as possible.

Statement 7 (XSD creation based on table)

```
① SELECT table_to_xmlschema('Course', true, false, '')

② <xsd:schema xmlns:xsd="http://www.w3.org/2001/XMLSchema">
   ...
   <xsd:complexType name="RowType.CourseDB.public.course">
      <xsd:sequence>
         <xsd:element name="cnr" type="VARCHAR"
nillable="true"></xsd:element>
         <xsd:element name="label" type="VARCHAR"
nillable="true"></xsd:element>
         <xsd:element name="description" type="XML"
nillable="true"></xsd:element>
      </xsd:sequence>
   </xsd:complexType>
   ...
```

If generating XML documents from database contents is mostly of ad hoc nature or randomly, a better solution could be to use a *native XML database* (cf. Sect. 2.4). Nevertheless, commercial systems offer automatic derivation techniques. In DB2®,[5] XML schemas can be registered within the XML repository (can be also used for later validation). In Altova MapForce®,[6] for example, different information on database tables and database statistics can be transformed into XML. This might yield valuable meta information for the documentation process and the generation of XML schema.

Conclusion Designing a mapping from a relational database to XML documents can be supported by using SQL/XML functions, but the design choices on how the resulting XML document is constructed remain the task of the designer. The "table-based method" (cf. [43]) can be applied for mapping a relational table to a data-centric XML document. The relational content to be transformed into an XML document might also result from any query result, e.g., joining tables with projection on certain attributes. Thinking of interoperability, the resulting XML documents might be designed in such a way that they adhere to the intended exchange structure (e.g., based on an XML schema). In the example depicted in Fig. 2.6, based on the tables on the left-hand side, an XML document should be constructed that adheres to the XML schema on the right hand, top, and looks like the document on the right hand, bottom. Note that for, for example, XML element NumberP, additional information about its semantics is necessary. In this example, NumberP reflects the number of participants in a specific course.

Statement 8 shows a possible solution. The subquery selects the information from the tables, including the number of participants. The "outer query" constructs the XML document as specified in the XML schema in Fig. 2.6.

---

[5] https://www.ibm.com/support/knowledgecenter/SSEPGG_11.5.0/com.ibm.db2.luw.xml.doc/doc/c0050643.html.

[6] https://www.altova.com/mapforce.

Participant	PNr	Name	Location
	143	Schmidt	Bremen
	145	Huber	Augsburg
	146	Abele	Senden

Course	CNr	Label	Description
	C11	Databases	XXX
	C12	Interoperability	YYY

Enrolled	PNr	CNr
	143	C11
	143	C12
	145	C11
	146	C12

```
<xs:schema ..>
<xs:element name="CourseOffering">
  <xs:complexType>
    <xs:sequence>
      <xs:element name="Course" maxOccurs="unbounded" minOccurs="0">
        <xs:complexType>
          <xs:sequence>
            <xs:element type="xs:string" name="Label"/>
            <xs:element type="xs:short" name="NumberP"/>
          </xs:sequence>
        </xs:complexType>
      </xs:element>
    </xs:sequence>
  </xs:complexType>
</xs:element>
</xs:schema>
```

```
<?xml version="1.0" encoding="utf-8"?>
<CourseOffering>
  <Course>
    <Label>Databases</Label>
    <NumberP>2</NumberP>
  </Course>
  <Course>
    <Label>Interoperability</Label>
    <NumberP>2</NumberP>
  </Course>
</CourseOffering>
```

Fig. 2.6 Mapping to XML (schema and document)

Statement 8 (Concluding example, SQL statement)
```
select xmlelement(name "CourseOffering",
   xmlagg(xmlelement(name "Course", xmlelement(name "Label", I.Label1),
      xmlelement(name "NumberP", I.NumberP)))) from (Select C.Label as
Label1, count(*) as NumberP
         from Course as C, Participant as P, Enrolled as E where
P.PNr=E.PNr and E.CNr=C.CNr group by C.Label) as I
```

2.4 Storing XML Data in Databases

This section discusses selected options as depicted in Fig. 2.7 to store, manage, and query XML documents in databases. Basically, XML documents can be stored as a whole, based on a generic storage of their structure, and through a mapping.

2.4.1 Storage in XML Databases

The first option is to store XML documents "as a whole" and subsequently in a generic way. Different methods to store XML documents in a relational database as a whole are discussed in Sect. 2.3, i.e., storing the XML documents as an attribute of type CLOB or an attribute of type XML. Storing XML documents as attribute of type XML enables queries in terms of an XML query language such as XPath or XQuery.

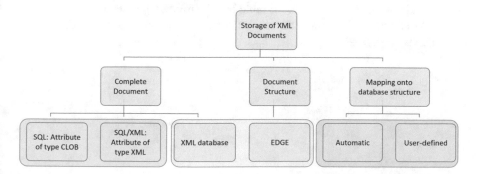

Fig. 2.7 Selected storage options for XML documents in relational databases (refined from [143])

Another option to store and manage XML documents as a whole is the usage of an XML database. In general, there is distinction between XML-enabled databases (such as DB2, Postgres, cf. Sect. 2.3) and native XML databases (also referred to as NDX) [43]. In the following, we refer to NDX. Although NDX have seen their high times years ago, they provide an elegant way to store and query one or several collections of XML documents and have raised interest again during the rise of NoSQL, i.e., *"nonrelational data store[s]"* [60]. Such NoSQL stores comprise, for example, key-value stores or document stores. A NDX can be seen as a document store, specifically storing XML documents and XML document collections. Other document stores such as MongoDB[7] focus on JSON documents (cf. Sect. 2.5).

In this section, we focus on NDX and take as an example BaseX[8] [108]. BaseX is open source and lightweight. The data model of a NDX is the XML document collection, and supported query languages are XPath and XQuery [43]. Figure 2.8 depicts the database `CourseDB` following up on the running example from Sect. 2.3. In detail, one can see the XML document (top, middle), the so-called tree map visualization of the hierarchical structure of the XML document (top, right), and the table-based representation (bottom). Moreover, an XPath query is shown where the results are highlighted in the tree map in red.

2.4.2 Generic Relational Storage

The basic idea is to not only store the "content" of the XML documents in the relational databases but also their structure in a generic way, resulting in the EDGE approach [85]. The EDGE approach requires to find a generic mapping of the hierarchical XML structure onto the "flat" structure of database tables. As the mapping is generic, it can be applied to arbitrary XML documents. Specific mappings of XML documents or their schema onto relational tables is conceivable, as well, and is discussed in Sect. 2.4.3.

Assume that a set of XML documents $D_1, \ldots, D_k$ is to be stored in the (relational) EDGE table. The EDGE table has the following structure:

`EDGE(DocID, ElementName, ElementID, Predecessor, ChildNo, Value)`

---

[7] https://www.mongodb.com/.

[8] https://basex.org/.

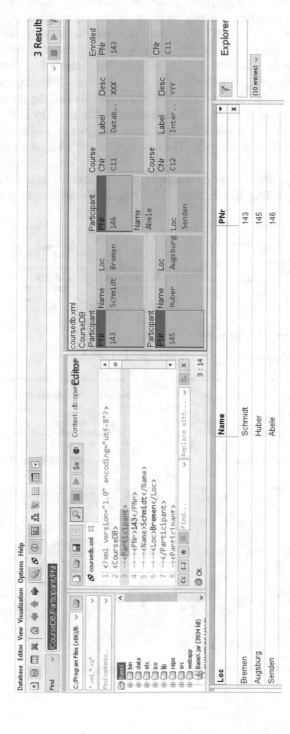

Fig. 2.8 CourseDB XML example file in BaseX with selection of participant 143

The DocID assigns to each XML document $X_i, i = 1, \ldots, k$ a document id. The ElementName attribute stores all element names, together with a unique ElementID. The ElementID is the key to store the structure of the XML document; it enables to store the direct predecessor of the element in the tree structure (attribute Predecessor) as well as the order of sibling elements (attribute ChildNo), i.e., children of the same element. Consider Fig. 2.9 that depicts an example XML document on the left-hand side and the underlying tree structure on the right-hand side. The elements would be stored in the EDGE table with their names. Elements hotelname, address, and desc point to their predecessor, i.e., hotelname. Their order is signified by the numbering in ChildNo.

Figure 2.10 augments the hotel example with a second XML document and shows the corresponding EDGE table. The two XML documents are assigned

```
<hotel>
    <hotelname>Hotel Stern</hotelname>
    <adress>
        <zip>89073</zip>
        <loc>Ulm</loc>
        <street>Hirschstrasse</street>
    </adress>
    <desc>
        From Stuttgart by train...
    </desc>
</hotel>
```

Fig. 2.9 Mapping XML documents to EDGE table (hotel example)

```
<hotel>
    <hotelname>Hotel Stern</hotelname>
    <adress>
        <zip>89073</zip>
        <loc>Ulm</loc>
        <street>Hirschstrasse</street>
    </adress>
    <desc>
        From Stuttgart by train...
    </desc>
</hotel>
```

```
<hotel>
    <hotelname>Sonne</hotelname>
    <adress>
        <zip>89075</zip>
        <loc>Ulm</loct>
        <street>Baumstrasse</street>
    </adress>
    <desc>
        From Stuttgart by train...
    </desc>
</hotel>
```

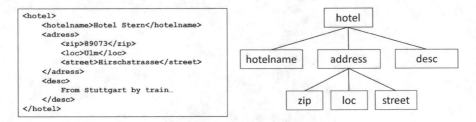

DocID	Element name	ID	Predecessor	ChildNo	Value
h001	hotel	101		1	
h001	hotelname	102	101	1	Hotel Stern
h001	address	103	101	2	
h001	zip	104	103	1	89073
h001	loc	105	103	2	Ulm
h001	street	106	103	3	Hirschstrasse
h001	desc	108	101	3	From Stuttgart...
h002	hotel	201		1	
h002	hotelname	202	201	1	Sonne

Fig. 2.10 Mapping XML documents to EDGE table (hotel example)

```
<hotel>
        <hotelname>Hotel Stern</hotelname>
        <adress zip = "89073" loc = "Ulm" street = "Hirschstrasse"
        </adress>
        <desc>
          From Stuttgart by train…
        </desc>
</hotel>
```

DocID	Attribute name	ElementID	Value
h001	zip	103	89073
h001	loc	103	Ulm
h001	street	103	Hirschstrasse

Fig. 2.11 Edge table with outsourcing of values

unique doc ids h001 and h002. The elements are stored with their element ids, e.g., for document h001, element hotelname is assigned element id 102 and element address element id 103. While element 102 stores a value, i.e., Hotel Stern, address has an empty value.

Figure 2.10 highlights that arbitrary XML documents can be stored in an EDGE table (even without schema information). On the downside, the mapping of the XML structure onto the table structure causes queries that are simple on the XML documents to become complex and costly on the EDGE table. Assume the query that selects all names of hotels in Ulm. The resulting query requires a self-join as shown in SQL code 9, i.e., the EDGE table is required twice, once for selecting the hotel name and once for selecting the location as "Ulm."

Statement 9 (SQL Query on EDGE Table)
```
select a.value
from elements a, elements b
where a.elementname = 'hotelname'
AND b.elementname = 'loc'
AND b.value = 'Ulm'
AND a.docid = b.docid;
```

A variant to the EDGE table depicted in Fig. 2.9 outsources the values of elements in separate tables, cf. Fig. 2.11. In detail, values are organized along their type in separate tables, e.g., for string values. The advantage of the outsourcing approach is that the value tables can be ordered and searched more easily.

In summary, the EDGE-based storage of XML documents is generic and can be applied for XML documents of arbitrary structure, i.e., also for documents with irregular structure. Specifically, no schema information is required. On the

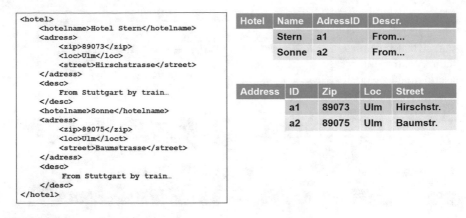

Fig. 2.12 User-defined relational mapping for data-centric XML document

downside, queries might require expensive self-joins, and reconstruction of the XML document can become complex too. Although the basic EDGE approach dates back 20 years, it is still considered a *"mainstream approach widely used while dealing with heterogeneous XML databases"* [87] and essential for the development of NoSQL databases [16]. Schema-oblivious approaches such as the EDGE approach are investigated for relational storage of data in other, more specialized formats such as JSON as well [21] (cf. Sect. 2.5).

2.4.3   Mapping-Based Storage

"Converting XML data into relational columns and rows is not an easy process" [93] and is also referred to as *shredding*. In contrast to the generic EDGE approach described in Sect. 2.4.2, shredding requires specifically designed database structures for each XML document, often defined based on a schema description (DTD or XML schema).

Basic considerations for defining a mapping from an XML document to a relational database are similar to the converse case depicted in Fig. 2.3. It depends on the type of XML document and how easy it is to find a relational mapping, i.e., for data-centric XML documents with regular structure, the definition of a user-defined mapping is more straightforward than for an XML document containing text and of irregular structure. Figure 2.12 shows a user-defined mapping for a data-centric XML document. The `address` element cannot be mapped into the `hotel` table with its elements `zip`, `loc`, and `street` but is stored within a separate table.

When assessing user-defined mapping approaches and comparing them to the generic EDGE approach (cf. Sect. 2.4.2), at first, user-defined mappings might typically enable simpler SQL queries by avoiding costly self-joins. Still, if the information contained in the XML documents has to be "distributed" over several relational tables, again joins become necessary. For the example depicted in Fig. 2.12, the query for selecting all hotel names in "Ulm" as described below Fig. 2.10 also requires a join of tables `Hotel` and `Address`. This might also affect the reconstruction of XML documents in a negative way. The real disadvantage of user-defined mappings is that they might have to be adapted each time an XML document with varying structure is to be stored, i.e., changes of the XML document affect the table structures.

Conclusion It can be recommended to use user-defined mappings for data-centric and stable XML documents. For all other XML documents, the generic EDGE table is more advisable. As a variant to both approaches, the difficulties with reconstructing XML documents can be addressed by redundant storage of these documents, e.g., in attributes of type XML.

2.5 Specialized Exchange Formats: JSON, YAML, BSON, MSGPACK

For interoperability applications, as well as any implementation, the credo always has to be the following: choose the right tool for the job. Aside from choosing the thing that one knows and has used before (thus leading to a perceived initial productivity boost), selecting specialized data representation format might yield huge benefits regarding one of several key aspects:

- **Readability** might improve the ability of programmers to debug and maintain an application.
- **Expressiveness** might reduce the size of information to be stored, as well as improve or reduce readability.
- **Compactness** might improve the throughput for distributed communication scenarios.
- **Serialization performance (SP)/deserialization performance (DP)** might heavily affect the overall performance/throughput your application can achieve.
- The impact of **special features** for custom application aspects like potentially required frequent changes of serialized data structures might be alleviated by relying on properties of a data representation format, such as for example the ability for partial serialization/deserialization, or techniques for reducing memory consumption when working with a format.

All of these key aspects involved when deciding for a data representation format are heavily influencing each other; thus, when optimizing for one, often, detrimental effects regarding different key aspects occur. Take for example XML, which has been introduced previously: It's very human readable; its high expressiveness (i.e., the way to describe concepts with elements and attributes) can be used in a way that negatively affects maintainability;[9] it's also not compact and has bad SP/DP.

Thus, in this section, we will discuss five additional data representation formats that cover a wide spectrum of needs that might arise when developing an application:

- **JSON** (JavaScript Object Notation) is simple tree-based serialization format that focuses on a few simple data types plus arrays and dictionaries. Like XML, it requires the decoration of the start and end of nested objects.
- **BSON** (Binary JSON) is a non-human readable, more compact version of JSON.
- **YAML** (YAML Ain't Markup Language) focuses on the same concepts as JSON but achieves nesting by indentation (not unlike python). While JSON has to be explicitly formatted to be human readable, YAML is always human readable. YAML also supports custom application scenarios, by introducing additional features to support progressive/partial deserialization and insertion of data.
- **MessagePack** (furthermore abbreviated MSGPACK) is a non-human readable like BSON but optimized toward compactness and serialization/deserialization speed.

Before diving deeper into syntactical properties of these data representation formats, it is useful to explore, rate, and discuss them regarding the above introduced key aspects. Consider the following simple example, both given in the JSON and XML data representation formats:

Listing 9 Initial example—a generic data structure

```
1 <book xmlns="rrrr">
2   <title >InterOp </title >
3   <chapters  a="12"><metric >1</metric ></chapters >
4   <references ><metric >2</metric ><metric >3</metric ></references >
5 </book>
6
7 ≡
8
9 {
10   "title ": "InterOp",
11   "chapters ": {
12     "metric ": 1
13   },
14   "references ": {
15     "metric ": [2,3]
16   }
17 }
```

Consider this data either present in the memory of an application, ready to be serialized, or available to the application as a string/byte array ready to be parsed in order to be present in memory.

While serialization/deserialization speed is pretty self-evident, readability and compactness are not. We define compactness as the number of bytes required to

---

[9] That is, see the discussion regarding when to use elements and when to use attributes in the XML section.

store a serialized version of a data structure. In the example given in Listing 9, the XML version has less lines and looks more compact, but in reality, the pretty printed JSON version is 1/3 smaller. It also becomes obvious that while XML focuses on representation that gives context to the data, with named elements, attributes, and nesting, JSON focuses more on the representation of data types. For example, in Listing 9, the JSON shows a differentiation between strings and numbers that is missing from the XML.

In general, it can be said that XML is a little bit more abstract than most data representation formats. This also includes certain degrees of freedom exist when translating between these data representation formats. As other data representation formats do not support attributes, translation might not be invertible. Another example for this is the potential presence of multiple elements with the same name on the same child axis: translation into a dictionary becomes impossible, but when all children have unique names, a dictionary is a very intuitive choice.

In order to make the comparison more realistic, we introduce a slightly bigger example (see Listing 10) that especially includes more numbers, which gives the binary formats an advantage, as they focus on the efficient encoding of floats, integers, and dates. In contrast, in JSON, YAML, and XML, everything is a string.

Listing 10 Initial example—more realistic comparison

```
1 <book xmlns=" rrrr ">
2   <title >InterOp </ title >
3   <chapters  a="12"><metric >111111111111</ metric ></ chapters >
4   <references ><metric >222222222222</ metric ><metric >333333333333</ metric ><
      ↪ metric >444444444444</ metric ><metric >555555555555</ metric ></
      ↪ references >
5 </book>
6
7 ≡
8
9 {
10    "title ": "InterOp ",
11    "chapters ": {
12      "metric ": 111111111111
13    },
14    "references ": {
15      "metric ": [222222222222,333333333333,444444444444,555555555555]
16    }
17 }
```

The example is selected so that the binary data representation formats have a chance to be more efficient (albeit by a small margin). This leads to the numbers shown in Table 2.1:

Apart from the formats discussed above, a XML row is included for comparison. Additionally, Table 2.1 also includes a row JSON-PP. JSON can be output either in a readable form (multi-line, indented) or in a more compact form (1-line). It is assumed that JSON is only selected over, e.g., BSON or MSGPACK for readability reasons. The performance for both is identical, but the JSON-PP is about 30% less compact (row **Length**). For both performance column, each operation was called 100000 times and averaged. The numbers show the potential **slowdown** regarding

Table 2.1 Performance

Format	Length	SP	DP
XML	310	31.92	11.24
JSON-PP	194	1.59	1.48
JSON	130	1.59	1.48
BSON	129	1.60	1.81
YAML	140	73.58	13.82
MSGPACK	97	1.00	1.00

Table 2.2 Rating

Key Aspects	XML	JSON	BSON	YAML	MSGPACK
Readability	4	4		5	
Expressiveness	5	4	4	4	4
Compactness	1	2	4	3	5
Serialization Speed	2	4	3	1	5
Deserialization Speed	2	4	3	1	5
Extra Features			1	5	

the best solution. MSGPACK is always the most performant version; thus, it comes in with 1.00; JSON-PP in comparison was 1.6 times slower for serialization.

Of course, these numbers have to be taken with a grain of salt, as they depend on the programming language/library that is used.Here especially, YAML might be much faster (for a more optimized implementation), as there is technical reason why it should perform worse than, e.g., XML (although it will be always slower than JSON/BSON for its inherent higher complexity).

Additionally, SP/DP are not the only deciding criteria: the loaded data also has to be traversed and searched. JSON, BSON, YAML, and MSGPACK deserialize to an in-memory data structure native to the programming language you use, which is parsed by custom code (written by you). This code might be slow (especially for complex filter operations). XML on the other hand deserializes into a special in-memory data structure. With the help of (heavily optimized) XPath complex, filter operations might be much faster. Especially when using XML/JSON in a browser, test carefully to come to an informed decision.

Table 2.2 shows structured table that rates each format regarding the above discussed key aspects. For JSON, the JSON-PP row in Table 2.1 is considered. Points from 1 to 5 are awarded (5 is the maximum). When a format does not support a particular key aspect, no value is awarded.

Table 2.2 shows that YAML is considered slightly more human readable than XML and JSON, while BSON and MSGPACK miss this aspect. XML is considered a little bit more expressive, but all the other formats are basically the same.

Compactness is hands down won by MSGPACK. BSON is badly represented in Table 2.1: although it wins against JSON/YAML by a hair, it has the potential to be much better for bigger and number heavy information. BSON actually can be considered to be more in a class with MSGPACK, although being not as

Table 2.3 Performance

Format	Length
XML	209
JSON-PP	123
JSON	73
BSON	95
YAML	75
MSGPACK	55

efficient. YAML and JSON (even the compact version, not the JSON-PP version) are surprisingly close in terms of compactness. Although one could expect YAML to be more on par with JSON-PP as both are indented, YAML is missing all the start/end decoration, which makes all the difference. XML is the clear loser regarding compactness.

Performance-wise, MSGPACK is closely trailed by JSON an BSON. XML can be considered slower by a factor 30. Here, YAML is the clear loser, although it should be not slower than XML. Your results regarding performance may of course vary, as the performance influenced by the used programming language and implementation.

When it comes to extra features, YAML is the king. Through blocks (multiple separately parseable YAML documents in one), comments, binary data, as well as references, an application developer can reap custom performance benefits. YAML can be used for, e.g., logging applications, as in contrast to all other formats, data can be appended to the end files without deserialization. BSON on the other hand allows in-place updates of values without deserialization, which makes it very efficient for its design purpose (in-database serialization format).

Just for the sake of curiosity, the lengths (basis for compactness) for the example in Listing 9 are given in Table 2.3.

Here BSON is much worse than JSON. The reason is that for strings and small numbers, BSON has to reserve the exactly same number of bytes but includes extra meta information to become parseable. As BSON is less compliant with JSON than MSGPACK, BSON should be only selected when in-place replacement of data without deserialization is a must (rare). All other formats are consistent with the results in 2.3.

For the remainder of this section, data representation formats will be discussed in more detail.

2.5.1   JSON

JSON (JavaScript Object Notation) is a lightweight data representation format used to store data as well as exchange data between different systems. It has support in most programming languages. It is easy for both humans to read and write and for machines to parse and generate. JSON is widely used in Web development and API communication (Web services) and for data storage.

2.5.2   BSON

BSON (Binary JSON) is a binary-encoded serialization format used to represent and exchange data in a binary form. It was designed to be more efficient in terms of storage compared to plain text formats like JSON and YAML. BSON has been developed in conjunction with MongoDB, a popular NoSQL database that uses BSON as its primary data storage format.

Real-world performance sadly is typically not better than current (heavily optimized) JSON implementations. BSON should in theory be faster to parse than JSON, but this depends on the size and types of data contained in your BSON.

2.5.3   YAML

YAML (YAML Ain't Markup Language) is a human-readable data serialization format often used for configuration files and data exchange. It is supported by most programming languages. Unlike JSON, which uses a nested array/dictionary representation with start/end decorations, YAML uses a more natural and expressive indentation-based syntax. Despite its advanced feature set in relation to JSON, it is considered more readable, understandable, and modifiable and thus preferred by developers and system administrators.

It is used in projects like Docker, Kubernetes, Ansible, and many others.

Performance will be always worse than JSON or BSON.

2.5.4   MSGPACK

MessagePack, is another binary serialization format that efficiently stores and exchanges data in a compact binary form. It is designed to be faster and more space-efficient than both JSON and BSON. Similar to BSON, MSGPACK is suitable for use in scenarios where data needs to be serialized and deserialized quickly and with minimal overhead.

It is supported by most programming languages. It excels for realizing communication in distributed systems and in high-performance applications (e.g., in-memory databases such as Redis).

2.6   Case Study: University Search System

The higher-education case study motivated in Sect. 1.3.1 will illustrate the concepts and technologies for Chaps. 2–4 in a combined way in Sect. 4.4.

2.7   Conclusion and Lessons Learned

The exchange of information between different information systems is essential for many business applications. One challenge is that the data in different information systems might be modeled and stored in different formats and following different modeling approaches. In this chapter, we address the challenge of dealing with different formats. The challenge of differences in modeling will be addressed in subsequent Chap. 3.

This chapter addresses the challenge of different formats based on the example of relational databases and XML due to the relevance of these formats. Moreover, the combination of both formats is informative in general for aligning data in different formats. XML data is hierarchically structured, and relational databases are flat. Hence, either hierarchical data has to be flattened into relational data or hierarchical data has to be constructed based on flat data. Also the query languages for both formats have different characters, i.e., set-oriented (SQL) for relational databases versus navigating (XPath, XQuery) for the XML world. These query languages play an important role in the transformation process.

Different possibilities exist to store XML documents in relational databases such as mapping the documents onto generic relations (e.g., using an edge table), defining specific mappings (e.g., by shredding) based on hybrid storage using the SQL/XML standard, or using native XML databases.

The exchange between relational databases and XML documents has been a research topic and has been also implemented in commercial systems (SQL/XML standard). In general, (relational) databases are often used as data sources and XML as exchange format. Hence, the combination of both techniques is a pillar in information exchange and interoperability. The techniques for mapping XML documents onto relational structure and vice versa can also be used for the transformation of exchange formats and integration format as to be discussed in Chap. 3. XML is only one format of choice, i.e., other exchange formats such as JSON, BSON, YAML, and MSGPACK exist. Here, it is crucial to make an informed decision on criteria such as readability and performance, depending on the requirements of the interoperability project.

Further Reading
1. Klettke, M., Meyer, H.: XML & Datenbanken Konzepte, Sprachen und Systeme. dpunkt.verlag, New York (2003). ISBN 3-89864-148-1
2. Moos, A.: XQuery und SQL/XML in DB2-Datenbanken. Vieweg+Teubner, New York (2008)

3. Møller, A., Schwartzbach, M.: An Introduction to XML and Web Technologies. Addison-Wesley, New York (2006). ISBN 0-321-26966-7
4. Schöning, H.: XML und Datenbanken. Hanser Verlag, New York (2002)
5. Kazakos, W., Schmidt, A., Tomczyk, P.: Datenbanken und XML, Springer, Berlin (2002)

Chapter 3
Transformation and Integration
of Exchange Formats

3.1 Motivation and Goals

This chapter aims at exchanging and integrating data between information systems. For this, technologies for schema transformation are introduced, and concepts for schema matching and mapping are provided (cf. Fig. 3.1).

The mix of conceptual and practical views furthers the understanding and application of how schemas and data in various formats can be exchanged between information systems, also in a concrete, hands-on manner.

Figure 3.2 displays a small example for managing the participants of a course database as introduced in Chap. 2 (cf. Fig. 2.3 and following figures) by two different information systems. Both applications use XML as format to manage the participants through the associated XML schemas.[1] In XML schema S1, element CourseDB can contain 1 to many elements Participant. Element Participant has an XML attribute PNr and contains XML elements Name, FirstName, Location, and Advance. In XML schema S2, element Courses can contain 1 to many elements Participant. Element Participant contains elements PNr, Name, City, and Advance.

Intuitively, one can see that schemas S1 and S2 describe the same situation but differ as indicated by arrows in Fig. 3.2. The first difference is the different labelling of elements CourseDB and Courses. The second difference is the structuring of their sub-elements. Where schema S1 has an attribute PNr, schema S2 an element, and also the name information is expressed by two elements in S1 and one element in S2. Finally, there is also a difference in the types of elements, i.e., for element Advance.

When we now aim at merging both schemas into one course participant application, first of all, we have to decide on the target schema. Here we can select one of

---

[1] An example for XML schema is provided in Chap. 2; more details can be found in Sect. 3.4.

© Springer Nature Switzerland AG 2024
S. Rinderle-Ma et al., *Fundamentals of Information Systems Interoperability*,
https://doi.org/10.1007/978-3-031-48322-6_3

Levels / Tasks	Syntactical	Semantic	Organizational
Exchange	Exchange formats, e.g., XML, relational databases, JSON, BSON, YAML, MessagePack; query languages: XPath, XQuery, SQL; transformation languages, e.g., XSLT	Schema matching and mapping; ontologies;	Message exchange; correlation
Integrate	SQL/XML standard; native XML databases; REST and GraphQL	Edge table, shredding; XML schema and RNG; schema and data integration; service integration	Correlation and choreography
Orchestrate	BPMN, Petri Nets, Workflow Nets, RPST, CPEE Trees, Colored Petri Nets	Verification, task and worklist design; service invocation; correlation; integration patterns and processes	Choreography

Fig. 3.1 Interoperability perspectives I: Chap. 3

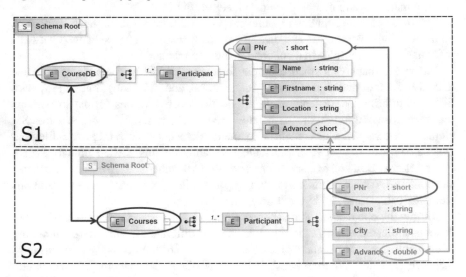

Fig. 3.2 XML schemas S1 and S2 describing the same real-world book collection (modeled using Liquid Studio®)

the two schemas S1 and S2 or create a third one. In any case, both existing schemas have to be matched, i.e., the differences in the schemas are to be resolved. In addition to the schema differences, there might also be differences in the data, i.e., in the corresponding XML documents, which cannot be spotted at the schema level. One example for a difference in the data is differing currencies for element Advance in both schemas. Another one is the difference in writing of the name information. All differences—at schema and data level—must be dealt with during schema matching, mapping, and integration into a target schema [94]. Moreover, the mapping results must be expressed in transformation rules, for example, if S1 is mapped onto S2, the transformation on how to map the different elements and attributes has to be specified. This necessitates transformation languages. In case of XML as exchange format, XSLT is the transformation language of choice. In Sects. 3.2 to 3.4, we lay the technological foundation for schema querying and transformation, while Sect. 3.5 presents concepts for schema mapping and matching.

3.2 XPath

The XPath language[2] uses a compact non-XML syntax to navigate, address, or query the structure of XML documents (i.e., its elements, attributes, texts, comments, ...). The name XPath hints at the way the language is structured, i.e., similar to addressing directories and sub-directories in a filesystem tree.

Listing 11 shows the XPath (in the caption) that selects the root element in the given XML document.

Listing 11 /book—The root element

```
1    <?xml version="1.0" encoding="utf-8"?>
2  ▶<book>
3       <paragraph/>
4       <title/>
5       <author/>
6       <author/>
7       <chapter/>
8          <paragraph/>
9       </chapter>
10   </book>
```

Please note that this XPath selects the whole element, from <book> to </book>, with all its children. Further XPaths can be utilized to search children inside this element. An XPath that starts with a slash (/) is called an absolute path or **absolute addressing**. This means that we always start searching from the root down. Please be aware that while there can be only one element below root (in this case <book>), in the anatomy of an XML document, other concepts such as comments are allowed before or after <book>. Addressing these concepts with /CONCEPT is possible.

---

[2] https://www.w3.org/TR/xpath.

3.2.1   Selecting Elements

Listing 12 shows the XPath (in the caption) for selecting all child elements
`<title>` of the root element `<book>` in the given XML document:

Listing 12 /book/title—A child element

```
1      <?xml version="1.0" encoding="utf-8"?>
2      <book>
3         <paragraph/>
4    ▶   <title/>
5         <author/>
6         <author/>
7         <chapter/>
8            <paragraph/>
9         </chapter>
10     </book>
```

This demonstrates the concept of addressing by separating the names of the
elements with slashes in a step-by-step way. In this particular case, the instruction is
as follows: go to the element book below root and then to a child (children) named
title.

In contrast to absolute addressing, there is also **relative addressing**. Whenever
an XPath starts with two slashes (*//*), all elements inside the XML tree are a potential
starting point for the search (not just the root). Listing 13 shows the XPath (in the
caption) for selecting all elements `<paragraph>` in the given XML document:

Listing 13 //paragraph—All elements named paragraph

```
1      <?xml version="1.0" encoding="utf-8"?>
2      <book>
3    ▶   <paragraph/>
4         <section>
5    ▶      <paragraph/>
6         </section>
7         <chapter>
8            <section>
9    ▶         <paragraph/>
10   ▶         <paragraph/>
11           </section>
12        </chapter>
13     </book>
```

In this case, the following search based on traversing the whole tree is performed:
search for `<paragraph>` inside (1) **root**, (2) `<book>` (1 hit), (3) `<paragraph>`,
(4) `<section>` (1 hit), (5) `<paragraph>`, (6) `<chapter>`, (6) `<section>`
(2 hits), (7) `<paragraph>`, (8) `<paragraph>`. Thus, in this case, four elements
(4 hits) are found.

As hits might be different concepts, e.g., elements, attributes, texts, or comments,
a hit is denoted as a **node**. Multiple nodes form a **nodeset**. Thus, in Listing 13, a
nodeset with four nodes (all elements) is returned.

In Listing 14, a more complex relative search (see XPath in caption) is demonstrated, i.e., for each element, we are looking for elements named `<section>`
and inside them for children named `<paragraph>`. As the first `<paragraph>`

is inside the root element <book> and not inside an element <section>, it is excluded from the returned nodeset. Thus, in this case, the nodeset contains three nodes (all elements).

Listing 14 //section/paragraph—Elements paragraph which are children of section

```
1      <?xml version="1.0" encoding="utf-8"?>
2      <book>
3        <paragraph/>
4        <section>
5  ▶       <paragraph/>
6        </section>
7        <chapter>
8          <section>
9  ▶         <paragraph/>
10 ▶         <paragraph/>
11         </section>
12       </chapter>
13     </book>
```

So far only named nodes have been addressed. In order to select arbitrary nodes, like in filesystems, a * can be used. Listing 15 returns all nodes below chapter (see XPath in caption).

Listing 15 /section/chapter/*—All children of chapter

```
1      <?xml version="1.0" encoding="utf-8"?>
2      <book>
3        <paragraph/>
4        <section>
5          <paragraph/>
6        </section>
7        <chapter>
8  ▶       <section>
9            <paragraph/>
10           <paragraph/>
11         </section>
12       </chapter>
13     </book>
```

This can also be combined with relative addressing, to select all descendants of chapter as demonstrated in Listing 16 (see XPath in caption).

Listing 16 /section/chapter//*—All descendants of chapter

```
1      <?xml version="1.0" encoding="utf-8"?>
2      <book>
3        <paragraph/>
4        <section>
5          <paragraph/>
6        </section>
7        <chapter>
8  ▶       <section>
9  ▶         <paragraph/>
10 ▶         <paragraph/>
11         </section>
12       </chapter>
13     </book>
```

Listing 17 shows how the * can also be used to search in arbitrary parent nodes (see XPath in caption).

Listing 17 /*/*/*/paragraph—Paragraphs on the fourth level

```
1    <?xml version="1.0" encoding="utf-8"?>
2    <book>
3      <paragraph/>
4      <section>
5        <paragraph/>
6      </section>
7      <chapter>
8        <section>
9  ▶        <paragraph/>
10 ▶        <paragraph/>
11       </section>
12     </chapter>
13   </book>
```

3.2.2 Restricting Selections: Predicates

Predicates are written in square brackets ([. . .]), with the goal to narrow or restrict
a selected nodeset. The simplest form of restriction is by putting a number inside
the square brackets: if multiple nodes are selected, then one particular node from the
nodeset is returned. **Important:** accessing the first element of the nodeset is done
by using [1] (one-based indexing)—in contrast to most programming languages,
where the first element is selected with [0] (0-based indexing). Listing 18 shows a
simple restriction to the second node in a resulting nodeset (see XPath in caption).

Listing 18 —Second child of book]/book/*[2]—Second child of book

```
1    <?xml version="1.0" encoding="utf-8"?>
2    <book>
3      <paragraph/>
4  ▶   <section>
5        <paragraph/>
6      </section>
7      <chapter>
8        <section>
9          <paragraph/>
10         <paragraph/>
11       </section>
12     </chapter>
13   </book>
```

In order to access certain nodes in a nodeset, it is also possible to utilize
predefined functions inside predicates. An immediate use-case that comes to mind
is selecting the last element in a nodeset, as demonstrated in Listing 19 (see XPath
in caption).

Listing 19 —Last child of book]/book/*[last()]—Last child of book

```
1    <?xml version="1.0" encoding="utf-8"?>
2    <book>
3      <paragraph/>
4      <section>
5        <paragraph/>
6      </section>
7  ▶  <chapter>
8        <section>
9          <paragraph/>
10          <paragraph/>
11        </section>
12      </chapter>
13    </book>
```

Inside predicates, it is also possible to use arithmetic operators, e.g., with [last()-1], it is possible to select the second last element (would be <section> in Listing 19). More examples for utilizing last can be seen in Listing 20 (see XPath in caption).

Listing 20 //paragraph[last()]: ▶ and //section[last()]/*: ▶

```
1    <?xml version="1.0" encoding="utf-8"?>
2    <book>
3      <paragraph/>
4      <section>
5  ▶    <paragraph/>
6      </section>
7      <chapter>
8        <section>
9  ▶      <paragraph/>
10 ▶▶      <paragraph/>
11        </section>
12      </chapter>
13    </book>
```

3.2.3 Restricting Selections: Logical Expressions

Each predicate can also contain logical expressions to further restrict a nodeset.

- Operands are XPaths or functions such as last() illustrated in Listing 20.
- Operands can be compared with = (equal), != (not equal), >=, >, <, and <=.
- Comparing operands by default compares their text content.
- Operands are not compared to something; their existence is checked.
- The result of expressions can be negated with not(...).
- Expressions can be connected with logical **or** and logical **and**.
- Expressions can be nested (XPaths with predicates inside predicates)

Listing 21 Logical expressions

```
1      <?xml version="1.0" encoding="utf-8"?>
2   ▶▶<book>
3         <paragraph>Second</paragraph>
4         <paragraph>First</paragraph>
5    ▶    <section>
6            <length>14</length>
7    ▶       <paragraph/>
8         </section>
9    ▶    <chapter>
10   ▶       <section>
11             <length>5</length>
12             <paragraph>dimidium</paragraph>
13   ▶         <paragraph>facti</paragraph>
14          </section>
15   ▶      <section>
16             <length>10</length>
17             <paragraph>qui</paragraph>
18             <paragraph>copit</paragraph>
19             <paragraph>habet</paragraph>
20   ▶         <comment>good</comment>
21          </section>
22       </chapter>
23    </book>
```

Listing 21 is the basis for demonstrating a wide range of expression capabilities:

- ▶ **/book[paragraph='Second']:** The root element book is selected, if it has a child element paragraph with text "Second" inside.
- ▶ **//*[section[length > 12] or position()=last()]:** Any element is selected, which (1) has a section element as its child, which in turn has a length element as its child with a number larger than 12 as its content, or (2) is the last element among its siblings.
- **/book/chapter[section/comment != 'good']:** Every chapter is selected, which has sections with comments that do not have the text "good" inside. In this case, only one section/comment exists, and it has the text "good" inside, so **nothing** is selected. If any other comment existed in either section that had any other text in it, the chapter would be selected.
- ▶ **//section[length and not(comment)]:** Every section is selected, which has a child element length but not a child element comment.

3.2.4 Attributes

It is possible to access attributes by prefixing its name with @. Attributes are handled like children of their containing elements, albeit with a special name.

An interesting question is: **when should I use child elements and when should I use attributes?** In general, it is a good idea to only use **attributes** when the data contained in them is **atomic**, i.e., it cannot be further split up. Typically when attributes contain numbers, e.g., id, age, or length, they are safe. When an attribute contains something like an address, which might in the future be further decomposed into, e.g., street, number, and apartment, it is advisable to use a child element instead of an attribute.

Further decomposition, if the address is contained in an attribute, would lead to the removal of the attribute and the creation of a child element <address> containing either individual address components as attributes or additional child elements for simple extensibility. Further decomposition, if the address is already an element, leads to similar results but relies on less modifications. The attribute name in Listing 22, for example, contains the value "Arthur Dent," which should be decomposed to child elements.

Listing 22 provides the XML document as basis for the following XPaths that especially select attributes:

- ▶//@*: Selects all attributes anywhere in the document.
- ▶//@orcid: Selects all attributes named *orcid* anywhere in the document.
- ▶//author/@orcid: Selects all attributes *orcid* of any author in the document.

Listing 22 Select attributes

```
1    <?xml version="1.0" encoding="utf-8"?>
2    <book>
3      <authors>
4        <author ▶id="1" ▶▶ orcid="0000-0002-6332-5801"/>
5        <author ▶id="2" ▶▶ orcid="0000-0001-5656-6108"/>
6        <author ▶id="3" ▶▶name="Arthur_Dent"/>
7        <author ▶id="4"/>
8        <author/>
9      </authors>
10   </book>
```

Listing 23 shows XPaths that select elements based on attribute restrictions. Attributes follow the same rules as elements when used as logical expressions, so their existence can be checked, or their content can be compared.

- ▶//author[@*]: Selects all elements <author> that have any attribute (in this case, the first four authors)
- ▶//author[@orcid]: Selects all elements <author> anywhere in the document that have an attribute *orcid*
- ▶//author[not(@*)]: Selects all elements <author> anywhere in the document that do not have any attributes
- ▶//author[@name or @orcid='0000-0001-5656-6108']: Selects all elements <author> anywhere in the document that either have an attribute name or an attribute orcid with a value of "0000-0001-5656-6108"

Listing 23 Restrictions based on attributes

```
1     <?xml version="1.0" encoding="utf-8"?>
2     <book>
3        <authors>
4  ▶▶        <author id="1" orcid="0000-0002-6332-5801"/>
5  ▶▶▶       <author id="2" orcid="0000-0001-5656-6108"/>
6  ▶▶        <author id="3" name="Arthur_Dent"/>
7  ▶         <author id="4"/>
8  ▶         <author/>
9        </authors>
10    </book>
```

3.2.5   Restricting Selections: Complex Operands

As already mentioned, operands in restrictions can be complex XPaths. Listing 24 serves as the example XML document of the following XPath:

```
//section[
    length\textless 12 and
    @author=(//author[@name='Arthur Dent']/@id)
]
```

This particular XPath focuses on selecting elements `<section>` with particular authors. Each section contains an attribute `author` which contains an id. The authors identified by this id are listed in an element `<authors>`, each of them in an element `<author>`. All elements `<section>` are selected, if they contain a child element named `<length>` with a value less than 12 and if their attribute *author* references any `<author>`, which has an attribute named `name` with a value of "`Arthur Dent`."

Thus, in this case, `//section/@author` references `//author/@id`.

Listing 24 Complex restrictions

```
1     <?xml version="1.0" encoding="utf-8"?>
2     <book>
3        <chapter>
4  ▶       <section author="3">
5              <length>5</length>
6              <paragraph>dimidium</paragraph>
7              <paragraph>facti</paragraph>
8           </section>
9        </chapter>
10       <section author="2">
11          <length>14</length>
12          <paragraph/>
13       </section>
14       <authors>
15          <author id="1" orcid="0000-0002-6332-5801"/>
16          <author id="2" orcid="0000-0001-5656-6108"/>
17          <author id="3" name="Arthur_Dent"/>
18       </authors>
19    </book>
```

3.2.6   Context Nodes and Axes

Throughout this section, we will give examples based on Listing 24. The context node denotes the selected current node, based on which further restrictions (`[...]`) can be applied. In each restriction (predicate), it is possible to implicitly or explicitly refer to the context node:

Implicit - `//*[name()='section']`:   The predicate, and with it the function **name**(), is applied to every node in selected by `//*`.

Explicit - `//*[./name()='section']`:   The dot explicitly refers to the current node; thus, the function **name**() is applied to each context node from the nodeset selected by `//*`. Both predicates yield exactly the same result.

The navigation in XPaths is done along axes. As an XML document is a tree, there are several directions:

- Relative to the node: with one dot (`.`), it is possible to refer to the current node, e.g., `/book/authors/./name()` is equivalent to `/book/authors/name()`.
- Toward the parent: with two dots (`..`), it is possible to navigate to the parent, e.g., `/book/authors/..` is equivalent to `/authors`.
- Toward children: a function or name after a single slash (`/`) refers to children of the node, e.g., `/book/authors/author` refers to elements `<author>`, which are children of an element `<authors>`, `//book/authors/author/@id` refers to an attribute id of an element `<author>`, and `//book/authors/author/text()` refers to the text inside an element (also a child).
- Toward siblings on the same level of the tree, i.e., before or after the current element.

Figure 3.3 depicts a set of axes that can be used to select nodes relative to the context node. A subset of notable examples includes:

- `.` is the short form of `self::*`.
  Figure 3.3a depicts an XPath akin to `/book/chapter/self::*`.
- `..` is the short form of `parent::*`.
  Figure 3.3b depicts an XPath akin to `/book/chapter/section/parent::*`.
- `/book` is the short form of `/child::book`, i.e., book is a child of the root node (`/`) of the document.
  Figure 3.3c depicts an XPath akin to `/book/chapter/child::*`.
- `//section` is the short form of `/descendant-or-self::*/child::section`.
  Figure 3.3g depicts an XPath akin to `/book/chapter/descendant-or-self::*`.
- An additional axis attribute exists, `@id`, which is the short form of `attribute::id`. Thus accessing an attribute author in our running example

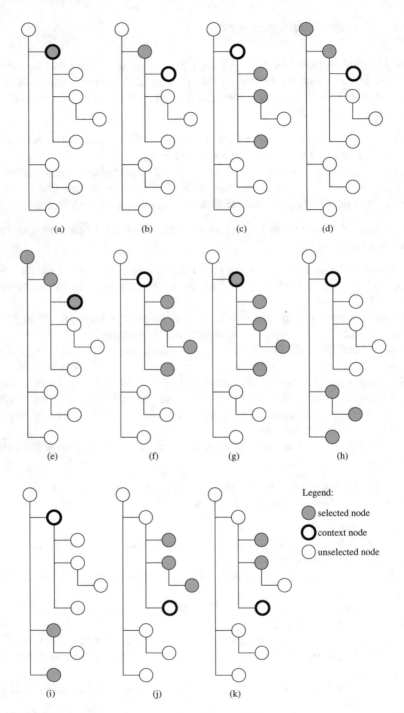

Fig. 3.3 XPath axes. (**a**) Self. (**b**) Parent. (**c**) Child. (**d**) Ancestor. (**e**) Ancestor-or-self. (**f**) Descendant. (**g**) Descendant-or-self. (**h**) Following. (**i**) Following-sibling. (**j**) Preceding. (**k**) Preceding-sibling

could be achieved by an XPath akin to `/book/chapter/section/attribute::author`, which is equivalent to `/book/chapter/section/@author`.

- An additional axis namespace exists, which allows to differentiate between nodes having different namespaces.

It has to be noted that the above examples often use `::*`. If `::node()` is used instead, not just children are selected but actually children, text nodes, and even comments. For example, `//section/length/child::node()` selects the text content of the element, while `//section/length/child::*` does not.

Another important remark centers around the ordering of nodes. When the **preceding** and **preceding-sibling** axes are used, the nodes can only be addressed in reverse order. Thus, `//authors/author[last()]/preceding-sibling::*[1]` in Listing 25 yields ▶, as the nodes are traversed from the context of `//authors/author[last()]/`. The overall nodeset returned by the XPath has the order as seen from the root node; thus, when putting the XPath into brackets, the result is different: `//authors/author[last()]/preceding-sibling::*[1]` in Listing 25 yields ▶.

Listing 25 Select attributes

```
1    <?xml version="1.0" encoding="utf-8"?>
2    <book>
3      <authors>
4  ▶     <author id="1" orcid="0000-0002-6332-5801"/>
5  ▶     <author id="2" orcid="0000-0001-5656-6108"/>
6        <author id="3" name="Arthur_Dent"/>
7        <author/>
8      </authors>
9    </book>
```

3.2.7 Unification of Results

Multiple XPaths can be combined with the pipe character (|) to unify the resulting nodesets. Like the term "set" in "nodeset" promises, unified nodesets will not contain the same node twice. Listing 26 shows a unification example (see XPath in caption).

Listing 26 //section[@author=2] | //section[@author=3]

```
1    <?xml version="1.0" encoding="utf-8"?>
2    <book>
3      <chapter>
4   ▶    <section author="3">
5          <length>5</length>
6          <paragraph>dimidium</paragraph>
7          <paragraph>facti</paragraph>
8        </section>
9      </chapter>
10  ▶   <section author="2">
11        <length>14</length>
12        <paragraph/>
13      </section>
14      <authors>
15        <author id="1" orcid="0000-0002-6332-5801"/>
16        <author id="2" orcid="0000-0001-5656-6108"/>
17        <author id="3" name="Arthur_Dent"/>
18      </authors>
19    </book>
```

3.2.8   XPath Functions

There exists a wide array of functions that can be used as part of XPaths. Every subsequent version of the XPath standard (version 3 as of 2023) adds new functions. In this section, the most common function and their usage will be discussed.[3]

Listing 27 XPath functions

```
1    <?xml version="1.0" encoding="utf-8"?>
2    <book>
3   ▶   <section author="2">
4         <length>0</length>
5         <paragraph/>
6       </section>
7       <chapter>
8   ▶      <section author="3">
9            <paragraph>dimidium</paragraph>
10           <paragraph>facti</paragraph>
11         </section>
12       </chapter>
13       <authors>
14         <author id="1" orcid="0000-0002-6332-5801"/>
15         <author id="2" orcid="0000-0001-5656-6108"/>
16  ▶      <author id="3" name="Arthur_Dent"/>
17       </authors>
18     </book>
```

- **last() : number**—returns the number of siblings in the current context, e.g., `//section[last()]`.
- **position() : number**—returns the index of a node among its siblings. As discussed above, the first node has the index 1. `//section[position()=2]`, for example, returns all elements `<section>` in a document, which are the second sibling in context to their respective parent and **NOT** the second section in the document. So for Listing 27, nothing is selected.

---

[3] Some functions have been used throughout this chapter already.

- **count(nodeset) : number**—returns the number of nodes in a nodeset.
    count(//section), for example, returns 2, and //section[count(*)=2] returns ▶ for Listing 27.
- **name(nodeset) : string**—returns the name of the first element or attribute if a nodeset is provided as a parameter. If no nodeset is given, it returns the name of the context node. name(//section), for example, returns the value "**section**"; if used in the context of a predicate such as //section[name()='section'], it will return the name of the context node, which can then be compared to another XPath or static string.
- **number(nodeset) : number**—returns the numerical representation of the first node in the nodeset. If the first node is an element or attribute, it tries to convert their text content. If the first entry in the nodeset refers to a text node, it directly tries to convert it. The result of the conversion can be a number or the value NaN (not a number).
- **string(nodeset) : string**—returns the string representation of the first node in the nodeset. If the first node is an element or attribute, it returns their text content; if the first entry in the nodeset refers to a text node, it directly returns it. If no text is found, it always returns an empty string.

A second group of functions specializes in Boolean values. The function boolean(object) : boolean operates on different objects:

- If object is a non-empty nodeset, boolean() returns true.
    boolean(//section/length), for example, returns **true** for Listing 27, as two <length> elements are in the nodeset.
- If object is a number, boolean() returns true for nonzero numbers.
    boolean(number(//section/length)), for example, returns **false** for Listing 27, as the content of the first selected length is **0**.
- If object is a string, boolean() returns true for nonzero length strings.
    boolean(string(//section/paragraph)), for example, returns **false** for Listing 27, as the content of the first selected element <paragraph> is empty.

The not(boolean) : boolean function on the other hand, is very simple, and just negates Boolean values. This is especially useful when checking the (non-)existence of nodes or when checking if nodesets are empty.
    //section[not(length)], for example, selects ▶ as, as the child length does not exist.

A final class of function deals with strings, as XML documents typically contain texts in attributes and many elements.

- **concat(string,string,...) : string**—combines all provided strings.
    section[concat('a',string(@author) = 'a3'], for example, selects ▶ for Listing 27.
- **starts-with(string,string) : boolean**—checks if the first string starts with the second.

`//author[starts-with(@name,'A']`, for example, selects ▶ for Listing 27.

- **contains(string,string) : boolean**—checks if the second string is contained in the first.

   `//author[contains(@name,'Dent']`, for example, selects ▶ for Listing 27.

- **substring(string,number,number) : string**—extracts a substring starting from the first number argument, with a length equal to the second number argument.

   `substring(//author/@name,8,4)`, for example, returns the value **"Dent."**

3.3   XSLT

The purpose of the extensible Stylesheet Language (XSL)[4] is to transform or present an XML document on different devices such as printers and screens (for humans), as well as for consumption by other software.

XSL consists of three main tools:

- **XPath** ... Navigation in XML Documents
- **XSLT** (XSL Transformation) ... transforming documents
- **XSL-FO** (XSL Formatting Objects) ... device independent formatting (similar to CSS for HTML but much more powerful, as e.g., PDF generation can be targeted)

XSLT, being the main focus of this section, is about transforming XML documents into different documents, including different XML documents, HTML, or just plain text documents. XSLT can only be used on XML source documents, and it utilizes XPath to navigate in XML documents. Transformation can encompass selection, reordering, filtering, and addition from different sources (i.e., XLink & Include). Applications include:

- Ensuring correct data input or data output for interoperability scenarios (e.g., a piece of code/Web service might require a certain XML input format or is required to produce a certain output format).
- Transforming XML into a HTML webpage (e.g., as part of content management systems or in the publishing industry).

XSLT is widely in use. In 2023, it is #61 of the most used programming languages on Github,[5] and as data-model-specific programming language, it is on par with SQL regarding usage. XSLT is in the special group of declarative languages, meaning it is defined as a set of rules called templates. It is inspired

---

[4] https://www.w3.org/Style/XSL.

[5] https://github.com/oprogramador/github-languages, last accessed 2023-06-01.

Fig. 3.4 XSLT processor

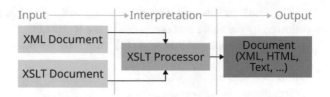

by functional concepts, where the templates are functions and produce some output, and can contain/call each other.

Although multiple versions of XSLT exist (V1.x to V3.x) with ever-expanding functionality, in this section, we will focus on the basic concepts that are the foundation of all versions.

XSLT is interpreted by an XSLT processor, as depicted in Fig. 3.4, creating output from an XML source and XSLT document. The XSLT processor, after loading all the templates, traverses the source tree, matches templates (which have associated XPaths) to the current position, and collects the output generated by the templates.

A desired transformation from source to target is depicted in Listing 28. The XML source (Lines 1–4) is to be transformed into an XHTML document (Lines 8–16).

Listing 28 Initial example, source and target

```
1    <book name="InterOp"> (1)
2        <chapter number="1">Intro</chapter> (2)
3        <chapter number="2">XSLT</chapter> (3)
4    </book> (1)
5
6        ↘
7
8        <html>
9            <head>
10               <title>InterOp – The Book</title>
11           </head>
12           <body>                                    (1)
13               <h1>Intro</h1> (2)
14               <h2>XSLT</h2> (3)
15           </body>
16       </html>    (1)
```

In the case of Listing 28, two templates are used. One realizes (1), and the second realizes (2) and (3). Listing 29 shows the first template (denoted as T1 in the following). T1(1) shows the element `<template>`, including an attribute `match` that contains an XPath T1(2) matching the root element (`<book>`) of the source document. Only if the source document contains root element `<book>` the template matches, and the contents of the template are considered for the output. The template T1(1) contains the fundamental `<html>` structure of the target. As the `<html>` is intended to hold the content of attribute `name` from the source document, the template contains a `<value-of>` element, which has the purpose to select and output its text content. The particular XPath T1(2) (in this case `@name`) operates relative to the path selected by the template.

The result of this selection as depicted in Listing 28, Line 10, is "InterOp," followed by the static text contained in the template: " - The Book."

It becomes apparent that all T1(2) values are XPaths.

Listing 29   Initial example, template 1

```
1   <xsl:template match="book"> (1)
2     <html> (3)              (2)
3       <head>
4         <title><xsl:value-of select="@name"/> - The Book</title>
5       </head>                         (2)  (5)
6       <body>
7         <xsl:apply-templates select="chapter"/>
8       </body>                     (2)   (4)
9     </html> (3)
10  </xsl:template> (1)
```

The `<apply-templates>` contained in T1(4) is the final important piece. It allows the second template to be recursively applied. Please note that the XPath "chapters" does not select one chapter from the source document but both chapters (see Listing 28 Lines 2 and 3). Thus, the second template is applied twice.

The second template is depicted in Listing 30, denoted as T2 in the following. Again element `<template>` contains an attribute `match` that contains an XPath T2(2), matching the chapters. In this case, the `<apply-templates>` T1(4) `select` attribute T1(2) has to be identical with the attribute match T2(2) of `<template>` T2(1). If the `<apply-templates>` T1(4) does not contain the attribute `select`, the XSLT processor would traverse the children of `<book>` recursively in the source document, checking if any template might match. However, as the attribute `select` is present, it can directly jump to the matching template (and it will only apply matching templates).

Listing 30   Initial example, template 2

```
1   <xsl:template match="chapter"> (1)
2       <h1><xsl:value-of select="text()"/></h1>
3   </xsl:template> (1)          (2)   (3)
```

T1(3) shows another `<value-of>` element, which serves the same purpose as before: it selects something and writes it in the target document, in this case inside the `<h1>`. The result can be seen in Listing 28, Lines 13 + 14.

3.3.1   Stylesheet Declaration

A XSLT stylesheet is itself an XML document and uses the namespace http://www.w3.org/1999/XSL/Transform. A basic stylesheet is depicted in Listing 31. The namespace is prefixed as **xsl:**, which was also used in the previous examples. It is important to use a special namespace to differentiate between XSLT-related "commands" and XML elements, which are just intended for the target document (such as `<h1>` in the example above).

Listing 31 XSLT declaration

```
1 <?xml version="1.0" encoding="utf-8"?>
2 <xsl:stylesheet version="1.0"
3    xmlns:xsl="http://www.w3.org/1999/XSL/Transform">
4      <!-- templates go here -->
5 </xsl:stylesheet>
```

3.3.2 Templates

As already described, the XSLT processor traverses the XML source file recursively starting with the root element and looks for templates that match these elements. If a matching template is found, it will be applied (and the children of the matching element will not be further traversed automatically).

The rules for template selection are quite complicated. Thus, it is advisable to follow the following tips when creating an XSLT file:

- Define a template for the root element.
- Control the application of further templates from this element.

In the example depicted in Listing 32, the template (2) matches the root element `<book>` (1) and outputs the value of an attribute selected with `<value-of>` (3). It furthermore outputs some static text (4) and the value of the child element `<chapter>` of `<book>`, also by again selecting it with `<value-of>` (5). The result in this case is plain text consisting of (3), (4), and (5).

Listing 32 Template usage

```
1    <book name="InterOp"> (1)
2       <chapter>Intro</chapter>
3    </book> (1)
4
5           ↘
6
7           <xsl:template match="/book"> (2)
8              <xsl:value-of select="@name"/> (3)
9              The first chapter is named: <xsl:value-of select="chapter"/> (5)
10          </xsl:template> (2)                        (4)
11
12               ↘
13
14              InterOp (3)
15              The first chapter is named: Intro
                                        (4)        (5)
```

3.3.3   Default Templates

The XSLT processor relies on some implicit/unseen templates, which are used when no templates are specified or when these specific templates are not overridden. The behavior of this templates is as follows:

- **Element:** Apply the default template for the root element and all of its children recursively.
- **Texts inside elements:** Copy them to output.
- **Attributes:** Ignore them.

Listing 33 depicts the behavior of the unseen templates. Although the root element is not explicitly mentioned in a template, its children are recursively traversed. When template (1) matches a particular `<chapter>`, its contents (3) are copied to the output. However, (4) being the text content of the remaining chapter also occurs in the output, although it has never been selected by any provided template. It appears because the unseen default template, which matches all elements, does its job.

As mentioned before, as soon as a template matches a particular element, there is no more automatic recursive traversal of the children of this element. As the function `text()` only selects the text inside the matched element,[6] and the element % in the first chapter is no longer traversed, the text "Good chapter" does not occur in the output.

Listing 33 Templates and default templates

```
1    <book name="InterOp">
2        <chapter id="1">Intro<comment>Good chapter</comment></chapter>  (1)
3        <chapter id="x">XSLT</chapter>
4    </book>
5
6          ↘
7
8            <xsl:template match="chapter[@id=1]">  (1)
9                <xsl:value-of select="text()"/>  (3)
10           </xsl:template>  (1)
11
12                 ↘
13
14                   Intro  (3)
15                   XSLT  (4)
```

The implicit/unseen default templates can be seen in Listing 34, and they also are present in all previous examples.

---

[6] In contrast to ., which would select the text inside all descendants of the element, as well.

Listing 34 Implicit/unseen default templates

```
1   <xsl:template match="*|/">
2     <xsl:apply-templates/>
3   </xsl:template>
4   <xsl:template match="text()">
5     <xsl:value-of select=".">
6   </xsl:template>
```

3.3.4 Template Matching

As discussed and demonstrated before (see Listing 33), whenever a template matches a node . . .

- . . . the template will be applied
- . . . the descendants of the node are by default not traversed, thus no more templates are applied.

Thus, from the templates/elements that match, it is necessary to have a means to (manually) control the traversal of descendant nodes and thus the matching of templates. For this, the <apply-templates> function exists. However, the <apply-templates> function matches ALL templates and also the unseen default templates and can thus lead to unexpected behavior. For example, Listing 35 demonstrates the following unexpected behavior:

- The chapter names are copied to output twice?!
- The comment is in the next line, and weirdly indented?!
- And anyways: did we ever specify to insert line breaks into to output!?

Listing 35 Template matching

```
1   <book name="InterOp">
2     <chapter id="1">Intro</chapter>
3     <chapter id="x">XSLT<comment>Good chapter</comment></chapter>
4   </book>
5
6           ↘
7
8           <xsl:template match="chapter">  (1)
9             <xsl:value-of select="text()"/>  (3)
10            </apply-templates>  (4)
11          </xsl:template>  (1)
12                                                    (2)
13          <xsl:template match="comment">
14            (<xsl:value-of select="text()"/>)
15          </xsl:template>  (2)                  (6) (5)
16
17             ↘
18                   (3)      (4)
19              Intro Intro
20                (Good Chapter)
21              XSLTXSLT        (6) (5)
                (3)    (4)
```

If one considers the existence of the default templates and the context of mixed content (see introduction to XML in Sect. 2.2), the explanation for this behavior becomes straightforward:

- **chapter names twice:** the default template `<template match="text()">` and the provided template `<template match="comment">` are both matched, when `<apply-templates>` (4). The match of `text()` function leads to the insertion of the contents of `<chapter>` a second time.
- **next line and indentation:** The `<template match="comment">` has mixed content, as it contains the brackets (). Thus all whitespace becomes significant, including the newlines and spaces. In order to avoid this, the special `<text>` function can be used, to ensure that the template has only elements as children, and thus whitespace is no longer significant.

Listing 36 demonstrates a solution that delivers the expected behavior. Here, new Line (6) is an explicit character and inserted after `<apply-templates>`, which only matches `<template match="comment">` as the default `<template match="text()">` has been deactivated. The mixed content issue with `<template match="comment">` has been fixed by inserting `<text>` functions, which only contain the desired characters and whitespace.

Listing 36 Template matching improved

```
 1   <xsl:template match="text"></xsl:template> (1)
 2
 3   <xsl:template match="chapter"> (2)
 4     <xsl:value-of select="text()"/> (4)
 5     </apply-templates> (5)
 6     <xsl:text>&#xa;</xsl:text> (6)
 7   </xsl:template> (2)
 8
 9   <xsl:template match="comment"> (3)
10     <xsl:text> (</xsl:text> (7)
11     <xsl:value-of select="text()"/> (9)
12     <xsl:text>)</xsl:text> (8)
13   </xsl:template> (3)
14
15         ↘
16              (4) (7)              (8)
17         Intro  (Good  Chapter)  (6)
18         XSLT                (9)
             (4)
```

Another way of achieving the result presented in Listing 36, Lines 19–21, is demonstrated in Listing 37. Here, the `<apply-templates select="comment">` has an attribute `select` that restricts which templates are allowed to match. Thus, this solves the duplication effect, but the default/unseen template `<template match="text()">` has still to be overloaded, as we do not match for the root element, and thus the default `<template match="text()">` is called there, and the whitespace contained before and after `<chapter>` elements is inserted, leading to empty lines before and after the texts.

Listing 37 Template matching with selection

```
1   <xsl:template match="chapter">
2     <xsl:value-of select="text()"/>
3     </apply-templates select="comment">
4     <xsl:text>&#xa;</xsl:text>
5   </xsl:template>
```

Listing 38 demonstrates a solution that uses the tips described above, mainly defining a template for the root element.

Listing 38 Template matching with reordering

```
1   <book name="InterOp">
2     <chapter id="1">
3       <title>Intro</title> (2)
4     </chapter>
5     <chapter id="x">
6       <comment>Good Chapter</comment> (3)
7       <title>XSLT</title> (2)
8       <comment>Best Chapter</comment> (3)
9     </chapter>
10  </book>
11
12      ↘
13
14      <xsl:template match="/book">
15        <xsl:apply-templates select="chapter"/> (1)
16      </xsl:template>
17
18      <xsl:template match="chapter">
19        <xsl:apply-templates select="title"/> (2)
20        <xsl:apply-templates select="comment"/> (3)
21        <xsl:text>&#xa;</xsl:text>
22      </xsl:template>
23
24      <xsl:template match="comment">
25        <xsl:text> (</xsl:text>
26        <xsl:value-of select="text()"/>
27        <xsl:text>)</xsl:text>
28      </xsl:template>
29
30      <xsl:template match="title">
31        <xsl:value-of select="text()"/>
32      </xsl:template>
33
34          ↘
35            (2)
36        Intro
37        XSLT (Good Chapter) (Best Chapter)
            (2)          (3)            (3)
```

`<apply-templates select="chapter">` (1) matches the root element, and by explicitly using `select` for (1), (2), and (3), we prohibit the matching of default templates. Furthermore, `<apply-templates select="title">` (2) and `<apply-templates select="comment">` (3) demonstrate how the output has a different order than the source document (Lines 6–8). While in the source the sequence is `comment`, `title`, and `comment`, the output needs a different order. This is achieved by matching `<title>` first (2) and only then % (3). So first the chapter names (2) are used, and only then the comments (3) are matched by the already known templates that add brackets.

A second concept to select a desired template is the attribute `mode`. In Listing 39, it can be seen that two templates with different `mode` attributes exist. In the presented case, the "**without**" is used, although both match. This allows to switch between versions with and without comments.

Listing 39 Template matching with mode

```
1    <book name="InterOp">
2      <!-- for book source XML see previous example -->
3    </book>
4
5         ↘
6
7         <xsl:template match="/book">
8           <xsl:apply-templates select="chapter" mode="without"/>(1)
9         </xsl:template>
10
11        <xsl:template match="chapter" mode="without">(1)
12          <xsl:apply-templates select="title"/>(2)
13          <xsl:text>&#xa;</xsl:text>
14        </xsl:template>
15
16        <xsl:template match="chapter" mode="with">(1)
17          <xsl:apply-templates select="title"/>
18          <xsl:apply-templates select="comment"/>
19          <xsl:text>&#xa;</xsl:text>
20        </xsl:template>
21
22        <!-- for title and comment templates see previous example -->
23
24            ↘
25                    (2)
26                 Intro
27                 XSLT
                    (2)
```

On the other hand, the mode can NOT be used to override default templates. If in Listing 39 `<apply-templates mode="without">` would be used without the `select` attribute, this does not mean that ONLY **mode="without"** templates match. Default templates without a **mode** could match as well,[7] leading again to the matching of the `<template match="text()">` default template and thus to the inclusion of spacing for the source XML document in the output. So if you override, the default template here including **mode="without"** should always have the desired effect. In contrast to that, if the **mode="with"** is removed from the second chapter template, it should nonetheless NEVER match if a mode is specified.

A final concept that can be utilized is the **priority** attribute with templates. If multiple templates match, then the one with the highest priority is selected. Internally, the XSLT processor ranks templates with priorities between -0.5 and 0.5, so manually set priorities should always be 1 or larger to ensure matches.

---

[7] There are some inconsistencies among XSLT processors. xsltproc, for example, which is included in most Linux, MacOS, and Windows (WSL) installations, behaves this way. Other processors behave differently.

3.3.5 Template Calling

Alternatively to matching a template, it is also possible to call a template explicitly. Listing 40 shows an example, of a template being called. Both the `<call-template>` and the `<template>` element (3) have to carry a **name** attribute. If a template is called, it inherits the same context node as the calling template (in this case `"/book"`). Thus, the XPath (2) utilized to copy from the source into the target document (1) has to be relative to **"/book"**.

Listing 40 Template calling

```
1    <book name="InterOp">
2      <chapter id="1">
3        <title>Intro</title> (1)
4      </chapter>
5      <chapter id="x">
6        <title>XSLT</title>
7      </chapter>
8    </book>
9
10       ↘
11
12       <xsl:template match="/book">
13         <xsl:call-template name="firstchapter"/> (3)
14       </xsl:template>
15                                    (3)
16       <xsl:template name="firstchapter">
17         <xsl:value-of select="chapter[1]/title/text()"/> (2)
18       </xsl:template>
19
20           ↘
21
22           Intro (1)
```

3.3.6 Creating XML Output

Including the already introduced `<text>` function, there are four special XML elements (XSLT functions) to create XML output:

- `<text>` just outputs verbatim text including whitespace and is utilized to avoid mixed content (i.e., producing unwanted indentation and linebreaks for formatted XSLT).
- `<element name='...'>` is used to created named XML elements. In order to avoid manually creating XML elements in the output by having to create `<`, `>`, start and end elements, `<element>` provides a convenient solution.
- `<attribute name='...'>` is utilized to create attributes for newly created named elements. As for `<element>`, the purpose is to provide convenient automatic formatting and escaping of text.
- `%` allows the simple creation of XML comments.

As stated, all of these elements are for convenience. Listing 41 demonstrates their use. From the source XML (1), (2), and (3) are copied into the target. The elements `<sects>` and `<sec>` (4) are created by utilizing the `<element>` (4) and the `<attribute>` (5) functions. Furthermore, XML comments (see Line 29) are created, which can be seen in Line 39 in the output (3). `<text>` is used twice (Line 26 and 28) to generate static text and spaces inside `<sec>` element.

Listing 41 Output creation

```
1    <book name="InterOp">
2      <chapter id="1">(1)
3        <title>Intro</title> (2)
4      </chapter>
5      <chapter id="x">(1)
6        <title>XSLT</title> (2)
7        <comment>Good Chapter</comment> (3)
8      </chapter>
9    </book>
10
11        ↘
12
13        <xsl:output method="xml" omit-xml-declaration="yes" indent="yes"/>
14
15        <xsl:template match="/book">
16          <xsl:element name="sects"> (4)
17            <xsl:apply-templates select="chapter"/>
18          </xsl:element> (4)
19        </xsl:template>
20
21        <xsl:template match="chapter">
22          <xsl:element name="sec"> (4)
23            <xsl:attribute name="num"> (5)
24              <xsl:value-of select="@id"/> (1)
25            </xsl:attribute> (5)
26            <xsl:text>Section </xsl:text>
27            <xsl:value-of select="title/text()"/> (2)
28            <xsl:text> </xsl:text>
29            <xsl:comment>
30              <xsl:value-of select="comment/text()"/> (3)
31            </xsl:comment>
32          </xsl:element> (4)
33        </xsl:template>
34
35            ↘
36                    (4)
37            <sects>       (1)              (2)
38              <sec num="1">Section Intro <!----></sec>
39              <sec num="x">Section XSLT <!--Good Chapter--></sec>
40            </sects>      (1)              (2)            (3)
                    (4)
```

Please also note the special function `<output>` inserted in Line 13. As we no longer want to produce text, but XML, the target format and its properties have to be specified. In our case, we omit the XML declaration (i.e., `<?xml version="1.0"?>`) and automatically indent (i.e., pretty print) the result.

The last available trick to simplify generation is to utilize { } inside attributes. It allows to use the result of XPath expressions. If it is necessary, for example, to use the text inside the `<title>` as the name of an output element, this could be achieved with { } as demonstrated in Listing 42 Line 30-24. The expression (1) has been inserted into the **name** attribute of the `<element>` function to achieve the desired effect. Please also note that the XML declaration is included in the output in Line 30 as we no longer require to omit the XML declaration in the `<ouptut>` element in line 12.

Listing 42 Output creation

```
 1   <book name="InterOp">
 2     <chapter id="1">
 3        <title>Intro</title>
 4     </chapter>
 5     <chapter id="x">
 6        <title>XSLT</title>
 7     </chapter>
 8   </book>
 9
10        ↘
11
12           <xsl:output method="xml" indent="yes"/>
13
14           <xsl:template match="/book">
15             <xsl:element name="s">
16               <xsl:apply-templates select="chapter"/>
17             </xsl:element>
18           </xsl:template>
19
20           <xsl:template match="chapter">      (1)
21             <xsl:element name="{title/text()}">
22               <xsl:attribute name="num">
23                 <xsl:value-of select="@id"/>
24               </xsl:attribute>
25             </xsl:element>
26           </xsl:template>
27
28                ↘
29
30               <?xml version="1.0"?>
31               <s>
32                 <Intro num="1"/>
33                 <XSLT num="x"/>
34               </s>
```

Another common usage of this approach is shown in Listing 43, demonstrating that { } can be used for string interpolation.

Listing 43 Mailto links

```
 1   <xsl:template match="person">
 2     <a href="mailto:{@email}">
 3       <xsl:value-of select="name"/>
 4     </a>
 5   </xsl:template>
```

3.3.7   Helper Functions

Despite solving everything with templates and matching, XSLT also provides more traditional functions:

- `<for-each select='...'>`: allows to iterate through the nodeset selected by an XPath context node. The context node inside `<for-each>` is the node from the current iteration of the nodeset.
- `<sort select='...' order='...'>`: can be placed inside `<for-each>` functions. When `<for-each>` selects a nodeset, the nodeset is by default in the order in which the nodes occur in the source document. Multiple `<sort>` statements can occur inside a document, in order realize different sort priorities (e.g., sort by last name; if the same last name, sort by first name).
- `<if test='...'>`: provides conditional execution of XSLT functions, thus conditionally adding to the output. There are NO `else` or `else-if` functions.
- `<choose>`, `<when test='...'>`, `<otherwise>`: provides a functionality similar to the `switch` statement in other languages. Multiple `<when>` statements can be selected, but only one `<otherwise>` can exist, and it is only selected when no `<when>` statement has been selected.

Listing 44   Output creation

```
1    <book name="InterOp">
2      <chapter id="3" length="255">
3        <title>XSLT</title>          (2)
4      </chapter>  (1)
5      <chapter id="1" length="100">
6        <title>Intro</title>
7      </chapter>
8      <chapter id="2" length="205">
9        <title>XML</title>          (2)
10     </chapter>(1)
11   </book>
12
13          ↘
14
15         <xsl:output method="text"/>
16         <xsl:template match="/book">
17           <xsl:text>Long chapters: </xsl:text>
18           <xsl:for-each select="chapter[@length>100]">
19             <xsl:value-of select="title"/>          (2)
20             <xsl:if test="position()!=last()">
21               <xsl:text>, </xsl:text>          (3)
22             </xsl:if>
23           </xsl:for-each>
24         </xsl:template>
25
26          ↘
27
28              Long chapters: XSLT, XML
                            (1) (3)  (1)
```

Listing 44 shows the usage of `<for-each>` and `<if>` to realize the creation of a list of chapters that contain all chapters (1) which are longer than 100 lines. In `<for-each>`, the attribute **select** contains an XPath (2) that selects the correct elements `chapter` based on the attribute **length** (2) in the source document. The result is a nodeset containing two nodes `<chapter>`. The content of `<for-each>` is thus invoked twice, once for each `<chapter>`. The `<value>` function first prints the contents of `<title>` (relative XPath, as the current context is `<chapter>`). After this, the `<if>` tests for the position of the node `<chapter>` in the nodelist (3). For every node that is not the last in the nodelist, a "," is added, to create a proper comma separated list. After the last node, the comma is omitted.

This time, the example includes an `<output>` function (line 15) explicitly specifying that the output is to be text.

For Listing 45, the goal is to improve upon the formatting of the list of chapters, by adding a "." (1) at the end of the output. While in Listing 44 the chapters were listed in the order in which they occurred in the source document, the goal in Listing 45 is to sort them by the attribute id contained in `<chapter>`.

Listing 45 Output creation

```
1       <chapter id="3" length="255">
2         <title>XSLT</title>
3       </chapter>
4       <chapter id="1" length="100">
5         <title>Intro</title>
6       </chapter>
7       <chapter id="2" length="205">
8         <title>XML</title>
9       </chapter>
10    </book>
11
12
13
14        <xsl:output method="text"/>
15        <xsl:template match="/book">
16          <xsl:text>Long chapters: </xsl:text>
17          <xsl:for-each select="chapter[@length>100]">
18            <xsl:sort select="@id" order="ascending"/>
19            <xsl:value-of select="title"/>
20            <xsl:choose>
21              <xsl:when test="position()!=last()">
22                <xsl:text>, </xsl:text>
23              </xsl:when>
24              <xsl:otherwise>
25                <xsl:text>.</xsl:text>
26              </xsl:otherwise>
27            </xsl:choose>
28          </xsl:for-each>
29        </xsl:template>
30
31
32
33              Long chapters: XSLT, XML. (3)
```

For this the `<sort>` function is used (Line 18) inside the `<for-each>`. The `<for-each>`, as discussed before, selects all nodes `<chapter>` from the source document. The attribute **select** (2) of `<sort>` instructs the built-in sorting algorithm to rely on the "id" attribute of each node in nodeset selected by `<for-each>`. Thus, the nodeset is reordered before the contents of `<for-each>` are invoked.

The second aspect of sorting is the order, as established by the attribute **order** (2) of `<sort>`. Order can be either "**ascending**" or "**descending**."

In the output, it can be seen that in comparison to Listing 44, in Listing 45, "XML" occurs before "XSLT."

The `<choose>` (2) contains the same condition (4) as the `<if>` in Listing 44 but inside a child element **<when>** (Line 21). But the `<choose>` also contains an `<otherwise>` (1), which is invoked when the last node in the sorted nodeset selected by `<for-each>` is reached: it inserts the dot (3) into the output at the end of the list displayed in the output.

3.3.8   Variables and Template Parameters

Like most programming languages, XSLT supports variables, which can occur in two forms:

- Global variables that are defined outside of templates and can be used in all templates.
- Local variables than can only be used within the template they have be defined.

Variables can be used in the attributes of all XSLT functions by prefixing them with a "**$**" (dollar) sign. For example:

- `<value-of select='$var'/>` writes the value of a variable into the output.
- `<for-each select='/boo/chapter[@length>$var]'/>` demonstrates the utilization of a variable in an XPath.
- `<value-of select='$a + $b'/>` demonstrates the utilization of XPath expression to concatenate strings contained in variables to calculate results, which can then be written to the output.

Variables can be defined through the function:
`<variable name='...' select='...'/>`.

Listing 46 demonstrates the use of variables to output the position of a chapter in relation to the overall number of chapters. Two global variables (1) are defined, the first named **size** containing the chapter length selection criteria. The variable **size** (2) is then used in the XPath of variable **num** to count the nodeset containing `<chapter>` elements with a length bigger than **size**. The variable **size** is then used in `<for-each>` as well, as here again we have to restrict the nodeset through the same criteria.

The output (3) containing the position information is then created using the **position**() function as well as the **num** variable.

Listing 46 Output creation

```
1     <chapter id="3" length="255">
2       <title>XSLT</title>          (2)
3     </chapter>
4     <chapter id="1" length="100">
5       <title>Intro</title>         (2)
6     </chapter>
7     <chapter id="2" length="205">
8       <title>XML</title>           (2)
9     </chapter>
10   </book>
11
12         ↘
13
14       <xsl:output method="text"/>
15
16       <xsl:variable name="size" select="100"/>
17       <xsl:variable name="num"
18                 select="count(//chapter[@length>$size])"/> (1)
19                                                        (2)
20       <xsl:template match="/book">
21         <xsl:text>Long chapters: </xsl:text>       (2)
22         <xsl:for-each select="chapter[@length>size]">
23           <xsl:sort select="@id" order="ascending"/>
24           <xsl:value-of select="title"/>
25           <xsl:text> (</xsl:text>
26           <xsl:value-of select="position()"/>
27           <xsl:text>/</xsl:text>
28           <xsl:value-of select="$num"/>
29           <xsl:text>)</xsl:text>    (1)            (3)
30           <xsl:if test="position()!=last()">
31             <xsl:text>, </xsl:text>
32           </xsl:if>
33         </xsl:for-each>
34       </xsl:template>
35
36         ↘
37
38           Long chapters: XSLT (1/2), XML (2/2) (3)
                                (3)
```

Like all functional programming languages, templates can have parameters. Templates take arbitrary parameters. In fact, a template cannot enforce the number or names of parameters it can receive. Parameters and their names are specified with `apply-templates` or `call-template`. Inside a template, parameters can be accessed like normal local variables.

Listing 47 creates the same output as Listing 46 but with parameter passing and thus a local variable **num**.

Listing 47 Output creation

```
1    <xsl:variable  name="s"  select="100"/>
2    <xsl:variable  name="n"  select="count(//chapter[@length>$s])"/>
3            .
4
5    <xsl:template  match="/">
6      <xsl:apply-templates  select="book">
7        <xsl:with-param  (1)   name="num">$n</xsl:with-param>
8        <xsl:with-param  (1)   name="size">$s</xsl:with-param>
9      </xsl:apply-templates>         (4)   (3)
10   </xsl:template>
11
12   <xsl:template  match="book">
13     <xsl:text>Long  chapters:  </xsl:text>      (4)
14     <xsl:for-each  select="chapter[@length>$size]">
15       <xsl:sort  select="@id"  order="ascending"/>
16       <xsl:value-of  select="title"/>
17       <xsl:text>  (</xsl:text>
18       <xsl:value-of  select="position()"/>
19       <xsl:text>/</xsl:text>
20       <xsl:value-of  select="$num"/>
21       <xsl:text>)</xsl:text>      (4)
22       <xsl:if  test="position()!=last()">
23         <xsl:text>,  </xsl:text>
24       </xsl:if>
25     </xsl:for-each>
26   </xsl:template>
```

The `<apply-templates>` function (Line 8) passes two parameters (1) to the template **book**. Parameters are passed through `<with-param>` inside the `<apply-templates>` (or the `<call-template>`). Two parameters named **num** and **size** (4) are passed, which are local variables inside the template **book**. They contain the values of the variables **n** and **s** (3). Again, the result should be restricted by the size of chapters (2), i.e., 100 lines.

3.4 XML Schema and RelaxNG

XML concentrates on representing data in a structured, coherent, and human-readable way. What it does not do (unlike data representation formats like JSON) is making assumptions about data types contained in its attributes and values. Furthermore, by default, the structure of an XML document is not pre-determined or defined: every element can contain arbitrarily named other elements and attributes (e.g., JSON by default can contain arbitrary keys and values).

It is considered the job of the application using the XML to check if the certain data representation can be processed by the application logic or if the application logic does not want to try, because the faulty XML will just lead to errors (see Fig. 3.5).

Describing the structure and data types contained in an XML is called describing the **schema** of the file. For the purpose of checking the schema of an XML, multiple

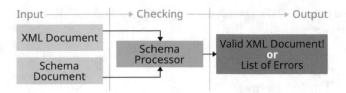

Fig. 3.5 XSLT processor

languages have been developed, and the most prominent are XML Schema and Relax NG. Both languages provide the ability to describe:

- Which elements are contained in an XML document.
- Which attributes are contained in an XML document.
- The association of attributes to elements.
- The nesting of elements.
- The order of elements.
- The number of elements.
- If elements or attributes are empty or contain values.
- Datatype for elements or attributes containing values.
- Default values for elements or attributes.

XML Schema (XS) is a W3C standard[8] and the older and more widely used of the two standards. The **Regular Language Description for XML New Generation** (RELAX NG, RNG) is an ISO/OASIS standard[9] and is younger, simpler, more powerful, better human-readable, and arguably better in all aspects than XS.

XS is written in XML, while RNG can be written in XML or in "Compact Syntax." For the purpose of this book, we will concentrate only on the XML syntax and convey both the similarities and differences of both languages.

While there is a standardized way of linking to an associated XS in an XML file, for RNG, there is no such mechanism. As depicted in Listing 48), first a namespace "http://www.w3.org/2001/XMLSchema-instance" with the identifier **xsi** has to be defined, and then with the attribute name **noNamespaceSchemaLocation**, the schema named **"book.xsd"** can be referenced.

Listing 48 Include XS in XML

```
1   <book xmlns:xsi="http://www.w3.org/2001/XMLSchema-instance"
2         xsi:noNamespaceSchemaLocation="book.xsd"           >
3      InterOp
4   </book>*@
```

Is this a disadvantage of RNG? Not necessarily: as application logic has to understand the structure of the XML in order to extract the correct data, most of the time, the schema is available to the application logic and tested when the XML

---

[8] http://www.w3.org/XML/Schema.

[9] ISO/IEC 19757-2, OASIS http://relaxng.org/.

is received (see Fig. 3.5), instead of being included in the XML (where it could be changed by the sender).

3.4.1 A Basic Schema

Listing 49 shows a simple source document (Line 1), just consisting of the element <book>, followed by basic XS and RNG definitions. While the root element for an XS is <schema>, a RNG typically uses <grammar>. Both use different namespaces. In RNG, additionally, an attribute datatypeLibrary is present. RNG has no built-in data types but instead reuses the data types defined for XS.

Listing 49 Basic schema structure

```
1    <book>InterOp</book>

        ↓ XS

2    <schema xmlns="http://www.w3.org/2001/XMLSchema">
3      <element name="book" type="string"/>
4    </schema>

        ↓ RNG

5    <grammar
6        xmlns="http://relaxng.org/ns/structure/1.0"
7        datatypeLibrary="http://www.w3.org/2001/XMLSchema-datatypes">
8      <start>
9        <element name="book">
10         <data type="string"/>
11       </element>
12     </start>
13   </grammar>
```

For XS, the <element> inside <schema> describes the root element of the document. It has a **name** and optionally a **type**.

An RNG <grammar> has to contain an element <start>, which in turn contains an <element> that describes the root element of the document. As for XS element has a **name**. The datatype is not defined as an attribute of <element> but in the form of a separate child element named <data>, which has an attribute **type**. As already mentioned, the RNG **type** always has the same value as its RNG counterpart, as the data types are shared between both languages.

At first glance, RNG seems more verbose and complicated than XS, but the initially higher structuredness will later on provide a strong foundation for simplified description of XML documents (see below).

3.4.2 Fixed and Default Values

As already discussed above, an element can either be required to have a value adhering to a certain data type definition (string, integer, float, date, or Boolean), or a fixed string can be defined.

Listing 50 Fixed values

```
1    <book>InterOp</book>
```

↓ **XS**

```
2    <element name="book" type="string" fixed="InterOp"/>
```

↓ **RNG**

```
3    <element name="book">
4      <choice>
5        <value>InterOp</value>
6      </choice>
7    </element>
```

In Listing 50, it becomes apparent that the mechanism for RNG is more flexible, as it readily allows for a set of fixed values by just adding `<value>`'s. For XS, a more complex path has to be pursued to achieve this, which will be discussed in subsequent sections.

The difference between a fixed value and a default value is simple: a fixed value has to be present, while a default value is used when the value is empty. So in the example presented in Listing 50, whenever in the XML document (Line 1) the value **InterOp** is changed to something different, the document is no longer compliant.

Listing 51 shows the implementation of default values for both schema languages.

Listing 51 Default values

```
1    <book></book>
```

↓ **XS**

```
2    <element name="book" type="string" default="InterOp"/>
```

↓ **RNG**

```
3    <element name="book"
4        xmlns:a="http://relaxng.org/ns/compatibility/annotations/1.0"
5        a:defaultValue="InterOp"/>
```

RNG by default does not support default values but instead relies on compatibility annotations (namespace) to provide information about default values. Both schema languages support setting default values for attributes and elements.

3.4.3 Attributes

Attributes are the second staple of XML besides element. For the definition of attributes, the difference in complexity between the two languages suddenly becomes clear. Listing 52 demonstrates the two approaches. XS operates based on data types, which have to be defined by the author. Thus, we had to introduce a namespace XS (instead of the default namespace) so that we can differentiate between standard data types (e.g., `xs:string`) and self-defined data types (e.g., `<complexType>` **booktype**). The following ways of defining types exist:

- `<simpleType>` for elements with no attributes and no child elements but content with a custom data type.
- `<complexType>` for elements with attributes and/or child elements and/or mixed content.

For a `<complexType>`, two different variations are possible:

- `<simpleContent>` for elements with attributes and no child elements but content with a custom datatype.
- `<complexContent>` for elements with attributes, child elements, and/or mixed content.

More details regarding `<extension>`, which is contained in `<simpleContent>`, will be given in subsequent chapters.

In contrast, the RNG approach (Listing 52, lines) is much simpler. An arbitrary number of `<attribute>` elements can exist inside `<element>`'s. Both `<attribute>` and `<element>` can contain on `<data>` element.

It becomes clear that for most basic concepts contained in an XML source, a simple to understand, readable, and consistent version can be produced by humans with a simple text editor. XS on the other hand, with its focus on data types with combinations of `<...Type>` and `<...Content>`, is hard to create without proper tool support (i.e., specialized XML toolchains; see subsequent sections).

A special topic is lists: attributes might contain multiple values, separated by space. Both languages support this through a `<list>` element. An example for restricting a list to a length of three integers is shown in Listing 53.

3.4.4 Modularity

XS relies mostly on data types and references to these data types (see previous section) for modularity. RNG, on the other hand, has much more generic support for reuse: `<define>` and `<ref>`. Its purpose is to serve as an envelope for arbitrary concepts, such as `<element>`, `<attributes>`, or `<data>` elements. Thus, it becomes simple to reuse the content of elements (i.e., attributes, child elements, data types), without additional complexity (see Listing 54).

Listing 52 Attributes

```
1    <book name=" InterOp "/>
```

↓ **XS**

```
2    <schema xmlns:xs=" http: //www.w3. org /2001/XMLSchema">
3      <xs:element name="book" type=" booktype "/>
4      <xs:complexType name=" booktype ">
5        <xs:simpleContent>
6          <xs:extension base=" xs:string ">
7            <xs:attribute name="name" type=" xs:string " name="name"/>
8          </ xs:extension>
9        </ xs:simpleContent>
10     </ xs:complexType>
11   </ schema>
```

↓ **RNG**

```
12   <grammar
13       xmlns=" http: // relaxng . org / ns / structure /1.0 "
14       datatypeLibrary=" http: //www.w3. org /2001/XMLSchema–datatypes ">
15     <start>
16       <element name="book">
17         <attribute name="name">
18           <data type=" string "/>
19         </ attribute>
20         <data type=" string "/>
21       </ element>
22     </ start>
23   </ grammar>
```

Each <define> has to occur as a child element for <grammar>. It has an attribute **name**, which also occurs at the <ref>. References can be recursive, i.e., <define> might <ref> itself or <ref> things that in turn <ref> it.

For XS, an additional modularity mechanism exists (which is not needed for RNG, as it is modularity is much for flexible), i.e., elements <attributeGroup name=" ... ">. With this mechanism, sets of attributes can be referenced and do not have to be defined over and over again.

3.4.5   Data Types

Restricting data types is an important part of describing valid documents and furthermore enforcing them. As RNG reuses the XS data types, they are very similar in this regard. The most commonly used data types are listed in Table 3.1. A variety of other (derived) data types exist.

Table 3.1 Regular expression basics

string	...	"..."
QName	...	valid namespace prefix + colon (:) + valid XML element name
boolean	...	true, false, 1, 0
anyURI	...	RFC 2396
decimal	...	-1.2, 23.9984, +10.0, 245
float, double	...	-1E4, 1234.4321E12, 12.7e-2A
dateTime	...	year, month, day, hours, minutes, seconds, timezone in the format YYYY-MM-DDTHH:MM:SS±HH:MM; trailing elements can be omitted, so YYYY-MM-DD is valid, but can then not include seconds without also including the elements before.
time	...	only the time part as specified above
date	...	only the date part as specified above
duration	...	in the format P.Y.M.D.TH.M.S, e.g., "P1Y2MT4H3S" means 1 year, 2 months, 4 hours, and 3 seconds
gYearMonth	...	only the year and month as specified above
gYear	...	only the year as specified above
gMonth	...	only the month in the format –MM–
gMonthDay	...	only the month and day in the format –MM-DD
gDay	...	only the day in the format —DD

Both solutions presented in Listing 56 reuse the same terminology for restricting integers to a range of values: **minInclusive/minExclusive** and **maxInclusive/maxExclusive**. While for XS, they have to be placed in a `<restriction>` inside a `<simpleType>` (or `simpleContent` for that matter); for RNG, they are just placed as `<params>` elements inside the `<data>` (see lines 11, 12).

Listing 53 Lists

```
1   <book chapters="1␣2␣3"/>
```

          ↓ **XS**

```
2   <xs:element name="book">
3     <xs:complexType>
4       <xs:attribute name="chapters">
5         <xs:simpleType>
6           <xs:restriction base="chapterlist">
7             <xs:length value="3"/>
8           </xs:restriction>
9         </xs:simpleType>
10      </xs:attribute>
11    </xs:complexType>
12  </xs:element>
13  <xs:simpleType name="chapterlist">
14    <xs:list itemType="xs:integer"/>
15  </xs:simpleType>
```

          ↓ **RNG**

```
16  <element name="person">
17    <attribute name="chapters">
18      <list>
19        <data type="integer"/>
20        <data type="integer"/>
21        <data type="integer"/>
22      </list>
23    </attribute>
24  </element>
```

Listing 54 Reuse

```
1   <book name="InterOp"/>
```

          ↓ **RNG**

```
2   <define name="booktype">
3     <attribute name="name"><data type="string"/></attribute>
4     <data type="string"/>
5   </define>
6   <start>
7     <element name="book">
8       <ref name="booktype"/>
9     </element>
10  </start>
```

The following restrictions are allowed:

- **enumeration:** List of allowed values for almost all data types (although often used for xs:string). This is similar in RNG to the <choice> solution presented in Listing 50 but less flexible as <choice> might combine <value> and additional <data> elements, to combine fixed values and restrictions on integers together. Nonetheless, the **enumeration** restriction should work for both, XS and RNG, and should look like this (XS syntax):

Listing 55 Attribute groups

```
1    <book id ="270777" name="InterOp"/>

     ↓ XS

2    <schema xmlns:xs="http://www.w3.org/2001/XMLSchema">
3      <xs:element name="book" type="booktype"/>
4      <xs:complexType name="booktype">
5        <xs:simpleContent>
6          <xs:extension base="xs:string">
7            <xs:attributeGroup ref="common"/>
8          </xs:extension>
9        </xs:simpleContent>
10     </xs:complexType>
11     <xs:attributeGroup name="common">
12       <xs:attribute name="id" type="xs:integer"/>
13       <xs:attribute name="name" type="xs:string"/>
14     </xs:attributeGroup>
15   </schema>
```

Listing 56 Default values

```
1    <book><pages>25</pages></book>

     ↓ XS

2    <xs:simpleType name="booktype">
3      <xs:restriction base="xs:integer">
4        <xs:minInclusive value="18"/>
5        <xs:maxExclusive value="99"/>
6      </xs:restriction>
7    </xs:simpleType>
8    <xs:element name="book" type="booktype"/>

     ↓ RNG

9    <define name="booktype">
10     <data type="integer">
11       <param name="minInclusive">18<param/>
12       <param name="maxExclusive">99<param/>
13     </data>
14   </define>
15   <element name="book">
16     <ref name="booktype">
17   </element>
```

Listing 57 Default values

```
1        <xs:restriction base="xs:string">
2          <xs:enumeration value="InterOp"/>
3          <xs:enumeration value="InterOperability"/>
4          <xs:enumeration value="Inter␣Operability"/>
5        </xs:restriction>
```

- **totalDigits:** The exact number of digits in a `xs:decimal` data type. This includes the digits, before and after the fraction character (dot), e.g., 5 for 1.2345. This restriction also works for `xs:integer`, `xs:byte` and other data types where it makes sense.
- **fractionDigits:** The maximum number of fraction digits for `xs:decimal` data type. For the example above (1.2345), the **fractionDigit** would be 4.
- **length:** The number of characters for `xs:string` data types or elements in `xs:list`. It also is applicable for binary, entity, name, and ID types.

- **maxLength, minLength:** Upper and lower limits for lengths, as defined above.
- **maxExclusive, maxInclusive, minExclusive, minInclusive:** Upper and lower limits for almost all data types, i.e., numbers, dates, and times.
- **whiteSpace:** How whitespace is handled in `xs:string` data types and sub-data types. It can have one of three values:

  - preserve (keep them all)
  - replace (replace them all with spaces)
  - collapse (replace all consecutive whitespace with one space, e.g., like in HTML)

- **pattern:** regular expressions. This works for number as well as string data types and is, for example, used instead of the totalDigit/fractionDigit combo.

Especially the **pattern** extension is very widely used and relies on its own flavor of regular expression (see Table 3.2).

Table 3.2 Regular expression basics

[abc]	. . .	characters Class (character can be a, b or c)
[^abc]	. . .	negative Character Class (everything except a,b,c)
*	. . .	match 0 or more times
+	. . .	match 1 or more times
?	. . .	match 1 or 0 times
{n}	. . .	match exactly n times
{n,}	. . .	match at least n times
{n,m}	. . .	match at least n but not more than m times
.	. . .	match any character
\w	. . .	match a "word" character (alphanumeric plus "_")
\W	. . .	match a non-word character
\d	. . .	match a digit character
\D	. . .	match a non-digit character
\.	. . .	escape a character with a special Meaning (., +, *, ?, . . .)
[^@]+	. . .	match any character that is not a @ 1 or more times
@	. . .	match exactly a @
[^.]+	. . .	match any character that is not a . 1 or more times
\.	. . .	match exactly a .
.+	. . .	match any character 1 or more times

3.4.6 Sequences of Elements

If an element is supposed to contain text as well as elements, the approaches are
different in the two languages. While in XS a **complexType** with the attribute **mixed**
is used, RNG just defines a data type and the elements nested inside the element
that should contain text and elements, as shown in Listing 58. Of course, the same
could again be done by employing `modularity concepts`, as described in the
previous section.

For RNG, the order in which `<elements>` occur directly affects the order in
which they are expected to occur in the XML source document.

Listing 58 Default values

```
1    <book>A detailed book about <strong>InterOp</strong> topics</book>

        ↓ XS

2    <xs:element name="book">
3      <xs:complextype mixed="true">
4        <xs:sequence>
5          <element name="strong" type="xs:string"/>
6        </xs:sequence>
7      </xs:complexType>
8    </xs:element>

        ↓ RNG

9    <element name="book">
10     <element name="strong"><data type="string"></element>
11     <data type="string">
12   </element>
```

So if for both versions additional elements are added, they have to exactly occur
in this order, exactly once. The `exactly once` condition can be circumvented:
in XS by adding **minOccurs** and **maxOccurs** attributes to the element and in RNG
by surrounding the elements by `<zeroOrMore>` or `<oneOrMore>`.

Again, the RNG solution is easily more flexible, because it can be utilized with
one or multiple elements inside. In XS, in order to repeat multiple elements in a
particular order (e.g., ABAB), the **minOccurs** and **maxOccurs** attributes can also
be added at to the `<sequence>` element.

An example of the different approaches is shown in Listing 59.

Listing 59 Sequences

```
 1   <book>
 2     <author>Stefanie</author><chapter>1</chapter>
 3     <author>Juergen</author><chapter>2</chapter>
 4   </book>
```

↓ **XS**

```
 5   <xs:element name="book">
 6     <xs:complextype>
 7       <xs:sequence minOccurs="1" maxOccurs="unbounded">
 8         <element name="author" type="xs:string"/>
 9         <element name="chapter" type="xs:string"/>
10       </xs:sequence>
11     </xs:complexType>
12   </xs:element>
```

↓ **RNG**

```
13   <element name="book">
14     <zeroOrMore>
15       <element name="author"><data type="string"></element>
16       <element name="chapter"><data type="string"></element>
17     </zeroOrMore>
18   </element>
```

Sometimes, such as in the example in Listing 59, it is important that the sequence of elements is fixed; in the example case, the elements **<author>** and **<chapter>** should always alternate in order to show which authors contributed to which chapter.

For the given example, each element must occur exactly once (or in XS terms: minOccurs='1' and maxOccurs='1'). For XS, the **minOccurs** and **maxOccurs** attributes at the element <author> could be used to express that multiple authors are allowed. For example, minOccurs='1' and maxOccurs='unbounded' can be used to express that one or more authors are allowed, which then are always followed by one element <chapter>. The same can be achieved in RNG by additionally wrapping the element <author> in an element <oneOrMore>. Again, we can conclude that RNG achieves the goals of a source document designer, with less constructs and in a more flexible and better understandable way.

But what if the order of elements is not important? For this, both languages provide different constructs: XS provides <all>, which replaces <sequence> in the examples above, and RNG provides <interleave>, which can wrap any number of elements.[10]

---

[10] It does not make sense that interleave is used for <attribute> elements, as the order of attributes is always non-deterministic, as per the XML standard.

3.4.7   Optional Elements

Making elements and attributes optional can be achieved in different ways. In RNG
wrapping, an `<element>` or `<attribute>` in a `<zeroOrMore>` element (as
already introduced before) can achieve this feat.

But what if an element is to appear exactly zero or one time, which corresponds to the definition of optional. In XS, this requires `minOccurs='0'` and
`maxOccurs='1'`. In RNG, an extra element **`<optional>`** exists, which can be
used to wrap any `<element>` or `<attribute>`.

For XS `<attribute>` elements, there exists the possibility to add the attribute
`use='optional'` (in contrast to `use='required'`, which is the default).

Both approaches of course work when elements have nested content inside.

3.4.8   Choices

Sometimes, it is useful to restrict a document to contain either one element or
another. For this case, both XS and RNG contain the `<choice>` element, which
works similar: one of the child elements of `<choice>` has to be present in the
source document.

For XS, the `<choice>` element has to be contained inside a `<complexType>`,
`<sequence>`, `<simpleContent>`, or `<complexContent>`. Elements might
have different sets of attributes (defined by own types as described above).

RNG again excels with simplicity. Any combination of `<element>`,
`<attribute>`, or even **datatypes** (see below) can be wrapped by `<choice>`.

3.4.9   Unions

In addition to specify data types (with optional restrictions) for single elements, it
is also handy to specify unions of data types, e.g., an element could contain strings
or integers. As can be seen in Listing 60, both languages follow their respective
approaches. While XS allows the definition of `<simpleType>` elements to be
combined with a `<union>` element, RNG follows the much simpler path of reusing
the `<choice>` element and just defining different elements with different data
types, of which one has to match the source document.

Please be aware that XS unions are only allowed inside `<simpleType>`
elements. Therefore, unions are restricted to only a handful of use cases. Some
people prefer to utilize the `<choice>` approach even for XS (analogous to RNG),
although for XS, that leads to much worse performance than unions.

The RNG approach in this case again is more straightforward, produces less
overhead, and is easier to understand by humans.

Listing 60 Unions

```
1  <book>
2    <chapter><title >Cl</ title ><length>512</length></ chapter>
3    <chapter><title >C3</ title ><length>not finished</length></ chapter>
4  </ book>
```

↓ XS

```
5  <xs:simpleType name="expression">
6    <xs:union memberTypes="words_not"/>
7  </ xs:simpleType>
8  <xs:simpleType name="words">
9    <xs:restriction base="xs:integer">
10     <xs:minInclusive value="0"/><xs:maxInclusive value="800"/>
11   </ xs:restriction>
12 </ xs:simpleType>
13 <xs:simpleType name="not">
14   <xs:restriction base="xs:string">
15     <xs:enumeration value="not_finished"/>
16   </ xs:restriction>
17 </ xs:simpleType>
18 <xs:element name="book">
19   <xs:complexType>
20     <xs:sequence maxOccurs="unbounded">
21       <xs:element name="chapter">
22       <xs:complexType>
23         <xs:sequence maxOccurs="unbounded">
24           <element name="title" type="xs:string"/>
25           <element name="length" type="expression"/>
26         </ xs:sequence>
27       </ xs:complexType>
28       </ xs:sequence>
29     <xs:complexType>
30 </ xs:element>
```

↓ RNG

```
31 <element name="book">
32   <zeroOrMore>
33     <element name="chapter">
34       <element name="title "><data type="string"/></ element>
35       <choice>
36         <element name="length">
37           <data type="integer">
38             <param name="minInclusive">0<param/>
39             <param name="maxInclusive">800<param/>
40           </ data>
41         </ element>
42         <element name="length"><choice><value>not finished</ value></ choice
              ↪ ></ element>
43       </ choice>
44     </ element>
45   </ zeroOrMore>
46 </ element>
```

3.4.10 Unique IDs and References to Them

For XS, it is possible to check if certain values, referenced by an element or attribute
are actually contained in the document. For this, XPath is utilized.

This is done by using the `<key>` and `<keyref>` elements, inside the root element. Luckily, this solution works independently of the rest of defined structure of the document. Listing 61 shows an example.

Listing 61 Referencing

```
1   <book>
2     <chapter id="1">...</chapter>
3     <chapter id="3">...</chapter>
4     <author idref="1">Stefanie</author>
5     <author idref="3">Juergen</author>
6   </book>
```

↓ **XS**

```
7   <xs:element name="book">
8     <xs:key name="chapterKey">
9       <xs:selector xpath="chapter"/>
10      <xs:field xpath="@id"/>
11    </xs:key>
12    <xs:keyref name="chapterRef" refer="chapterKey">
13      <xs:selector xpath="author"/>
14      <xs:field xpath="@idref"/>
15    </xs:keyref>
16    ...
17  </xs:element>
```

Sadly RNG does not support this directly. Instead, it utilizes a separate language called Schematron[11] to achieve this. Schematron is a rule-based language (XML syntax, utilizing XPath) that is more powerful than the XS mechanism presented above, as it cannot just check refs but do any content consistency checks. In fact, it can be used in conjunction with XS and RNG (and other languages). Simply put: each Schematron rule is an XPath that is checked. So for the example above, two rules reusing the XPaths shown above would suffice.

3.4.11 Tool Support

The most widely used tool for checking RNG is **libxml2** with its commandline utility `xmllint`, which is included in most Linux distributions, MacOS, and Windows (through WSL) out of the box.

Although this tools claims XS support, XS support is actually limited to a subset of the standard and reliably only checks data types (but might fail at checking the structure of the document). In order to get full XS support with this tool, we propose to use XSLT to transform the XS into an RNG, which can than be checked reliably. Multiple transformations exists; one example can be found here.[12]

---

[11] https://www.schematron.com/.

[12] https://raw.githubusercontent.com/epiasini/XSDtoRNG/master/xsdtorngconverter/XSDtoRNG.xsl, last accessed: 2023-08-24.

3.5   Schema Integration: Matching and Mapping Concepts

Sections 3.2 to 3.4 have introduced several technologies that can be used to transform and exchange XML documents and also build the basis for realizing the integration of schemas describing data structures (see XML Schema and Relax NG) as well as integration of the data.

Consider again the example of the two XML schemas S1 and S2 depicted in Fig. 3.2 with the goal to integrate them. The "good thing" in this case is that both schemas are in the same format, i.e., XML. It could also be possible that one schema is, for example, relational and the other one is XML-based. We will come back to the challenge of heterogeneous formats in the sequel. For the moment, we assume XML-based schemas to be integrated.

The main "instrument" for integration is schema matching, i.e., " *identifying semantically corresponding elements in two or more schemas*" [170]. Based on the semantic correspondences, a *schema mapping* can be defined. According to Definition 3.1 provided in [94, p. 110], a schema mapping is a function m that takes two schemas S_1 and S_2 as input and maps them to a set of tuples representing the corresponding elements in the schemas. The mapping takes the result of the matching as input, where the matching results can still be adapted/extended/reduced. Especially at the presence of a large number of schemas to be integrated, the (semi-) automatic support for matching by tools can be helpful.

For finding correspondences between elements in schemas, several matching techniques based on different similarity measures can be employed [33]. One commonly used approach is a *linguistic matching* of the element labels, e.g., label Advance is used for an element in both schemas depicted in Fig. 3.2. Hence, employing a similarity metric such as string edit distance (cf., e.g., [183]), both elements would be assessed as matching with a similarity of 1. Note that label similarity might not work in all cases, in particular, at the presence of synonyms and homonyms. Here, the utilization of *ontologies* can be helpful. Moreover, *attribute-based matching* can be used where the similarity between the elements is measured based on their attribute sets. *Structure-based matching* considers, for example, the relations between the elements. This is related to *graph matching* techniques, in combination with graph-based metrics such as *graph edit distance* [44] that measure the similarity of graphs based on the number of edit operations (e.g., inserting nodes) that are necessary to transform one graph into the other.

Based on the chosen similarity metric and matching techniques, for the given schemas S_1 and S_2, the cross-product between all elements of S_1 and S_2 is built, and the similarity of each pair in the cross product is calculated. A mapping is then chosen/built based on the most similar pairs, e.g., above a certain threshold.

Going back to the example in Fig. 3.2: Schema S1 has elements CourseDB, Participant, Name, Firstname, Location, and Advance. Schema S2 has elements Courses, Participant, PNr, Name, City, and Advance. Assume that we use label matching. Building the cross-product of all attributes between S1 and S2, we arrive at {(CourseDB, Courses), (CourseDB,

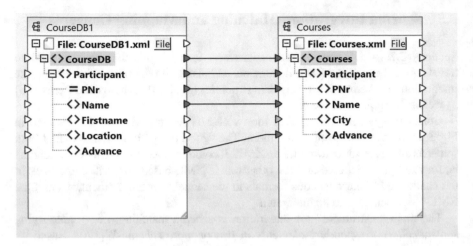

Fig. 3.6 Matching result for the XML schemas depicted in Fig. 3.2 using Altova MapForce®

Participant), (CourseDB, PNr), (CourseDB, Name), (CourseDB, City), (Participant, Courses), (Participant, Participant), ...}. Assume that we use a threshold of 0.75 for label matching.[13] Then, the matching results in (CourseDB, Courses, 0.75), (Participant, Participant, 1), (Name, Name, 1), (Advance, Advance, 1)} where the triples contain element from S1, element from S2, and the similarity value.

This matching result leaves elements unmatched, i.e., Firstname and Location for schema S1 and PNr and City for schema S2. If we include XML attributes into the matching, attribute PNr in S1 can be matched to element PNr in S2 with a similarity of 1.

Figure 3.6 shows the result of the automatic matching performed using Altova MapForce.[14] The elements and attributes connected by green lines have been matched. This result corresponds to the result created manually above.

In addition to matching based on the element and attribute labels, Altova MapForce suggests matchings based on the types, indicated by the yellow triangle for element City demanding for a matching input of type xs:string. In the example, all unmatched elements are of type xs:string; hence, this does not really help for finding another matching. If we apply domain knowledge and/or consult an ontology, we can manually match Location to City as displayed in Fig. 3.7. The only unmatched element then is Firstname. One could think of matching it together with Name from S1 into Name in S2. Altova MapForce does not allow more than one matching input. A reason for this can be that from an

---

[13] For calculating the string similarity, we use https://turboframework.org/en/app/stringutils/compare-similarity-between-two-strings (last accessed: 2023-08-29).

[14] https://www.altova.com/mapforce.

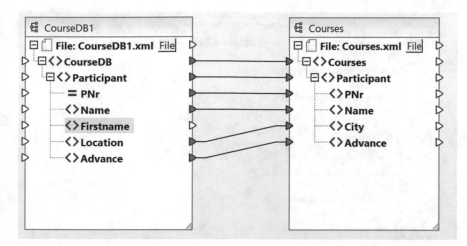

Fig. 3.7 Extended matching result for the XML schemas depicted in Fig. 3.2 using Altova MapForce®

instance point of view, i.e., when looking into the XML documents corresponding to the XML schemas, a rule must be defined on how to match the information from the two elements `Name` and `Firstname` onto one XML element `Name`, for example, `'Smith'`, `'Angela'` onto either `'Angela Smith'` or `'Smith, Angela'` or `'A. Smith'` and so on.

With the mapping, we only know which element is mapped onto which other element. A mapping can contain more information, especially, the code on how to transform one schema into the other one using XSLT (cf. Sect. 3.3). Figure 3.8 shows the XSLT code that transforms XML documents of XML schema S1 into XML documents of XML schema S2. Note that highlighted by the light-blue box, the mapping of elements `Firstname` and `Name` in S1 to element `Name` in S2 has been specified, i.e., content `<Firstname>Angela</Firstname>` `<Name>Smith</Name>` in S1 is transformed into content `<Name>Angela Smith</Name>` in S2. Note that other options to specify the transformation code are conceivable such as XQuery.

Matching and mapping can be done in a one-step process, in particular, if two schemas are to be integrated or if multiple schemas are integrated in one go (one-shot strategy), cf. [31]. Rahm and Peukert [169] differentiates the *pairwise* integration of two schemas (also denoted as *binary* approach in [31]) from the *holistic* integration of more than two schemas. For holistic schema integration, in addition to the one-shot strategy, several other strategies exist, ranging from iterative pairwise/binary integration [31] to clustering and grouping of the schemas [169]. Clustering of XML documents can be done based on their hierarchical structure, using, for example, tree similarity metrics such as tree edit distance [59]. For other formats such as JSON (cf. Sect. 2.5), clustering based on JSON edit distance has been proposed in [110].

```xml
<xsl:stylesheet version="1.0" xmlns:xsl="http://www.w3.org/1999/XSL/Transform"
xmlns:xs="http://www.w3.org/2001/XMLSchema" xmlns:fn="http://www.w3.org/2005/xpath-functions"
exclude-result-prefixes="xs fn">
  <xsl:output method="xml" encoding="UTF-8" byte-order-mark="no" indent="yes"/>
  <xsl:template match="/">
    <Courses>
      <xsl:for-each select="CourseDB/Participant">
        <Participant>
          <PNr>
            <xsl:value-of select="@PNr"/>
          </PNr>
          <Name>
            <xsl:value-of select="Firstname"/>
            <xsl:text> </xsl:text>
            <xsl:value-of select="Name"/>
          </Name>
          <City>
            <xsl:value-of select="Location"/>
          </City>
          <Advance>
            <xsl:value-of select="Advance"/>
          </Advance>
        </Participant>
      </xsl:for-each>
    </Courses>
  </xsl:template>
</xsl:stylesheet>
```

Fig. 3.8 XSLT code for matching result for the XML schemas in Fig. 3.2

The general process of schema integration—especially when to integrate more than two schemas—comprises the following phases according to [31]:

1. *Pre-integration:* In this phase, the schemas to be integrated are identified and analyzed w.r.t. their elements, relations between the elements, and structure. Moreover, the *integration strategy* is determined, including one-shot or iterative approaches. If the strategies involve clustering and/or grouping of schemas, this is also part of the pre-integration. Note that typically, schemas that are integrated earlier in the process have a higher impact on the result as schemas that are considered later.
2. *Schema comparison (↦ schema matching):* This phase corresponds to or applies techniques of schema matching, i.e., conflicts between entities in the schemas are detected and tried to be resolved. One type of conflict is *naming conflicts* based on the use of homonyms or synonyms. These can be resolved using ontologies or based on domain knowledge. *Structural conflicts* arise due to different choices on the structuring of the XML documents. In the example (cf. Fig. 3.7), the names of the participants are modeled using two elements in schema CourseDB1 and using one element in schema Courses. More conflicts can arise, for example, w.r.t. conflicting integrity constraints [33].
3. *Schema conforming (↦ schema mapping):* This phase corresponds to or applies techniques of schema mapping, i.e., the goal is to resolve the conflicts detected in the schema comparison phase. This can comprise the resolution of naming conflicts by re-labelling elements and restructuring of the schemas in case of structural conflicts. In the example shown in Fig. 3.7, the conflict between using an attribute PNr in schema CourseDB1 and an element PNr in schema Courses can be resolved by transforming the attribute into an element in

schema `CourseDB1`. In this case, the values of attribute `PNr` can be directly mapped onto the corresponding element information. Resolving the conflict between element `Firstname` and `Name` in schema `CourseDB1` and element `Name` in schema `Courses` can be addressed by splitting `Name` into elements `Firstname` and `Name` for schema `Courses` at schema level. For the values, the necessary transformation can be achieved using XSLT using, for example, the code depicted in Fig. 3.8.

4. *Schema merging and restructuring:*   At first, all schemas to be integrated are merged into one schema based on the results of the schema comparison and conforming phases. Then the resulting schema is restructured in order to meet the following quality criteria: (i) *completeness*, which means that all objects within the participating local schemas have to be present in the global schema as well; (ii) *minimality*, which means avoiding redundancies, i.e., every element is present just once; and (iii) *understandability*, demanding the documentation of each transformation step, possibly supported by tools. [170] demands for *effectiveness* referring to the identifying the correspondences between schema elements during schema matching in a correct and complete way.

Overall, the process of schema integration as described above is iterative, i.e., merging and restructuring might be done in an iterative way, and it is even possible that from the phase of merging and restructuring, one has to go back to schema comparison and conforming. Overall, schema integration is an art, highly complex, and done in a mostly manual way [129]. This is particularly true if a multitude of schemas with different formats are involved where the formats also influence which query language(s) can be used to access the schemas and the stored information (referred to as *technical heterogeneity*), which is paramount for integration [129]. The techniques for exchanging information between relational databases and XML documents as presented in Chap. 2 can be used for integration as well. Consider Fig. 3.9 where a relational database (a) is to be integrated with the XML document (b). One way to go is to utilize the techniques for extracting and publishing content from the relational database as corresponding XML document (c) and, by doing so, transferring the problem to the integration of two XML documents again. A possible mapping using Altova MapForce is shown in (d).

At this point, we want to mention *process model matching* (cf., e.g., [67, 128]), where the goal is to match two or several process models. We will introduce the basics of process modeling in Sect. 5.2 and comment on the usage of process model matching techniques for creating process choreography models in Sect. 8.3.

Integration at the Instance Level In addition to challenges with integrating schema information, challenges at the instance level, i.e., with the data, might arise, including errors in the data (e.g., typos), different data formats such as price in dollar vs. price in Euro, inconsistencies (e.g., zip code does not match city), and duplicates [129]. These data challenges often correlate with data quality challenges. Data quality has several dimensions including credibility of the data sources, relevance of the data, and completeness. For completeness—similar to completeness of the

a) Database to be integrated

Participant	PNr	Name	Location	Advance
	143	Schmidt	Bremen	100
	145	Huber	Augsburg	150
	146	Abele	Senden	180

b) XML document to be integrated

```
<?xml version="1.0" encoding="utf-8"?>
<CourseDB>

    <Participant>
        <PNr>143</PNr>
        <Name>Schmidt</Name>
        <Loc>Bremen</Loc>
    </Participant>
    <Participant>
        <PNr>145</PNr>
        <Name>Huber</Name>
        <Loc>Augsburg</Loc>
    </Participant>
    <Participant>
        <PNr>146</PNr>
        <Name>Abele</Name>
        <Loc>Senden</Loc>
    </Participant>

</CourseDB >
```

c) Derived XML document

```
<?xml version="1.0" encoding="utf-8"?>
<CourseDB>
    <Participant>
        <PNr>143</PNr>
        <Name>Schmidt</Name>
        <Loc>Bremen</Loc>
        <Adv>100</Adv>
    </Participant>
    <Participant>
        <PNr>145</PNr>
        <Name>Huber</Name>
        <Loc>Augsburg</Loc>
        <Adv>150</Adv>
    </Participant>
    <Participant>
        <PNr>146</PNr>
        <Name>Abele</Name>
        <Loc>Senden</Loc>
        <Adv>180</Adv>
    </Participant>
</CourseDB >
```

d) Mapping

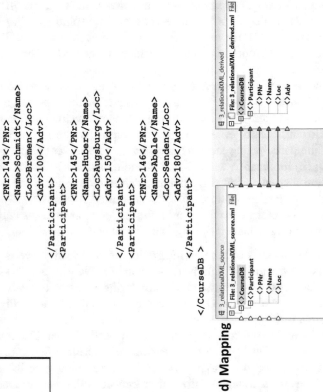

Fig. 3.9 Example for mapping a relational CourseDB database to an XML document structure, partly using Altova MapForce®

integrated schema—one can ask whether all real-world objects considered and all attributes have values.

There are several ways for dealing with data errors, also referred to as *data cleaning* or *data scrubbing* [129]. *Profiling* includes the statistical analysis of the data, typically on numeric values, e.g., comparing the distributions of the values of two data elements, and pattern analysis. Profiling is mostly conducted by the domain expert. *Assessment* is based on the definition of certain conditions on the data values, e.g., age <15. Using profiling and assessment, errors in the data can be detected and fixed, and possibly, erroneous data sources can be removed. Furthermore, *duplicates* in the data can be detected during data cleaning. In the *data fusion* phase, duplicates can be handled, either by removing them or adding associated information to data sources. *"Data fusion is the process of fusing multiple records representing the same real-world object into a single, consistent, and clean representation."* [39]. The goal is to achieve minimality and completeness at the same time. Overall, it is vital, to implement the continuous monitoring of the data quality in order to avoid errors from the beginning, but also data errors that might be injected when data sources change. Note that more recently, the term data fusion is used in the context of merging sensor data, e.g., in Internet of things (IoT) applications (cf., e.g., [116]). We will comment on this interoperability challenge in Chap. 9.

On top of detecting and fixing data errors, data values can be aligned in order to be integrated with other data sources. Many techniques for aligning data values (*data normalization*) are already implemented in commercial databases [129] and comprise capitalization and de-capitalization; alignment of abbreviations and spelling, e.g., A. Smith and Smith, Angela; stemming, i.e., reducing string values to their word stem; as well as transformation of dates, scales (e.g., dollar to Euro), and coding, e.g., 0 and 1 in FALSE and TRUE.

3.6 Case Study: University Search System

The higher-education case study motivated in Sect. 1.3.1 will illustrate the concepts and technologies for Chaps. 2 to 4 in a combined way in Sect. 4.4.

3.7 Conclusions and Lessons Learned

In general, preparing data is THE prerequisite for many applications including business intelligence and machine learning projects and is often a complex and expensive task [94] consuming up to 80% of the entire project time. Schema and data transformation and integration constitutes a major part of the data preparation phase and poses many challenges due to the heterogeneity of the schema information and the data. This chapter has discussed these challenges and provided strategies and technologies how to overcome them. The main focus was on XML-based technologies as major exchange format in practice. Combined with the techniques from Chap. 2, also relational database schemas and data can be integrated.

In any case, due to the complexity of the transformation and integration tasks, sufficient time and manpower should be dedicated. Moreover, schema and data integration demand for domain knowledge. Ontologies and domain models can help resolve semantic conflicts when, for example, matching schema elements. However, not all of these conflicts might be covered by existing ontologies; hence, domain expert knowledge is indispensable (also to check the feasibility of an established integration).

Another advise for transformation and integration projects is to document every step of the integration process. This is inevitable for reproducibility, transparency, and maintainability as we have to keep in mind that data sources might change, even quite frequently. For documentation purposes, tool support can be helpful, e.g., modeling the integration process using existing tools such as Pentaho[15] or Altova MapForce. In [94], an overview on open-source data preparation pipelines for business intelligence projects can be found.

Further approaches are conceivable for schema and data integration, for example, approaches based on *3-Ways merge*. 3-ways merge is typically applied in version control systems in software development such as SmartGit (cf., e.g., [147]). 3-ways merge assumes that two schemas are integrated where a common ancestor of both schemas is known.

Further Reading
1. Doan, A.H., Halevy, A.Y., Ives, Z.G.: Principles of Data Integration, pp. I-XVIII, 1–497. Morgan Kaufmann, Burlington (2012). ISBN 978-0-12-416044-6
2. Bellahsene, Z., Bonifati, A., Rahm, E.: Schema Matching and Mapping. Data-Centric Systems and Applications. Springer, Berlin (2011). ISBN 978-3-642-16517-7
3. Grossmann, W., Rinderle-Ma, S.: Fundamentals of Business Intelligence. Data-Centric Systems and Applications. Springer, Berlin (2015), pp. 1–327. ISBN 978-3-662-46530-1
4. Bleiholder, J., Naumann, F.: Data fusion. ACM Comput. Surv. **41**(1), 1:1–1:41 (2008)

---

[15] https://tinyurl.com/y97rxdtn (last accessed: 2023-08-29).

Chapter 4
Service Interoperability

4.1 Motivation and Goals

Services solve two interoperability aspects: (a) a service provides abstract access to complex (legacy) functionality or data, and (b) a service fosters reusability. In this chapter, at first, foundations for service realization using current technologies such as REST and GraphQL are introduced and compared (cf. Fig. 4.1). Then the chapter rounds off by discussing (a) and (b) based on a case study from the higher-education domain that also covers the concepts and technologies presented in Chaps. 2 and 3.

Service-oriented architectures (SOAs) are one of the staples of interoperable software design, as they facilitate a couple of important properties:

- **Loose coupling:** Traditionally, a clean and minimal API design is responsible for the degree of coupling. This leads to less complicated dependencies in the code, less crashes, and better maintainability. SOAs have the additional advantage that individual components interact through message passing. Individual components crashing will not bring down the whole system, errors are localized, and interactions can be introspected through independent mechanisms (e.g., log network traffic). This leads to more resilient software.
- **Scalability:** Components can be distributed to different nodes, can employ load-balancing (distribute work to multiple components that provide the same functionality) and fail-over (when a component crashes, redirect requests to a component with the same functionality).
- **Reusabililty:** Independent components are provided for other software development teams to be used but, as they are network based, without any extra installation/deployment costs.
- **Flexibility, modularity, agility:** Again, SOAs promote these properties by providing independent components, which can be changed and adapted to changing requirements independently.

© Springer Nature Switzerland AG 2024
S. Rinderle-Ma et al., *Fundamentals of Information Systems Interoperability*,
https://doi.org/10.1007/978-3-031-48322-6_4

Levels ,.. / Tasks ⤸	Syntactical	Semantic	Organizational
Exchange	Exchange formats, e.g., XML, relational databases, JSON, BSON, YAML, MessagePack; query languages: XPath, XQuery, SQL; transformation languages, e.g., XSLT	Schema matching and mapping; ontologies;	Message exchange; correlation
Integrate	SQL/XML standard; native XML databases; REST and GraphQL	Edge table, shredding; XML schema and RNG; schema and data integration; service integration	Correlation and choreography
Orchestrate	BPMN, Petri Nets, Workflow Nets, RPST, CPEE Trees, Colored Petri Nets	Verification, task and worklist design; service invocation; correlation; integration patterns and processes	Choreography

Fig. 4.1 Interoperability perspectives I: Chap. 4

- **Efficient monitoring:** As stated above, having a set of components interacting over the network allows monitoring these interactions without building mechanisms into the software itself, which decreases the complexity and coupling of the overall system and also allows to improve maintenance aspects of the software without touching the software itself.

Of course, other prominent traditional properties apply as well, such as **discoverability** (i.e., the possibility to register services in service directories, which is deemed a less important aspect in the context of this book).

A multitude of technologies for realizing such services exists, ranging from binary legacy technologies such as CORBA (Common Object Request Broker Architecture) and SOAP (Simple Object Access Protocol) to more lightweight and transparent approaches such as REST (Representational state transfer) and GraphQL, which will be discussed in the remainder of this chapter.

Typically, each of these technologies covers two questions:

- What methods, functions, or data does the API expose?
- What is the protocol in which the client and the server communicate with each other?

In this chapter, we try to answer these questions, based on two prevalent service technologies, their differences and similarities.

4.2 REST

As defined by Fielding [82] *"REST components communicate by transferring a representation,"* e.g., an HTML document for a GET request. The different components (in our case, services) interact with each other by interpreting the representation at runtime. A representation includes all the information to allow for further interaction with a resource. In the case of an HTML document, the semantic of the included information is to be understood by a human. However, of course, the HTML document can be replaced with something altogether different and easier to parse by machines, such as JSON or HTML.

Whatsoever, a (well-desired) characteristic of a REST service is that it reveals several ways of interacting with it at runtime, i.e., when using, for example, a Web browser to browse a service, it can will reveal the data contained within and ways to interact (e.g., delete) with it. This is called HATEOAS (Hypermedia As The Engine Of Application State). Sometimes, HTML might transport all the information that is necessary to understand the structure of a REST service, but of course, this information can be contained in any data structure.

A REST service dealing with the writing of a book, for example, might upon request of the structure of the book respond with the answer given in Listing 62. In this particular example, the description of a chapter, besides the obvious details, holds a list of **links** to read or modify particular aspects of this chapter. As can be seen in Listing 63, this list of **links** no longer contains the **todos** when a particular chapter is finished. This example also shows that the **Application State** (as in HATEOAS) is communicated as XML document, which is easy to parse (in comparison to parsing HTML) by software using the API.

Listing 62 HATEOS 1

```
 1    <book>
 2      <chapter id="1" status="unfinished">
 3        <title>Introduction</title>
 4        <links>
 5          <authors>/1/authors</authors>
 6          <title>/1/title</title>
 7          <todos>/1/todos</todos>
 8        </links>
 9      </chapter>
10      ...
11    </book>
```

4.2.1 HTTP Basics

As REST is tightly connected with the HTTP standard, understanding HTTP is imperative. HTTP is stateless, i.e., a client sends a request, the server sends a response, and then the connection is terminated. There is no means at the protocol level to exchange multiple messages between client and server. This does not mean that a client cannot tell the server with each request (1) who he is or (2) provide context about previous interactions. But this all happens as part of the content of the interaction. As a consequence, while HTTP is **stateless**, the applications communicating over HTTP (can) have an **Application State**.

Listing 63 HATEOS 2

```
1    <book>
2      <chapter id="1" status="unfinished">
3        <title>Introduction</title>
4        <links>
5          <authors>/1/authors</authors>
6          <title>/1/title</title>
7        </links>
8      </chapter>
9      ...
10   </book>
```

HTTP messages are essentially text files sent over a lower-level network protocol (such as TCP) and consist of three important parts, as depicted in Listing 64.

- The **request line** (Line 1) contains the operation (e.g., GET), resource (i.e., path), and protocol (e.g., HTTP/1.1). For responses from the server, this is called the **status line** (Line 5) and contains the protocol and HTTP status code. The status code is a standardized means (in IETF RFC 7231[1]) for the server to convey the nature of the response, e.g., 2xx if everything went well, 3xx if requested resources moved, 4xx if the request was somehow bad, and 5xx if could for internal reasons not complete the request.
- The **headers**—key/value pairs that describe expectations and properties of the interaction between a client and a server. This can, for example, contain an ID describing the identification of the context (or Application State) in the form of a **Cookie** header or application-specific header. There also exists a list of standardized headers, one of which is **Accept**, which, as part of a request, tells the server if it should respond with, e.g., HTML or XML. This can be used to realize HATEOAS in the form of HTML for humans and JSON/XML for machines.
- The **content** contains everything else, e.g., XML/JSON or any other form of text or binary document to be sent between client and server. The type of content has to be identified by a standardized header **Content-type** containing a **MIME-type** description (standardized in IETF RFC 2046[2]) such as `application/json`.

---

[1] https://datatracker.ietf.org/doc/html/rfc7231 (last accessed: 2023-08-24).

[2] https://datatracker.ietf.org/doc/html/rfc2046 (last accessed: 2023-08-24).

Listing 64 HTTP Basics

```
1   GET /book/chapters/4/authors HTTP/1.1
2   Host: www.interopbook.work
3
4
5   HTTP/1.1  200  OK
6   Content-Type: application/json
7
8   [ 'Stefanie' ]
```

Listing 64 also shows that (1) in order to separate headers from content, a simple empty line is used, (2) request and response are just one continuous text stream, and (3) request and response are separated again through a newline. If no content is given, as in the request of the current example, two newlines are present. If the content contains newlines, it either has to be encoded (e.g., BASE64) or a Content-length header has to be carried.

4.2.2 Resources and Operations

It is important to note that REST exposes data and access to this data. It does not expose operations, functions, or methods. Calculating $1 + 1$, for example, is an operation, and is thus not a prime REST candidate. Not every API that is exposed through HTTP is a REST API. While other mechanisms such as SOAP, CORBA, or RPC concentrate on providing means to expose own operations, REST relies on a set of standard operations, called resources.

Always think about REST as exposing a complex tree data structure and allowing to modify it.

Listing 65 shows an XML document representing the data structure and a list of REST resources, which allow to access individual parts of this data structure. Thus, for REST (as really for any good software design), it is important to first design the data structure and then decide on the operations and means to filter the data.

As can be seen, whenever more than one element with the same name exists, it has to be identified with an ID, in order to make it accessible through a unique path. Otherwise, URLs are roughly XPath expressions that allow to access one particular aspect of the data. Please note that even if at the level of <book> only <chapter> elements existed, it would still be wise to represent chapter as its own resource (and not go for /book/4), as in the future at any level, there might be the need for extending the API. Defensive design will save you time and effort in the future.

4.2.3 Reading Data

Reading any of the resources in Listing 65 should be possible and yield different results. While it is up to the designer what a resource returns, one common

convention has to be followed in order to fulfill the HATEOAS requirement: each
resource has to return a list of sub-resources and how to access them.

Listing 65   Data Structure and Resources

```
1    <book>
2      <authors>
3        <author id="S">Stefanie</author>
4        <author id="J">Juergen</author>
5        <author id="D">Daniel</author>
6      </authors>
7      <chapter id="4">
8        <title>Service Tech</title>
9        <length>500</length>
10       <authors>
11         <author id="1">Juergen</author>
12         <author id="2">Stefanie</author>
13       </authors>
14     </chapter>
15       ...
16   </book>

                ↓ Resources

17   /book
18   /book/authors
19   /book/authors/S
20   /book/authors/J
21   /book/authors/D
22   /book/chapters
23   /book/chapters/4
24   /book/chapters/4/title
25   /book/chapters/4/authors
26   /book/chapters/4/authors/1
27   /book/chapters/4/authors/2
```

For example, /book has to return that a book has **authors** and **chapters**.
Reading /book/chapters has to reveal the existence of /book/chapters/4
(and others), i.e., the list of resources representing these chapters.

The HTTP operation for reading data is **GET**. It is the equivalent of
typing the resource into the address bar of a Web browser. The standard
HTTP filtering mechanism (question mark) might be used, but the API
designer has to be careful to expose the exact usage. In the current example,
/book/chapters?length_bigger_than=200 might be a way to only
show certain chapters, but the parameter **length_bigger_than** is custom, and
its existence should thus be exposed when calling /book/chapters (i.e.,
HATEOAS). Communicating the knowledge of this parameter just through separate
documentation of the API might work for certain scenarios, but it is obviously
negatively affecting the properties of the SOA.

4.2.4   Adding New Data

Adding data is mostly done through the HTTP **POST** operation. As new data is
added to the data structure, this operation has always to be called at the level where

data is to be inserted. If a new **chapter** is to be inserted, for example, the **POST** has to occur at /book, and if a new **author for a particular chapter** has to be inserted, the **POST** has to occur at /book/chapters/4.

In order to insert data, a client typically obeys the following rules:

- Select the correct resource where the data has to be inserted (see above).
- Send the data to be inserted.
- Receive the ID for the data.

So for the current example, a request such as shown in Listing 66 might result in an additional resource as depicted in Line 11.

Listing 66 POST

```
1    POST /book/chapters/4/authors HTTP/1.1
2    Content-type: text/xml
3    Host: www.interopbook.work
4
5    <author>Daniel</author>
6
7    HTTP/1.1 200 OK
8    Content-Type: application/json
9
10   { "id": 3 }
                ↓ Resources
11   //book/chapters/4/authors/3
```

Alternatively, the HTTP operation **PUT** can be used, but it is different from POST: it modifies data in place and, as a side effect, creates data if it does not exist. So in comparison to the previous case, the resource where to add the data (including the ID) has to be explicitly specified in the request. It is not foreseen to dynamically get an ID assigned as before. Listing 67 shows an example where the **chapter author** with the ID **7** is explicitly added to **Chap. 4**. If the chapter author with the ID 7 would have already existed, it would have been replaced.

Listing 67 PUT To Add Data

```
1    PUT /book/chapters/4/authors/7 HTTP/1.1
2    Content-type: text/xml
3    Host: www.interopbook.work
4
5    <author>Daniel</author>
6
7    HTTP/1.1 200 OK
                ↓ Resources
8    //book/chapters/4/authors/7
```

4.2.5 Changing Data

Changing data comes in two forms: HTTP **PUT** and **PATCH** operations. Please note that replacing a resource is supposed to also replace all data in the tree below. Both operations operate directly on the resources that have to be changed, but the difference lies in how the data is changed:

- **PUT** replaces all data. Thus, e.g., when calling PUT on /book, all authors, and chapters, the chapter lengths, chapter authors, and chapter titles have to be provided. All the old data is gone and replaced by the new data.
- **PATCH** changes all existing data and deletes nothing but also adds new data. Thus, e.g., when calling PATCH on /book, but not providing the <authors> in the XML content, and only providing <title> inside <chapter id="4">, only title is replaced (or added if it does not exist). All other chapters and authors are left alone.

Both ways of changing data are useful in different scenarios, but PATCH is obviously much more difficult to implement. If GET returns proper HATEOAS, it can often avoid showing the structure and contents of the full sub-tree, which can be very big. In order to support people using PUT and PATCH, some form of describing the schema of the full sub-tree is useful, as traversing all resources just to find out potential structure is neither good for performance nor for client code complexity.

4.2.6 Deleting Data

Deleting data is straightforwardly mapped to the HTTP **DELETE** operation. It has to be called for the resource that is to be deleted and will result in the deletion of all data (including everything beneath the resource in the tree structure).

4.2.7 Richardson Maturity Model (RMM)

The idea of the RMM is to classify the relation between different Web service implementation technologies and REST but, in doing so, also allowing to classify "How much REST" something is. The four different levels in this model are depicted in Table 4.1.

RMM thus provides a means to classify the quality of a supposed REST API. Anything below Level 4 cannot be considered REST, as it violates the conventions that REST proposes. Violation of these conventions makes the API harder to use (especially when calling it REST), as it behaves in an unexpected manner.

Table 4.1 RMM Levels

Level 0	...	Plain	...	SOAP, RPC, many old services. Use mostly POST. Often use resources like operations with custom parameters. Often provides a single resource that behaves differently with different parameters
Level 1	...	Resources	...	Correct usage of multiple resources but mostly using the POST operation
Level 2	...	Operations	...	Correct usage of GET, POST, PUT, PATH, DELETE, with often multiple operations per resource possible
Level 3	...	HATEOAS	...	Correct usage of HATEOAS when using GET on different resources

Please also note than in our experience, it is much better to have multiple small REST services, than to pack everything into one big service during implementation.

4.3 GraphQL

GraphQL in contrast to REST does not purely rely on HTTP semantics but tries to improve on some REST shortcuts by introducing a number of new concepts. Most of these concepts can be implemented for REST services, but as they are not explicitly defined, developers will invent slight deviations of these concepts, thus requiring client developers to explore and understand certain aspects of particular REST APIs over and over again.

GraphQL does not rely on different resources but on JSON and POST for all requests and allows arbitrary responses (but JSON again is a very common response). It is thus much more like an RPC mechanism, but data-oriented like REST. Other aspects defined by GraphQL are:

- A `type system`, which describes which parameters for data queries and which types these parameters might have. All queries are checked against this schema.
- `Queries` allow to only return the data that is needed. For REST, often, data is returned that is not needed, unless there is a custom filtering mechanism (which not always exists). While REST `/book/chapters/4`, for example, might return title, length, and all authors, in GraphQL by default, data (especially in sub-trees) can be restricted.
- `Mutations` serve for inserting, updating, and deleting data.
- `Subscriptions` allow to be notified when something changes on the server. They are commonly implemented as WebSockets (IETF RFC 6455 [3]).

---

[3] https://datatracker.ietf.org/doc/html/rfc6455 (last accessed: 2023-08-24).

In the remainder of this section, we will look at these concepts in more detail and also discuss shortcomings of GraphQL in comparison to REST.

4.3.1 Type System

The type system is expressed as a custom language. At the root of the type system is the **type** Query. Example Listing 68 shows the schema that is intended to provide a similar functionality as the REST example given in Listing 65.

Listing 68 GraphQL Schema

```
1    type Query {
2        authors: [Author]
3        chapters: [Chapter]
4    }
5    type Chapter {
6        id: ID!
7        title: String!
8        length: Int!
9        authors: [Author]
10   }
11   type Author {
12       id: ID!
13       name: String!
14   }
15
```

Basic types such as **String**, **Int**, **Float**, **Boolean**, and **ID** are available. Whenever an exclamation mark is added at the end of the type, the field is required. Additionally, it is possible to define lists of types by putting them in brackets (**[...]**).

4.3.2 Queries

The purpose of a GraphQL query is to define which data is required from the server. It has to match the schema and is sent via POST to the GraphQL resource. Example Listing 69 shows a query and its result for the schema defined above.

As can be seen, a custom JSON is returned, which only contains the title, as defined in the query. Queries themselves allow for arbitrary restrictions of related objects, using a wide variety of self-explanatory operators, including equality (_eq, _ne), comparison (_gt, _gte, _lt, _lte), regex (_regex), and lists (_in).

Listing 69 GraphQL Query

```
1   query longChapter {
2     chapters(where: { length: { _gt:  200 } } ) {
3       title
4     }
5   }
```

↓ **Query Result**

```
6   {
7     data: {
8       chapters: [
9         {
10          title: "Service Tech"
11        }
12      ]
13    }
14  }
```

One important advantage in comparison to REST is that filtering at multiple levels of the query is possible. While for REST it is not possible in one request to filter for chapters longer than 200 words and authors starting with the letter "A" (unless there is a custom mechanism to use both restrictions at the level of /book/chapters), for GraphQL, this would be straightforward.

4.3.3 Mutations

Mutations define how in GraphQL data is created, updated, or deleted. Mutations contain variables that are then passed as an object field to the server. Example Listing 70 shows mutation to insert chapter 99 for the schema defined above. Each mutation also defines the data returned to the user after the data is inserted.

As can be seen, the query object field contains the list of variables needed for updating the data.

4.3.4 Subscriptions

Subscriptions are a means to get live updates and rely on the keyword **subscription**. They are basically queries and yield a response whenever data matching the query is inserted.

Subscriptions are a subject to change and improvement in GraphQL so it's worth to watch out for substantial updates.

Listing 70 GraphQL Mutation

```
1    mutation createChapter($title: String, $authors: [Author]) {
2      inserted {
3        chapters(where: { title: { _eq:  $title } } ) {
4          title
5          authors
6        }
7    }
```

↓ **Query Object Field**

```
8    {
9      title: "99 Problems",
10     authors: [
11       { name: "Roy" }
12     ]
13   }
```

↓ **Query Result**

```
14   {
15     data: {
16       inserted: {
17         chapters: [
18           {
19             title: "99 Problems",
20             authors: [
21               { name: "Roy" }
22             ]
23           }
24         ]
25       }
26     }
27   }
```

4.3.5 Current Shortcomings

As a general rule of thumb, the following applies: GraphQL gives users a structured but restricted way. REST is more flexible but messier and harder to apply.

REST can use the following HTTP mechanisms for REST, which are prohibited for GraphQL due to its usage of a generic endpoint (all requests go to a single resource):

- Quotas and rate limiting: determining the difference between queries or mutations in GraphQL in GraphQL means analyzing the queries themselves. While it is not impossible, it definitely results in lots of overhead and a bloated GraphQL framework. For REST on the other hand, configuration based on resources and HTTP operations is straightforward and built into Web servers (separation, i.e., loose coupling).
- Caching: repeated requests do not have to be answered. In REST, again, this is simple based on HTTP status codes and built into many Web servers. For GraphQL, the same argumentation as above applies—yes, but lots of overhead.

- DDoS detection: again REST has the advantage that for different resources and operations, traffic is easy to analyze. Again GraphQL has problems described above—yes, but lots of overhead.
- Analytics tooling: tracking of service usage. For REST, even basic tracking for operations and resources yields great results and a wide variety of analysis tools based on Web server logs. For GraphQL, again, such functionality has to be supported in the framework and again produces lots of overhead.

REST is very mature and flexible as a concept. It can be implemented with minimal tooling and overhead. Unless you have a case that supports GraphQL, REST is the more mature and more flexible option. GraphQL frameworks on the other hand have to be much bigger to support the same concepts as REST. GraphQL is still relatively new. Tooling will improve so it will be interesting to see how the situation changes. REST on the other hand often requires much more data filtering on the client side, although this can be avoided if the server is properly designed.

4.4 Case Study: University Search System

The higher-education case study motivated in Sect. 1.3.1 illustrates the concepts and technologies for Chaps. 2–4 in a combined way.

The real-world system, which is the basis for this study, has been available under https://ufind.univie.ac.at/[4] since 2016 and during peak times has about 40.000 page views a minute.[5]

The overall design goal of the system was as follows: create a user interface that provides a compound search and browsing experience similar to modern search engines. Included in this design goal were the following set of interoperability goals and interoperability challenges, stemming from the heterogeneous organization structure of this particular university (but really is generic for large organizations).

- The data to be available through such a system is available through heterogeneous sources, in different formats, and sometimes hard to transform, combine, and connect.
- The legacy systems (in this case a database) do provide neither the performance nor the functionality to realize such as system.
- The data volume (>5 terabyte) and potential amount of users (>100000) are huge, demanding for aggressive scalability measures.

---

[4] last accessed: 2023-08-28.

[5] One page view: a user loads a page in the browser, resulting in about 30–40 requests (hits) to the Web server for a variety of resources such as icons, style sheets, JavaScript libraries, and the displayed data.

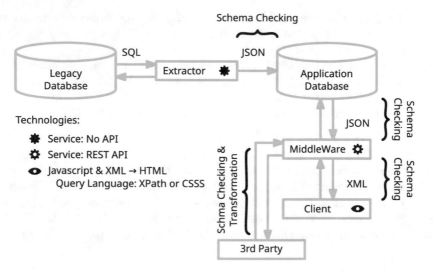

Fig. 4.2 University search service

- The system is to be actively integrated into a large number of other backend (through an API) and frontend systems due the heterogeneous nature of the organization.

The architecture of the system is displayed in Fig. 4.2. It entails the following components:

- The **Legacy Database(s)**, which holds data about courses, exams, and curricula back to the year 1995, as well as information about employees, teachers, and the organization structure.
- **Extractor** backend services, which provide no API. Their purpose is to extract, transform, and connect the data artifacts from legacy sources (which include multiple databases but also APIs of partner organizations).
- The **Application Database** (AD) (in this particular case ElasticSearch to realize fuzzy search for the huge dataset at hand) serves as an intermediate storage. It is periodically, i.e., every 10 minutes, updated from the legacy database, and is basically read-only from the point of view of the application. The AD provides REST, an interface which utilizes JSON for all of its communication purposes.
- The **MiddleWare** (MW), which provides a public REST API, which allows to (1) filter data for (a) one or (b) multiple of the abovementioned data categories and (2) allows to browse courses, staff, and curricula by different perspectives (e.g., units). The API and its specification are available under https://m-ufind.univie.ac. at/?riddl-description[6] and intended to be used by third-party applications inside

---

[6] last accessed: 2023-08-13.

as well as outside of the university. The MW orchestrates requests to the AD and prepares the data in the form of XML documents.

- The **Client**, which solely uses the same API as any other **third party**. The client contains ALL application logic and just requests XML data from the MW, which is then filtered and transformed into the presented UI.

From an interoperability standpoint, this architecture embodies best practice, as everything is loosely coupled. The MW exposes abstract search and browsing capabilities, as it exposes a certain view on the AD, which in turn stores the data in a way that is optimized for search. At no point is the design of the MW influenced by formatting requirements of the client.

All the XML and JSON exchanged throughout the architecture is defined by publicly available schemas, as can be seen in the MW link above.

The REST interface, as it is loosely coupled to all other components, is easily scalable. In fact, 64 instances of the same service are deployed over multiple nodes. The client randomly selects node for its sub-requests. The AD (also a REST service) is served from eight nodes.

The MW ensure proper function (and prevents misuse) by checking the data format of all incoming data against schemas (i.e., RNG for XML). Third-party applications transform the XML with XSLT to provide different views for different applications.

The question remains why the MW provides XML and not JSON. This decision was made for two particular reasons that affect both interoperability and maintenance of the software. For JSON, custom code has to be written to extract and filter information from potential MW returns. In XML, both XPath and browser-based CSS selectors (CSSS) (which are very similar to XPath) can be utilized to reduce code and make the extraction more universally understandable for developers (and even more performant across different browsers). For XML, much more standardized high-performance tooling is available, e.g., XSLT, XPath, and RNG.

The high scalability (AD, MW) is also achieved through aggressive caching. Whenever a user visits the client with a browser, most static content is not delivered, only making requests to MW necessary. MW requests, on the other hand consist of two types: (1) browsing requests and (2) search requests. Browsing requests can be handled through normal caching mechanisms in the MW Web server (no logic in MW needed), but search requests are handled by some caching logic in the MW.

As demonstrated, REST services work well for providing different views on data, both for AD and MW. The MW is a further abstraction for the AD, limiting the way data can be queried and connected, and ensures consistent performance. The detection of distributed denial-of-service (DDos) and rate limiting are handled through normal Web server functionally on the MW level.

Summing up the use case, the SOA properties are affected by the architecture as follows:

- **Loose coupling:** Independent services at all levels can be maintained, refined, and improved by independent development teams, as long as the public API is kept stable. Communication about the API and its structure is limited to a minimum between development teams.

- **Scalability:** The system is scaling at multiple layers (AD, MW) and can be linearly scaled up further if necessary. Fail-over is handled in each layer, providing a high robustness of the overall system.
- **Reusability:** The very nature of the architecture fosters reusability. It is imperative to not provide an internal and an external API but use layers and let all clients use the same API (to ensure that this one API is in the best shape possible).
- **Flexibility, modularity, agility:** They are fostered through the choice of layered architecture.
- **Monitoring:** The system utilizes no custom monitoring tools but relies on standard network and Web server monitoring tools.

4.5   Conclusion and Lessons Learned

Interoperable system design is fostered by relying on services and highly interoperable formats and approaches. The creation of a sustainable system architecture is improved by (1) utilizing loosely coupled services and (2) defining the granularity of services based on guiding interoperability principles such as:

- Flexible and modular data representation (by means of technologies such as XML, JSON, and YAML).
- Simple data transformation.
- Usability (easy and flexible accessibility through REST and GraphQL).
- Accountable data structures (schema checking; multiple schemas for multiple versions).

Chapter 4 addresses the creation of services, the correct service granularity, and how to foster interoperability between services. Subsequent Chap. 5 explains about how to make services interact. While it is of course possible to write code to aggregate data from different services, and pass data between services, this also means that the application logic is then hard-coded. This, in turn, means that whenever a change is required, programmers have to adapt this code. Change can come in two forms: (1) change to the API of services that are coordinated and (2) change in how the unchanged services interact. In subsequent chapters, we explore how to further abstract this application logic and thus further improve maintainability, flexibility, and agility of an overall system.

Further Reading

1. Bussler, C.: B2B Integration: Concepts and Architecture. Springer, Berlin (2003). ISBN 3-540-43487-9, pp. I-XXII, 1-418
2. Alonso, G., Casati, F., Kuno, H.A., Machiraju, V.: Web Services—Concepts, Architectures and Applications. Data-Centric Systems and Applications. Springer, Berlin (2004). ISBN 978-3-540-44008-6

Chapter 5
Process Orchestration: Conceptual Design

5.1 Motivation and Goals

Process orchestrations enable and realize the integration of application programs/services, data, as well as human tasks in a process-oriented way, i.e., along with a well-defined process logic that reflects the underlying business logic. The conceptual design of process orchestrations based on BPMN and their verification based on Petri Nets is discussed in Chap. 5.1 (cf. Fig. 5.1).

Subsequent Chap. 6 will focus on the execution design of process orchestrations, based on their conceptual design. Moreover, verification techniques will be described in order to guarantee the correctness and soundness of the conceptual process orchestration design at an time. This constitutes a crucial precondition for the execution of the process orchestration and the established interoperability. Process orchestrations model and realize business processes, capturing the business logic of companies and organizations. From an interoperability point of view, process orchestrations have a strong integration aspect as they connect process tasks along a well-defined process logic. The process tasks, in turn, describe and realize task logic, i.e., have input and output data, invoke application program/Web services, and interact with users. Hence, overall, process orchestrations constitute an elegant way for realizing interoperable and integrated applications.

Consider the following use case describing a customer complaint process:

Customer Complaint Process: Customers state their complaint via an online form. The form contains the insurance number, the amount of damage, and a description of the damage. If the amount of damage is ≤ 100 Euro, an automatic plausibility check is conducted, and the complaint is approved.

(continued)

© Springer Nature Switzerland AG 2024
S. Rinderle-Ma et al., *Fundamentals of Information Systems Interoperability*,
https://doi.org/10.1007/978-3-031-48322-6_5

Levels ⸍ / Tasks ⸗	Syntactical	Semantic	Organizational
Exchange	Exchange formats, e.g., XML, relational databases, JSON, BSON, YAML, MessagePack; query languages: XPath, XQuery, SQL; transformation languages, e.g., XSLT	Schema matching and mapping; ontologies;	Message exchange; correlation
Integrate	SQL/XML standard; native XML databases; REST and GraphQL	Edge table, shredding; XML schema and RNG; schema and data integration; service integration	Correlation and choreography
Orchestrate	BPMN, Petri Nets, Workflow Nets, RPST, CPEE Trees, Colored Petri Nets	Verification, task and worklist design; service invocation; correlation; integration patterns and processes	Choreography

Fig. 5.1 Interoperability perspectives I: Chap. 5

The customer is informed via email, and the money transfer is initiated. If the damage amount is above 100 Euro, a clerk checks the complaint. The customer is informed about the decision via email. If the complaint is rejected, the customer is offered an optional meeting.

Only from this small example, different integration aspects become obvious. First of all, the text covers different *process perspectives*, i.e., the functional aspect, e.g., function `check complaint`; the data aspect, e.g., data element `form`; the organizational aspect, e.g., role `clerk`; and the process perspective. The functions seem to follow a specific order, e.g., `plausibility check` is followed by `sending an email`. The functions to be modeled as tasks together with the order and further information such as `optional` build the control flow of the process to be modeled. If we assume that certain functions or tasks are associated with an application program or service, then we can also see from the text that these application programs/services are to be integrated with each other. One example is task `plausibility check` and the subsequent task `sending an email`. For both tasks, we assume an invoked service, and we further assume that the result of the `plausibility check` is to be passed on to task `sending an email` as this task needs the result of the `plausibility check` to decide on the content of the email. In general, data is exchanged along the process, e.g., data element `loan amount` for the different plausibility checks. Moreover, there are also human tasks, e.g., `customer meeting`.

This chapter will describe how to develop process orchestrations from scratch, illustrated based on transforming the use case (in natural language text) into a process orchestration that is correct and can be implemented and executed. We will emphasize interoperability and integration aspects. We will start with the conceptual design of the process orchestration in Sect. 5.2, using the standard Business Process Modeling and Notation (BPMN). We will show the potential of chatbot-based conversational process modeling in Sect. 5.3. This is followed by explaining methods and languages for the verification of the model in Sect. 5.4, based on Petri Nets. The conceptual design of process orchestrations serves as basis for their execution design as presented in Chap. 6.

Chapters 5 and 6 reflect the following stack of notations and languages to be utilized for a complete top-down process orchestration design and development. Note that a selection of these languages will be discussed and illustrated based on the running use case example for each of the layers in this book. For the other languages, we refer to the provided references:

- Semantic or conceptual process modeling notations and languages:

  - Business Process Modeling and Notation (BPMN) [95] ($\rightarrow$ Chap. 5)
  - Event-driven process chains (EPC) [5]

- Logic, formal languages:

  - Petri nets [157] ($\rightarrow$ Chap. 5)
  - Refined Process Structure Tree (RPST) [218] ($\rightarrow$ Chap. 6)

- Graphical programming, execution languages:

  - Workflow Nets [9] ($\rightarrow$ Chap. 6)
  - Cloud Process Execution Engine Trees (CPEE-Trees) [138], cpee.org ($\rightarrow$ Chap. 6)
  - Business Process Execution Language for Web Services (BPEL) [104]
  - Well-Structured Marking Nets (WSM-Nets) [176]

Approaches for transforming one notation into another one exist, e.g., [68], to transform BPMN models into Petri Nets or the www.workflowpatterns.com initiative, which models typical patterns in process models, e.g., sequence or decision, as Petri Nets in order to equip them with a formal execution semantics. The transformation is not always straightforward due to differences in the expressivity, mostly regarding the modeling of different process perspectives.

5.2 Conceptual Design

The integration of application programs and services through process orchestrations has the advantage of a model-driven approach, i.e., the "integration logic" can be specified based on well-known and understandable process modeling notations such as BPMN. In this book, we will use BPMN for the conceptual process design, but we will not provide an extensive discussion of BPMN concepts (please refer to the website bpmn.org and the book by M. Weske [220] for details).

Recall the use case on the customer compliance process, which is in the following presented with underlined keywords for establishing the control flow model of the process by identifying and specifying the process tasks and their order, including decision rules.

Customer   Complaint   Process-Control   Flow   Perspective: Customers upload their complaint via an online form. The form contains the insurance number, the amount of damage, and a description of the damage. If the amount of damage is ≤100 Euro, an automatic plausibility check is conducted and the complaint is approved. The customer is informed via email, and the money transfer is initiated. If the damage amount is above 100 Euro, a clerk checks the complaint. The customer is informed about the decision via email. If the complaint is rejected, the customer is offered an optional meeting.

Figure 5.2 depicts the process model for the customer complaint use case in Business Process Modeling and Notation (BPMN) [95]. More precisely, the process model reflects the control flow aspect, i.e., the process tasks, their order, and decision rules at alternative branchings. In detail: after an instance for a specific customer is created and started (*start* $\bigcirc$), process task upload complaint information (*task* $\boxed{}$) is executed. The order between start event and process task is represented by a *sequence flow* (────▸). The task is followed by an XOR gateway $\diamondsuit$) expressing an alternative branching depending on the amount of damage (see question attached to the XOR split). The outgoing edges are labelled with the possible decisions, i.e., >100 and ≤100 where the option >100 is the default path. This means that this path is chosen if none of the decision alternatives evaluates to true and is indicated by the little bar attached to the edge. If the damage amount is ≤100, two process tasks, check plausibility (automatic) and approve complaint and inform customer and initiate money transfer, are conducted. If the amount is >100, tasks check plausibility and decide on complaint and inform customer are executed in sequence, followed by another (nested) XOR branching, depending on the result of the check. The default path is to reject the complaint and to offer a meeting. Alternatively, the complaint is approved, and task initiate money transfer is executed. Then, all alternative branches are synchronized by the corresponding XOR joins, and the process ends with an end event ($\bigcirc$).

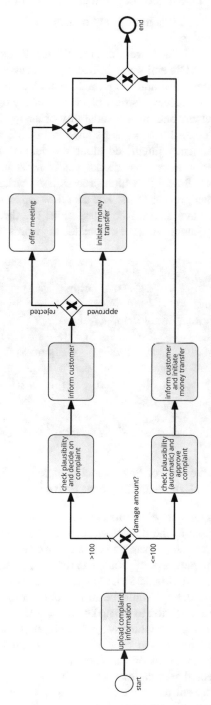

Fig. 5.2 Customer complaint process: BPMN-based process model, control flow perspective (using SAP Signavio®)

Note that this process model does not contain a parallel branching, denoted by parallel (AND) gateway ⊕. Tasks in different branches of a parallel branching can be executed in arbitrary order.

As modeling quality guidelines, we aim at achieving *block-structured* process models, i.e., parallel and XOR splits are joined by associated parallel and XOR joins. Specifically, the alternative and the parallel blocks do not overlap; they can only be nested. Doing so, we achieve (strict) *block structuring* of the process model, contributing to the correctness and understandability of the model.

We can see from the control flow model shown in Fig. 5.2 which process tasks are connected and consequently integrated along the defined process logic. What cannot be seen from the control flow model yet is how the process tasks are connected in terms of data flow, i.e., which process tasks write data elements that are read/consumed by other process tasks. The data flow aspect of a process realizes data exchange and results in a data-driven integration. The data flow aspect of the use case is emphasized by underlining the associated keywords in the following text.

Customer Complaint Process-Data Flow Perspective: Customers state their complaint via an <u>online form</u>. The form contains the <u>insurance number</u>, the <u>amount of damage</u>, and a <u>description of the damage</u>. If the <u>amount of damage</u> is ≤100 Euro, an automatic plausibility check is conducted and the <u>complaint</u> is approved. The customer is informed via <u>email</u> and the <u>money transfer</u> is initiated. If the <u>damage amount</u> is above 100 Euro, a clerk checks the <u>complaint</u>. The customer is informed about the <u>decision</u> via <u>email</u>. If the <u>complaint</u> is rejected, the customer is offered an optional meeting.

Figure 5.3 augments the control flow model depicted in Fig. 5.2 with the data flow perspective. In BPMN, the data flow perspective is modeled using, i.e., *data objects* (⬚) describing the data elements and *message flows* (○- - -▷) describing the read and write accesses to the data flow objects by process tasks. As we can see, two data objects exist, i.e., `complaint` and `decision`. Compared to the textual description, the parameters of `complaint`, i.e., `insurance number`, `amount of damage`, and `description of the damage`, are "hidden." The alternative way of modeling would be to model each of these parameters as a data object. Then their connection to `complaint` would not be visible anymore. We are not saying at this point which way is right or wrong. However, when envisioning a subsequent realization of the process as running process-oriented application, the precise definition of the data flow is of utmost importance as instances of process-oriented applications are running program code. Missing input parameters, for example, lead to errors and problems during runtime and should be avoided at design time. Note that at this point, we are still at the conceptual

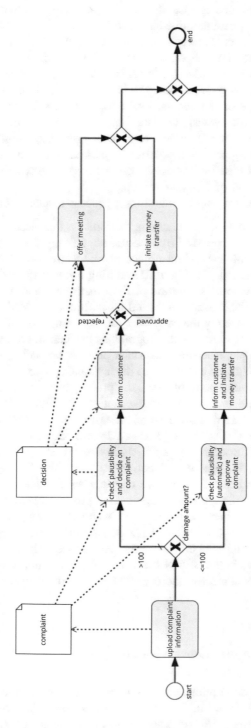

Fig. 5.3 Customer complaint process: BPMN-based process model, control and data flow perspective (using SAP Signavio®)

modeling phase. Precise and consistent definition of data flow often only happens in the execution design phase described in Sect. 5.4.

In the example, data object complaint is written by process task upload complaint information and read by process tasks check plausibility and decide on constraint and check plausibility (automatic) and approve complaint. The direction of the message flow indicates the type of the access, i.e., a write access based on a message flow directed from process task to data object and read access based on a message flow directed from data object to process task. Accordingly, data object decision is written by process task check plausibility and decide on complaint and read by process tasks inform customer, initiate money transfer, and offer meeting.

Note that an alternative way of initiating a process instance could be to start with a message start event (✉), indicating that process instances are started upon receiving a customer complaint request (cf. Fig. 5.4) from a separate customer process. In this case, data object complaint would be sent to the instance as message instead of being written during instance execution. As shown in Fig. 5.4, the organizational separation of the customer and the insurance can be expressed in BPMN using pools and lanes. Message-based events play an important role in the context of the *correlator* (cf. Sect. 6.6) and *interorganizational processes* realized through *process choreographies* in Chap. 8. For the use case, we could model, for example, a separate customer process, uploading all information and sending the complaint via a message to the insurance process.

From an interoperability point of view, the process tasks in the process model depicted in Fig. 5.3 are *orchestrated* along a given process logic, e.g., process task upload complaint information is executed before either process tasks check plausibility and decide on complaint or check plausibility (automatic) and decide on complaint, and data element complaint is "passed on" between these tasks. The interoperability and integration aspects become even more visible when considering the functional aspect of the tasks, i.e., the services or application programs invoked by the tasks, as described in Sect. 6.6, because the invoked Web services/application programs are also integrated in a process-oriented manner. As indicated in Fig. 5.4, process orchestrations between different process participants reflected by different roles and the corresponding lanes in the BPMN-based model can be connected via message exchanges. This results in *process choreographies* that will be discussed in detail in Sect. 8.

5.3 Conversational Process Modeling

Transforming process descriptions given in natural language such as the customer complaint use case described in Sect. 5.2 into process models expressed in, e.g., BPMN, so far, has required an interaction between domain expert and process

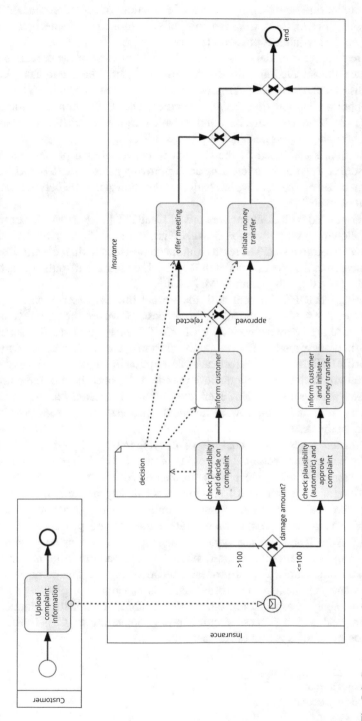

Fig. 5.4 Customer complaint process: BPMN-based process model, control and data flow perspective, inter-organizational view (using SAP Signavio®)

designer. Supporting the (semi-)automatic extraction of process models from process descriptions [3, 222], from the point of view of the process designer, might reduce the necessary interactions with the domain expert. Empowering the domain expert to create process models [161], from the point of view of the domain expert, might reduce the interaction with the process designer. The latter has received a recent push by the advent of AI-powered chatbots such as ChatGPT[1] offering multiple opportunities for *"the design, operation, and application of information systems"* [212]. More precisely, how and to which degree can chatbots replace the interaction with the process designer in process modeling?

This question is addressed by the concept of conversational process modeling *"which describes the process of creating and improving process models and process descriptions based on the iterative exchange of questions/answers between domain experts and chatbots"* [120].

We experimented with different versions of ChatGPT [120]. If we, for example, insert the following prompt `"create BPMN model: A follows B,"` Chat-GPT creates a twofold result. The textual output comprises a textual description how to create and depict the process model in BPMN. The "graphical" output is actually a self-drawn, textual graph, but no BPMN model.

Apparently, ChatGPT can deal with the textual process description and para-phrase it into a description of modeling the process. However, the graphical aspect of BPMN modeling is not supported by ChatGPT. Hence, an idea is to generate a BPMN-based process model in a non-graphical format, e.g., an XML-based format, in the case of BPMN, the `.bpmn` format. A description in .bpmn format can then be uploaded in tools such as SAP Signavio® in order to display them in the graphical BPMN-based process model. However, the output we created has not included the necessary information on how to layout the process model, e.g., positioning information on the tasks.

We conducted a systematic analysis of existing AI-based tools and chatbots for their support in conversational process modeling [120]. Table 5.1 summarizes the results along the life cycle phases process discovery, process analysis, and process redesign. Moreover, [120] provides a set of key performance indicators to measure the quality of the AI-generated output as well as a real-world data set containing real-world process orchestration models and process descriptions for testing.[2] Note that there are typically more process life cycle phases such as process implementation, but these phases would require a combination of ChatGPT and other tools, e.g., a process execution engine. The same holds for quantitative analysis, i.e., in the process analysis and redesign phases, we focus on qualitative analysis aspects. For quantitative analysis, the chatbot functionality can be combined with a process simulation environment, e.g., CPNTools.[3] This combined usage of tools is part of future work.

---

[1] https://chat.openai.com/.

[2] https://zenodo.org/record/7783492.

[3] https://cpntools.org/.

Table 5.1 Chatbot tasks along the process life cycle as in [70] (Table adapted from [120])

# application	input	output	chatbot task
1. gather information	process description	process description	paraphrase
2. process modelling	process description	process model, process description	extract
3. assure model quality	process model, process description, process modelling guidelines and metrics	quality issues, refined process model, refined process description	compare and assess
4. select redesign method	collection of process models and process descriptions	redesign method, selection of process models and process descriptions	select method, query models
5. apply redesign method	collection of process models and process descriptions, redesign method	collection of process models and process descriptions	query and refactor models

What can be concluded from Table 5.1 is that chatbots such as ChatGPT are strong in working with textual process descriptions, e.g., paraphrasing them and creating descriptions of how to model processes. Figure 5.1, for example, depicts the modeling "recipe" created by ChatGPT for the use case of customer complaints. Note that this output differs from the manually created BPMN model as depicted in Fig. 5.2. The chatbot output suggests, for example, a loop back to task Clerk Review after the customer meeting, which is not present in the manually created model. This shows that, first of all, there is always room for interpretation when transforming text into models, and in this case, the chatbot output should be analyzed with care (Fig. 5.5).

Creating process models with and without support of chatbots must not necessarily result in correct process models. As reported by Mendling et al. in [145], more than 5% of analyzed reference models contained errors, resulting in, for example, deadlocks. For process-oriented integration, it is mandatory to achieve correct process models and orchestrations at all times in order to avoid any problems or inconsistencies caused by flaws in the process model. In the following Sect. 5.4, we will discuss how structural and behavioral correctness of process model can be verified in a systematic way.

5.4 Verification of Process Behavior

In this section, we explain the notions and concepts of structural and behavioral correctness of process models and subsequently the executable process orchestrations and illustrate them based on the running example.

Explanation:

* The process starts with a "Start Event" that represents the beginning of the process.
* The "Customer Complaint" task represents the step where the customer fills in the online form to upload their complaint. This task has three input data: the insurance number, the amount of damage, and the description of the damage.
* The "Gateway" is used to split the process into two branches: one for complaints with a damage amount of 100 Euro or less, and one for complaints with a damage amount above 100 Euro.
* For complaints with a damage amount of 100 Euro or less, the process goes to the "Automatic Plausibility Check" task, where an automated check is conducted to verify the plausibility of the complaint. If the complaint is approved, the process goes to the "Inform Customer" task, where the customer is notified via email that their complaint has been approved and the money transfer is initiated. If the complaint is rejected, the process ends with an "End Event".
* For complaints with a damage amount above 100 Euro, the process goes to the "Clerk Review" task, where a clerk checks the complaint. If the complaint is approved, the process goes to the "Inform Customer" task, where the customer is notified via email that their complaint has been approved and the money transfer is initiated. If the complaint is rejected, the process goes to the "Optional Meeting" task, where the customer is offered an optional meeting to discuss their complaint. After the meeting, the process goes back to the "Clerk Review" task. If the customer doesn't want to have a meeting or if the complaint is still rejected after the meeting, the process ends with an "End Event".
* The "End Event" represents the end of the process.

↻ Regenerate response

Fig. 5.5 Customer complaint process: paraphrased description of the process of process modeling using ChatGPT

Most of the process modeling notations such as BPMN or Petri Nets come with structural correctness criteria, i.e., constraints and requirements inherent to the process meta model that must be followed by the process models and, if followed, guarantee certain properties. Examples comprise requirements on the number of start and/or end nodes and the connectedness of the process elements. Having a single, well-defined start node, for example, results in a well-defined start point of process instances. Connectedness prevents isolated nodes such as process tasks and, in turn, unclear semantics when these process tasks are to be executed.

Behavioral correctness refers to the runtime behavior of the processes that are executed based on the process models. The goal of checking behavioral correctness is to foresee possibly undesired behavior at the model level, i.e., during design time,

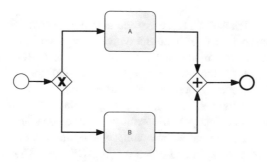

Fig. 5.6 Simple deadlock situation (using SAP Signavio®)

and before putting the process models into execution, i.e., before runtime. This can prevent undesired behavior and avoid follow-up costs or other consequences. A prominent example for undesired behavior is a *deadlock*, i.e., a situation where the process cannot be executed further and would, during runtime, just block without any further explanation or notification. Figure 5.6 depicts a simple and "classical" example for a deadlock (cf. [220]). The start event is followed by an XOR gateway ⊗, resulting in a choice between either executing process task A or process task B, i.e., only one thread of control is chosen. This alternative branching is synchronized by a parallel gateway ⊕, requiring that both threads of control are arriving. As this is impossible in the given model, a deadlock is caused (XOR split/AND join problem; cf. [9]).

While for the simple process model in Fig. 5.6 we can still relatively easy spot the deadlock based on the process model, for more complex process models, a manual inspection becomes hard, and potential problems might be overlooked easily. Hence, an automatic and systematic way of analysis is preferable. For this, an algorithmic approach is needed, which, in turn, requires a formal process meta model. Here, *Petri Nets* have proven themselves as a formal way of modeling and analyzing processes (cf., e.g., [11]).

The model in Fig. 5.7a depicts the process model from Fig. 5.6 represented as Petri Net. We can see that basically two types of elements are used, i.e., *transitions*

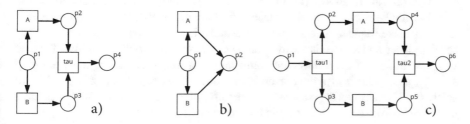

Fig. 5.7 Simple deadlock situation presented as Petri Net Model (**a**); solution with alternative branching (**b**); solution with parallel branching (**c**)

◻ and *places* ◯. Transitions represent the *active* elements of the process model and places the *passive* ones. Transitions typically represent process tasks, cmp. A and B. Places are used to model states or conditions in a process model. We can say that, for example, p1 represent the start state or condition and p4 the final state or condition of the process model. Transitions and places are connected by a flow relation, i.e., directed edges (———→), for example, place p1 to transition A.

Figure 5.7b and c depicts possible solutions for the deadlock. The Petri Net in Fig. 5.7b represents an alternative branching where either A or B are executed and place p1 serves as XOR split and place p2 as XOR join. The Petri Net Fig. 5.7c represents a solution based on a parallel branching where tau1 and tau2 serve as AND split and AND join and transitions A and B are executed in parallel during runtime.

Formally, the structure of a Petri Net is defined as follows:

Definition 5.1 (Petri Net (cf., e.g., [11, 157])) A Petri Net PN is defined as PN:=(P, T, F, W) with

- P denotes the (finite) set of places
- T denotes the (finite) set of transitions
- $P \cap T = \emptyset$
- F denotes a flow relation; $F \subseteq (T \times P) \cup (P \times T)$
- $W : F \mapsto \mathbb{N}$ is a function assigning to each edge $f \in F$ a weight; the default value for the weight of an edge is 1.

Note that in addition to the weight function given in Definition 5.1, a *capacity function c* might be defined to assign each place $p \in P$ a natural number reflecting the maximum number of tokens allowed in this place. The default capacity is ∞.

For the Petri Net shown in Fig. 5.7c, for example, its set-based definition turns out as follows:

- P = {p1, p2, p3, p4, p5, p6}
- T = {tau1, A, B, tau2}
- F = { (p1, tau1), (tau1, p2), (tau1, p3), (p2, A), (p3, B), ..., (tau2, p6)}
- $W(f) = 1 \forall f \in F$

Based on flow relation F (cf. Definition 5.1), we can see a structural correctness criterion for Petri Nets, i.e., that places and transitions always have to be ordered in an alternate manner. This means that a transition is always connected to one or several places and a place is always connected to one or several transitions. In other words, a transition must never be connected to a transition and a place never to another place. This is also the reason to introduce *silent* transitions tau, which are solely used for structuring reasons. Specifically, silent transitions do neither process data, invoke Web services, nor write entries to any log file.

For Fig. 5.7, middle, place p1 triggers the decision between firing transition A or firing transition B. Place p2, in turn, synchronizes the alternative execution of the threads. Hence, p1 serves as XOR split and p2 as XOR join.

For Fig. 5.7, right side, tau1 triggers the execution of both outgoing threads of control, and symmetrically tau2 synchronizes the threads, i.e., tau1 serves as the AND split and tau2 as AND join. We can note that places can be used to represent XOR splits/joins (see p1), and transitions can be used to represent AND splits/joins (see tau).

To present a more complex example, we translate the BPMN process model depicted in Fig. 5.2 into a Petri Net (cf. Fig. 5.8). The Petri Net starts with input place start, followed by an XOR split represented by place p1.

Either transition check plausibility and decide on complaint or check plausibility (automatic) and decide on complaint can then be executed in the sequel. After executing check plausibility and decide on complaint, transition inform customer becomes activated. This branch comprises a subsequent alternative branching, triggered by the XOR split p3. Through p3, the decision on the complaint is reflected, resulting in either execution of transition initiate money transfer or transition offer meeting. After executing transition check plausibility (automatic) and decide on complaint, transition inform customer and initiate money transfer becomes activated. The XOR split place p3 is "matched" by XOR join place p4 and p1 by p7. In order to not violate the alternating order of transitions and places, p4 and p6 are separated from p7 by silent transition tau1. Silent transition tau2 is not absolutely necessary as transition inform customer and initiate money transfer could be directly connected with place p7.

So far, we have introduced the formal definition of the structure of Petri Nets (cf. Definition 5.1). However, we have not explained how to express the *dynamic behavior* of a Petri Net. Basically, the dynamic behavior of a Petri Net is realized by changing the *state* of the net. The state of a Petri Net is reflected by the (sub) set of places P that are currently *marked*, i.e., if the places represent conditions, marked places reflect conditions that are currently fulfilled, and if the places represent states, marked places reflect states the system is currently in. How can places be marked? For Petri Nets, a marking is determined by *tokens* (●), i.e., a place that is not marked does not carry a token ($\bigcirc$) and a marked place carries a token ($\bigodot$), formally:

Definition 5.2 (Marking, Marking Function of a Petri Net [11]) Let PN = (P, T, F, W) be a Petri Net. The a marking on P is defined as a function $M := P \mapsto \mathbb{N}_0$, i.e., for a place $p \in P$, M(p) denotes the number of tokens assigned to p.

Different classes of Petri Nets exist that can be distinguished based on the number of tokens that are allowed on one place at maximum. *Event/Condition (E/C) Nets* restrict the maximum number of tokens per place to 1, i.e., a place can either carry 0 or 1 token. Note that accordingly, the edge weights are 1 for all edges in an E/C Net. The interpretation of the place is that of a condition, and a place marked with

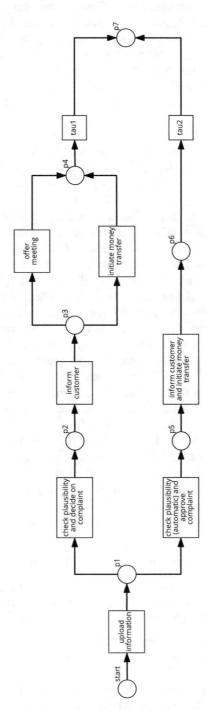

Fig. 5.8 Customer complaint process: Petri Net-based process model, control flow perspective (using SAP Signavio®)

0 tokens represents a condition that is currently not fulfilled, and a place carrying 1 token represents that the assigned condition is fulfilled. Here, marking M can be refined to $M : P \mapsto \{0, 1\}$ or, for the interpretation as conditions, $M : P \mapsto \{FALSE, TRUE\}$.

Another class of Petri Nets is *Place/Transition (P/T) Nets*. Here, a place can basically carry an arbitrary number of tokens. In order to restrict the number of tokens, a *capacity function* C can be defined, i.e., $C : P \mapsto \mathbb{N} \cup \infty$, where for a place $p \in P$, C(p) defines the maximum number of tokens that p can carry, i.e., $M(p) \le C(p)$ must hold $\forall p \in P$. The default capacity is ∞.

Another restriction that holds for both E/C Nets and P/T Nets is that we assume tokens to be *anonymous*, i.e., tokens that cannot be distinguished. In Chap. 7, we will introduce *Colored Petri Nets (CPN)* as a Petri Net class for which tokens can be distinguished based on their color, e.g., a red token can be distinguished from a blue token. The color extension can be also interpreted as tokens carrying data, e.g., a token carrying the patient information of John Smith from a token carrying the patient information of Jane Smith. Colored tokens constitute an instrument to augment Petri Nets with data flow.

Executing a Petri Net is based on the transition from one possible marking to another possible marking on the net; these transitions are actually realized by firing the actual transitions of the net. Take Fig. 5.9 where an alternative branching represented by a Petri Net is depicted, together with two possible markings on the net. On the left-hand side, the marking is defined as M(p1) = 1 and M(P2) = 0 and the marking on the right-hand side as M(p1) = 0 and M(p2) = 1.

The transition between markings is realized by *firing enabled transitions*. For this, we have to define (a) when a transition is enabled, i.e., can fire, and (b) what happens when the transition fires, i.e., which marking results from the firing of the transition (cf. Definition 5.3).

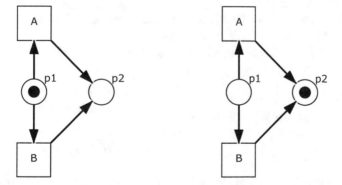

Fig. 5.9 Alternative branching represented as Petri Net with enabled transitions and firing sequences (using SAP Signavio®)

Auxiliary Definition 1 (Preset, Postset of a Transition [11]) *Let PN = (P, T, F, W) be a Petri Net. Then we define two auxiliary sets as follows:*

- *Preset of a transition $t \in T$:* $\bullet t := \{p \mid (p, t) \in F\}$
- *Postset of a transition $t \in T$:* $t\bullet := \{p \mid (t, p) \in F\}$

Definition 5.3 (Marking and Firing on Petri Nets, cf., e.g., [11]) Let PN = (P, T, F, W) be a Petri Net and let M: P $\mapsto$ $\mathbb{N}_0$ be the marking function on PN. Then the following transitions between markings can be defined:

- $M \xrightarrow{t} M'$: by firing $t \in T$, the state of PN changes from M to M'
- $M \rightarrow M'$: $\exists t \in T$ with $M \xrightarrow{t} M'$
- $M_1 \xrightarrow{*} M_n$: $\exists$ firing sequence $t_1, t_2, \ldots, t_{n-1}$ such that $M_i \xrightarrow{t_i} M_{i+1}$ for $i = 1, \ldots, n$
- M' is reachable from M $\Longleftrightarrow$ $M \xrightarrow{*} M'$

Definition 5.3 provides notions for markings and their transitions based on firing transitions. The first case describes the firing of transition t in marking M, resulting in marking M'. In the second case, marking M' is directly reachable from marking M as we know that there exists a transition t that by firing leads from M to M'. The third case describes the transition of a marking M_1 into a marking M_n by firing a sequence of transitions where the firing of a single transition in this sequence results in an "intermediate" marking. The fourth case is the most general one and makes an important statement about *reachability* of markings, i.e., a marking M' is reachable from another marking M if we can find a firing sequence of transitions that starting from M—via intermediate markings—results in M'. Definition 5.4 describes how the firing of a transition is actually working, i.e., when a transition can fire (i.e., is *enabled*) and what the effects of firing the transition are.

Definition 5.4 (Enabling/Activation/Firing of Transitions in E/C Nets) Let PN = (P, T, F, W) be an E/C Net.
Enabledness, Activation of Transitions: A transition $t \in T$ is enabled or activated if $\forall p \in \bullet t : M(p) = 1 \land \forall p \in t\bullet \setminus \bullet t : M(p) = 0$.
Firing of Transitions: Let M, M' be two markings on PN. Then:

$$M \rightarrow M' \text{ with } M'(p) = \begin{cases} 0 & p \in \bullet t \setminus t\bullet \\ 1 & p \in t\bullet \setminus \bullet t \\ 1 & p \in \bullet t \cap t\bullet \\ M(p) & p \notin \bullet t \cup t\bullet \end{cases} \tag{5.1}$$

Let us have a closer look at Definition 5.4. At first, it defines when a transition is enabled or activated. This is the case if for all places of the preset of the transition there is one token (i.e., the preconditions of the transition are fulfilled) and for all places of the postset there is no token except for those places that are also in the preset (i.e., all post conditions of the transition that are not preconditions at the same time are not fulfilled). The first condition that all preconditions should be fulfilled is intuitive. The second condition on the post conditions follows from the requirement of E/C Nets that no place carries more than one token.

To explain the last statement on the post conditions in more detail, let us have a look the second part of Definition 5.4 on the firing of transitions. When a transition fires, basically, all tokens of the places of the preset of the transition are removed, and one token is put on each of the places in the postset of the transition. For E/C Nets, the interpretation is that before firing, all preconditions of the transition are fulfilled, and after the firing, all post conditions are fulfilled.

Coming back to the post conditions: if the firing of the transition means to put a token in each of the places of the postset and if there would be already one token, then more than one token would result for this place, which is forbidden by the basic definition of E/C Nets, i.e., that each of the places of an E/C Net carries zero or one token.

Consider the Petri Net on the top left in Fig. 5.10 as an E/C Net. Which of the transitions is enabled? According to Definition 5.4, transition `tau1` is the only transition for which there is a token in all of the places of the preset, i.e., one token in place `p1`. There is no token in each of the places in the postset of `tau1`. Hence, it follows that `tau1` is enabled and can fire. If `tau1` fires, all tokens from the places of the preset, i.e., `p1` are removed, and a token is put on each of the places of the postset, i.e., `p2` and `p3`. The resulting marking is depicted next to the original net. Here, two transitions are enabled, i.e., A and B, which reflects the execution semantics of the parallel branching, i.e., the firing of `tau1` represents the activation of two parallel branches.

Figure 5.10 depicts all markings that are reachable from the initial marking on the net on the top left. All of these markings reflect the execution of the entire net and the process behind. The final marking is shown in the net on the bottom right where there is one token in place `p6`. In this case, no transition is enabled anymore. Formally, this means that we have reached a *deadlock*. For Petri Nets that represent processes, this can be a "desired" deadlock, i.e., the final state of the process.

Figure 5.11 shows a case for an "undesired" deadlock, consisting of an alternative split combined with a parallel join, modeled based on an E/C Net. The XOR split and AND join are represented by places p_1 and p_4, respectively. Consider the marking on the E/C Net on the left side where a token is in place p_1. In this marking, both transitions A and B are enabled and can fire. The decision as to which of the two transitions actually fires is non-deterministic, i.e., without any further information such as a decision rule, it cannot be decided. For the verification of the net, we anyway determine all reachable states, i.e., we follow both variants, the first one for which A fires (marking on top right) and the second one for which B fires (marking on bottom right).

In both cases, either A or B fires, putting a token in either place p_2 or p_3. AND join `tau` requires a token in each of both places p_2 and p_3 to be enabled. This is impossible; hence, for both markings in Fig. 5.11, right-hand side, an undesired deadlock is reached.

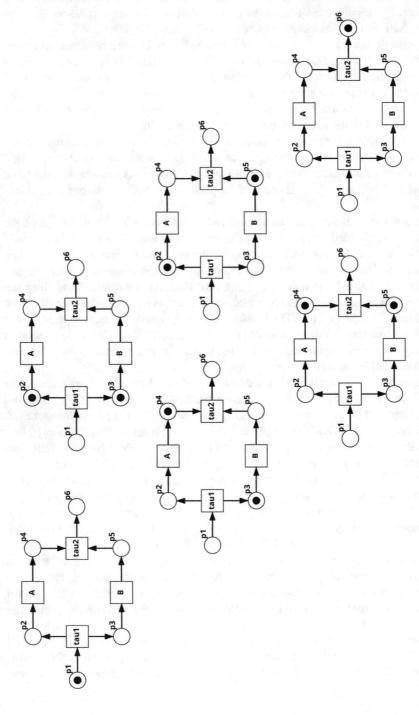

Fig. 5.10 Parallel branching represented as Petri Net with enabled transitions and firing sequences (using SAP Signavio®)

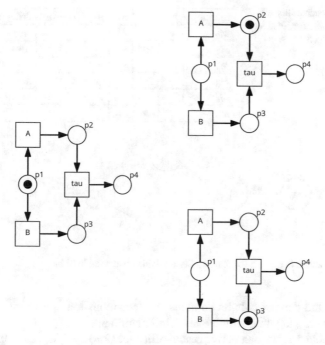

Fig. 5.11 Branching containing deadlock represented as Petri Net (using SAP Signavio®)

The firing and marking rules become more complex for P/T Nets as (i) more than one token can be in a place and (ii) as indicated by the weight function W, more than one token can be consumed and produced when a transition fires. Specifically, for (ii), weight function W determines how many tokens are consumed based on the weight assigned to the incoming edges of the transition and how many tokens are produced based on the weight assigned to the outgoing edges. Moreover, capacities defined on places have to be respected. Hence, the firing and marking rules for P/T Nets are driven by the weight and capacity function.

The basis for verification of the runtime behavior of Petri Nets is hence to determine all reachable markings, starting from an initial marking M_0, collected in a *reachability set* as defined as follows:

Definition 5.5 (Reachability Set, cf. [49]) Let M_0 be an initial marking of a Petri Net. Then $[M_0\rangle$ denotes the set of all possible markings, which can be reached starting from M_0 (for an E/C Net, e.g., using the firing rules as defined in Definition 5.4). $[M_0\rangle$ is denoted as reachability set of the Petri Net. For any marking M_i, $[M_i\rangle$ denotes the set of markings which can be reached from M_i.

For calculating the reachability set for a given Petri Net with initial marking M_0, it is recommended to use a table of the following form: the first column denotes the marking that is currently investigated, the following columns represent the places

Table 5.2 Reachability set captured as table for E/C Net depicted in Fig. 5.10

Marking	p_1	p_2	p_3	p_4	p_5	p_6	firing transitions
M_0	×						tau1 $\rightarrow M_1$
M_1		×	×				A $\rightarrow M_2$, B $\rightarrow M_3$
M_2			×	×			B $\rightarrow M_4$
M_3		×			×		A $\rightarrow M_4$
M_4				×	×		tau2 $\rightarrow M_5$
M_5						×	

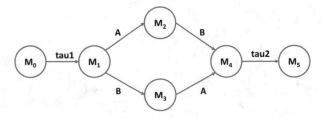

Fig. 5.12 Reachability graph for reachability analysis conducted in Table 5.2

of the net, and the last column contains the transitions that are enabled under the current marking, together with the resulting marking.

From Table 5.2, we can derive reachability set $[M_0\rangle = \{M_0, \ldots, M_5\}$ with the respective markings for the E/C Net depicted in Fig. 5.10. The reachability set can also be represented as *reachability graph*, defined as follows:

Definition 5.6 (Reachability Graph, cf. [11]) The reachability graph G(PN) of a Petri Net PN with reachability set $[M_0\rangle$ is defined as follows:

$$G(PN) := \{(M_1, t, M_2) \in [M_0\rangle \times T \times [M_0\rangle \mid M_1 \overset{t}{\rightarrow} M_2\}$$

Figure 5.12 depicts the reachability graph for the reachability analysis conducted in Table 5.2. What can be directly seen from the reachability graph is the dead state reached in M_5 as this node has no outgoing edges. M_0 is the initial state as it has no incoming edges.

Can we say more about the properties of a Petri Net with respect to its runtime behavior? An important notion in this context is *liveness* of (i) transitions and (ii) the entire Petri Net. For (i), liveness states whether or not a transition can at all fire during runtime and whether a transition can fire again and again (eventually). For (ii), liveness states whether the Petri Net contains a deadlock or at least one transition can fire again and again (eventually) or all transitions can fire again and again (eventually).

Definition 5.7 (Liveness, According to [157]) Let PN = (P, T, F, W) be a Petri Net with initial marking M_0. $[M_0\rangle$ denotes the set reachability set of PN and $L(M_0)$ the set of all possible firing sequences from M_0.
Then: PN is L_k-live if $\forall t \in T : t$ is L_k-live, $k \in \{0, \ldots, 4\}$:

- t is L_0-live if t can never fire in any $L(M_0)$
- t is L_1-live if t can fire at least once for a sequence in $L(M_0)$

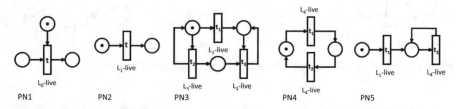

Fig. 5.13 Example of Petri Nets with different levels of liveness

- t is L_2-live if t can fire a finite number of times for a sequence in $L(M_0)$
- t is L_3-live if t can fire an infinite number of times for a sequence in $L(M_0)$
- t is L_4-live if t can fire an infinite number of times for $[M_0\rangle$

Based on the L_k-live notions, we can define the following liveness properties for PN:

1. PN is live or strong-live in $M_0 \Leftrightarrow \forall t \in T : t$ is L4-live
2. PN is weak-live or quasi-live (cf. [83]) in $M_0 \Leftrightarrow \exists t \in T: t$ is L4-live $\wedge$ $\exists t\prime \in T: t\prime$ is L0-, L1-, L2-, or L3-live.
3. PN is strictly L_k-live if it is L_k-live, but not L_{k+1}-live, $k \in \{1, \dots, 3\}$

We can interpret Property 3 in such a way that the liveness of a Petri net is determined by the transition(s) with the minimal L_k-liveness in the net. According to [157], L_4-liveness implies L_3-liveness, L_3-liveness implies L_2-liveness, and L_2-liveness implies L_1-liveness.

Figure 5.13 illustrates the different liveness levels of transitions and Petri Nets PN1, ... PN5. For PN1, the only transition t in the net can never fire and hence is L_0-live (dead). Consequently, PN1 is L_0-live. For PN2, the only transition t in the net can fire exactly once; then a deadlock is reached. Hence, t and PN2 are L_1-live. PN2 is neither weak nor strong live. PN3 consists of three transitions t_1, t_2, and t_3. t_1 is L_1-live as it can fire exactly once if it fires first in the given initial marking. Then no transition can fire anymore, and a deadlock has been reached. Otherwise, if t_2 fires first, t_1 can fire at least once, given the number of times t_2 fires. t_2 can fire an infinite number of times, given that t_1 does not fire, i.e., for a given firing sequence. Specifically for this reason, t_2 is L_3-live and not L_4-live. t_3 can fire a finite number of times as each of the firings of t_3 depends on the firing of t_2. Hence, t_3 is L_2-live. For PN4, both transitions t_1 and t_2 are L_4-live as they can fire an infinite number of times for all reachable markings, i.e., for $[M_0\rangle$. Hence, PN4 is L_4-live and strong live. For PN5, transition t_1 is L_1-live as it can fire exactly once. Transition t_2 is L_4-live as it can fire an infinite number of times for any reachable marking in $[M_0\rangle$. Overall, PN5 is weak live.

Another behavioral property of interest is *boundedness* (cf. Definition 5.8). Boundedness means that the number of tokens in certain places cannot become infinite. For E/C Nets, boundedness is guaranteed by design as the maximum number of tokens per place can be 1 at maximum. For P/T Nets, the number of

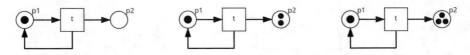

Fig. 5.14 Example of P/T Net with unbounded place (using SAP Signavio®)

tokens can become infinite by being "pumped" up when firing transitions (see P/T
Net shown in Fig. 5.14): every time transition t fires, a token is put on places p_1 and
p_2. While the token on p_1 is consumed when firing t again, the number of tokens in
p_2 increases. In order to control the number of tokens for the P/T Net, for example,
a capacity could be assigned to p_2. However, after reaching the capacity, then the
P/T Net reaches a deadlock while it has been L_4-live/strong live before.

Definition 5.8 (Boundedness, cf. [157]) Let PN = (P, T, F, W) be a Petri net with
initial marking M_0 and let $k \in \mathbb{N}$. Then:

$$\text{PN is bounded} \Leftrightarrow \forall M \in [M_0\rangle, \forall p \in P : M(p) \leq k$$

Effects of Behavioral Properties on Interoperability/Integration Aspects In
this section, the behavioral properties of liveness and boundedness have been
discussed for Petri nets, which can be verified during their design time. Liveness
allows statements on the executability of certain transitions and the entire net.
Specifically, we can determine dead states and deadlock situations. This can be
important if, for example, certain transitions represent the sending of messages that
are expected by partners. If these transitions cannot fire or only fire an insufficient
number of times, this can have severe impacts on the interoperability with partners.
This aspect will be deepened for process choreographies in Chap. 8. Moreover,
process orchestrations integrate tasks, services, and human workers and realize data
flow. If, for example, a task will never be executed and hence a mandatory data
element is missing for a subsequent task, the data flow and data integration to
be realized by the process orchestration fail. Boundedness enables to control the
number of tokens at certain places. Pumping up the number of tokens can translate,
for example, to sending an infinite number of messages to partners which, in turn,
can severely affect the interoperability with the affected partner if this partner is not
expecting and not able to process an infinite number of messages.

In summary, Petri Nets are utilized as formalism to systematically analyze process orchestration models regarding properties such as liveness and boundedness,
which might crucially influence interoperability. Basically, Petri Nets can be also
utilized to execute process orchestrations, i.e., for their execution design. However,
as already mentioned, higher Petri Net classes (when compared to E/C Nets and P/T
Nets) have to be used in order to distinguish process orchestration instances (e.g.,
using Colored Petri Nets) and to express process perspectives such as time and data.
Workflow Nets as a higher Petri Net class will be introduced in the next section on
execution design, along with other execution languages.

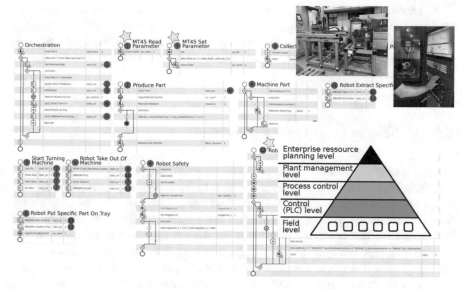

Fig. 5.15 Interoperability and integration challenges in manufacturing orchestrations

5.5   Case Study: Manufacturing Orchestration

The orchestration of manufacturing processes offers several advantages with respect to interoperability and integration of systems, humans, machines, and sensors. Figure 5.15 displays a network of process orchestrations with the main process called `Orchestration` invoking several sub-processes, e.g., starting the machining of a part or reading parameters. The orchestration enables the interoperability between the involved machines, sensors, and human workers (e.g., domain experts) and integrates the involved systems across the levels of the traditional automation pyramid (also depicted in Fig. 5.15).

We have orchestrated and implemented 16 process scenarios at seven manufacturing companies using the manufacturing orchestration engine centurio.work [161] based on open-source process execution engine CPEE.[4] The success of the CPEE is underpinned by more than 680.000 downloads,[5] complemented by add-ons such as connecting machines using standard format OPC-UA with more than 37.000 downloads.[6] The execution of a (fully automated) process orchestration for production of a metal rook is shown in this video.[7]

---

[4] cpee.org.

[5] https://rubygems.org/profiles/eTM, accessed 2023-05-04.

[6] https://rubygems.org/profiles/eTM, accessed 2023-05-04.

[7] https://lehre.bpm.in.tum.de/~mangler/.Slides/media/media1.mp4, last accessed: 2023-05-04.

In a nutshell, we assume a graph-based process model containing nodes reflecting tasks and edges reflecting the order of how the tasks are executed. Then, a mapping between to process models is based on mapping the labels of the tasks, the task attributes, and the context of the tasks, i.e., how they are embedded in the overall process model/graph [67].

5.6 Conclusion and Lessons Learned

Chapter 5 shows how (work) tasks can be orchestrated in a process-oriented manner, i.e., following an explicitly defined process logic. Doing so constitutes the first step toward developing interoperable process applications in a model-driven way. Special attention is paid to structural and behavioral soundness of the developed orchestrations. This builds the foundation for the implementation and realization of execution design and code in Chap. 6. In summary, process orchestrations enable the integration and hence the interoperability of systems, services, human work, and physical devices such as machines and sensors. Application areas range from office environments, e.g., loan applications in the financial domain, to production, logistics, and healthcare process.

Further Reading
1. van der Aalst, W.M.P., Stahl, C.: Modeling business processes—a Petri net-oriented approach. In: Cooperative Information Systems series. MIT Press, New York (2011). isbn 978-0-262-01538-7
2. Klievtsova, N., Benzin, J.-V., Kampik, T., Mangler, J., Rinderle-Ma, S.: Conversational Process Modelling: State of the Art, Applications, and Implications in Practice., arxiv 2023. https://doi.org/10.48550/arXiv.2304.11065
3. Murata, T.: Petri nets: properties, analysis and applications. Proc. IEEE **77**(4):541–580 (1989)
4. Weske, M.: Business Process Management—Concepts, Languages, Architectures, 3rd edn. Springer, Berlin (2019), pp. 1–417. ISBN 978-3-662-59431-5

Chapter 6
Process Orchestration: Execution Design

6.1 Motivation and Goals

The conceptual design of process orchestrations has been addressed in Chap. 5. Section 6.1 takes up the conceptual process orchestration models and provides execution design concepts, including process execution languages, task and worklist design, and correlation mechanisms (cf. Fig. 6.1). Regarding the overall embedding in the book, in Chap. 7, we discuss the patterns and processes for (enterprise) application integration (EAI) in more detail. In Chap. 8, the integration of processes of different partners through process choreographies will be explained.

In Chap. 5, we presented the fundamentals of conceptual process orchestration model design, including the verification of the behavior set out by these orchestration models. We modeled a use case from customer complaint management using BPMN and Petri Nets. We repeat the use case description, together with the corresponding Petri Net model (control flow only):

> **Customer Complaint Process** Customers state their complaint via an online form. The form contains the insurance number, the amount of damage, and a description of the damage. If the amount of damage is ≤ 100 Euro, an automatic plausibility check is conducted, and the complaint is approved. The customer is informed via email and the money transfer is initiated. If the damage amount is above 100 Euro, a clerk checks the complaint. The customer is informed about the decision via email. If the complaint is rejected, the customer is offered an optional meeting.

© Springer Nature Switzerland AG 2024
S. Rinderle-Ma et al., *Fundamentals of Information Systems Interoperability*,
https://doi.org/10.1007/978-3-031-48322-6_6

Levels ... / Tasks ↓	Syntactical	Semantic	Organizational
Exchange	Exchange formats, e.g., XML, relational databases, JSON, BSON, YAML, MessagePack; query languages: XPath, XQuery, SQL; transformation languages, e.g., XSLT	Schema matching and mapping; ontologies;	Message exchange; correlation
Integrate	SQL/XML standard; native XML databases; REST and GraphQL	Edge table, shredding; XML schema and RNG; schema and data integration; service integration	Correlation and choreography
Orchestrate	BPMN, Petri Nets, Workflow Nets, RPST, CPEE Trees, Colored Petri Nets	Verification, task and worklist design; service invocation; correlation; integration patterns and processes	Choreography

Fig. 6.1 Interoperability perspectives I: Chap. 6

The Petri Net depicted in Fig. 6.2 is equipped with one token in place `start`. Starting from this initial marking, the control flow can be executed. Firing sequence `upload information`, `check plausibility (automatic) and approve complaint`, `inform customer and initiate money transfer, tau2`, for example, reaches the final marking with a token in place `p7`. This illustrates the formal execution semantics of Petri Nets (more precisely an E/C Net in this case), which makes them basically ready for being executed as process orchestrations. However, basic Petri Net classes such as EC-Nets lack means to capture (i) multiple process instances to be executed on a process orchestration model; (ii) process perspectives such as data flow, resources, and time; and (iii) invocation of services and human work. Hence, this chapter provides further notations that are more geared toward process execution than (basic) Petri Nets, i.e., Workflow Nets [9]. Moreover, Petri Net notations are complemented by discussing the power of tree-based notations for process execution using the refined process structure tree [218] and CPEE trees [138].

For all presented notations, this chapter introduces execution and interoperability aspects of process orchestration control flow (cf. Sect. 6.2) and data flow (cf. Sect. 6.3). Following the development cycle of a process orchestration—and independently of a specific notation—task design aspects will be presented in Sect. 6.4 and worklist design aspects in Sect. 6.5. The technical realization via correlation is discussed in Sect. 6.6, and the chapter is rounded off by a real-world use case from the manufacturing domain in Sect. 6.7.

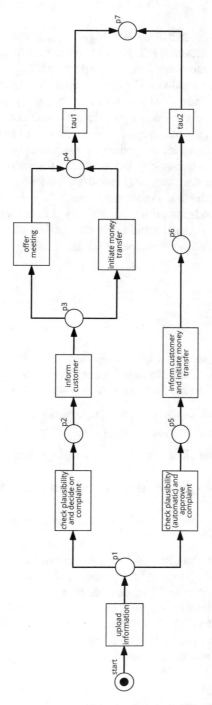

Fig. 6.2 Use case loan insurance claim modeled as Petri Net (using SAP Signavio ®)

6.2   Control Flow

In this section, we start with a Petri Net based notation that extends the basic
Petri Net classes of EC-nets and P/T Nets as introduced in Sect. 5.4 toward the
execution of process orchestrations. Let us here directly follow up on the behavioral
property of liveness (cf. Definition 5.7) to be checked on Petri Nets in the previous
section. (Strong) liveness means that for every marking, every transition can always
eventually fire. However, if we look at process orchestrations, the strong liveness
property goes too far, i.e., process orchestrations demand for being executable, and
every transition should be enabled for some firing sequence (otherwise they are not
contributing to the process execution), but also a well-defined end state should be
reached. For an example, see the process model depicted in Fig. 6.2. Technically
speaking, when reaching the final event end, a deadlock is reached.

Hence, for process orchestrations, we want to differentiate between *desired
deadlocks* such as end states and *undesired deadlocks*, i.e., states where the process
behavior blocks in an unintended manner, e.g., the XOR Split/AND join example
depicted in Fig. 5.6.

6.2.1   Workflow Nets

Basic Petri Net classes such as EC-Nets and P/T Nets have been extended by
Workflow Nets (cmp. [9]) in order to meet process orchestration specificities such as
reaching an end state as "desired" deadlock. Workflow Nets are defined as follows:

Definition 6.1 (Workflow Net, Based on [9]) A Petri net PN = (P, T, F)[1] is called
Workflow Net (WF Net for short) if and only if the following conditions hold:

- There is a distinguished place $i \in P$ (called initial place) that has no incoming
  edge, i.e., $\bullet i = \emptyset$
- There is a distinguished place $o \in P$ (called final place) that has no outgoing
  edge, i.e., $o\bullet = \emptyset$
- Every place and every transition is located on a path from the initial place i to
  the final place o

The claims set out in Definition 6.1 impose requirements on the structure of
a Workflow Nets and can be entirely checked on the process model (*structural
soundness*). For the soundness of the behavior of a Workflow Net, intuitively, the
execution should be deadlock-free except for reaching the final place o. Reaching o
reflects a "desired" deadlock, i.e., the end state of the process execution. Moreover,
no other tokens should be left in the Workflow Net when o is reached. Such "left
over" tokens result in an unclear execution semantics as they might trigger the

---

[1] In the definition of Workflow Nets, the weight function W (cf. Definition 5.1) is omitted.

Fig. 6.3 Workflow Net example (left) and its extension (right)

firing of transitions even though the end state and hence the end of the process execution has already been reached. Imagine, for example, a medical treatment process where the end of the treatment has been reached for patient X, but suddenly the examination starts over again. Definition 6.2 summarizes these behavioral soundness requirements.

Definition 6.2 (Behavioral Soundness, Workflow Nets, Based on [9]) Let PN = (P, T, F) be a Workflow Net. Let further M_i be the initial marking, i.e., one token in initial place i and no other tokens in PN, and M_o be the final marking, i.e., one token in the final place o and no other tokens in PN. PN is sound $\Leftrightarrow$

- Option to complete: $\forall M \in [M_i): M_o \in [M)$
- Proper completion: $\forall M \in [M_i): M \geq M_o^2 \implies M = M_o$
- No dead transitions, i.e., $\forall t \in T \exists M, M' \in [M_0)$ with $M \xrightarrow{t} M'$

The following Lemma 6.1 brings together the behavioral soundness requirements set out in Definition 6.2 and the notion of strong liveness (cf. Definition 5.7). The basic idea is to add a silent transition τ to a Workflow net that connects the final place o to the initial place i.

Lemma 6.1 (Extension of Workflow Net, Behavioral Soundness, Liveness, Boundedness, Based on [9]) *Let PN = (P, T, F) be a Workflow Net with inital place i, final place o, and initial marking M_i and $\bar{PN} = (\bar{P}, \bar{T}, \bar{F})$ the extended Workflow Net with $\bar{P} = P, \bar{T} = T \cup \{\tau\}$, and $\bar{F} = F \cup \{(o, \tau), (\tau, i)\}$. Then:*

- *PN sound $\implies$ $\bar{PN}$ with initial marking M_i is (strong) live*
- *PN sound $\Leftrightarrow$ $\bar{PN}$ with initial marking M_i is (strong) live and bounded*

For a proof of Lemma 6.1 we refer to [9]. Figure 6.3 illustrates the extension (depicted on the right-hand side) proposed by Lemma 6.1 based on a simple Workflow Net example (depicted on the left hand side). It can be easily seen that the extension is (strong) live, i.e., L_4-Live, and bounded. The original Workflow Net is structurally sound (one input place i, one output place o, connected net) as well as behaviorally sound (no dead transitions; the final marking in o is reachable from every marking reachable from the initial marking, and if the final marking in o is reached, no tokens are left in any of the other places).

---

[2] Let M, M' be two markings on a Workflow Net PN. Then: $M \geq M' \Leftrightarrow M(p) \geq M\prime(p)$ $\forall p \in$ P.

Lemma 6.1 nicely illustrates the relation between general behavioral properties of Petri Nets such as liveness and boundedness and the soundness property for formalisms geared toward describing process behavior such as Workflow Nets.

A tool for checking different properties on Workflow Nets is Woflan.[3] Here, Workflow Nets can be imported in the .tpn format and checked for several properties, also beyond the ones discussed in this book.

A powerful tool to model and simulate Petri Nets is CPN Tools,[4] continued as CPN IDE,[5] where CPN stands for Colored Petri Nets. As mentioned in the previous section, the coloring of tokens makes them distinguishable, which is an important feature to represent the execution of more than one process instance at a time. Colored Petri Nets and CPN tools will be explained in more detail in Chap. 7.

Workflow Nets are designed for process execution, and several options for "syntactic sugaring" exist, including icons for input and output places, as well as for XOR splits/joins and AND splits/joins. A Workflow Net-based process model can be imported and executed in the process management system YAWL[6] (Yet Another Workflow Language), which is open source. Nonetheless, as we will discuss in this section for data flow and the following sections for task and worklist design, several further specifications have to be made in order to achieve a fully functional process orchestration execution.

6.2.2   Refined Process Structure Trees

Workflow Nets can be seen as a bridge between formal languages to verify process orchestration models, i.e., Petri Nets, and executable languages. Another bridge formalism is the *Refined Process Structure Tree (RPST)* [218]. Refined process structure trees constitute a formal language for (i) the verification of process orchestrations, (ii) the basis for executing (interpreting) a process orchestration model, and (iii) transformation of a process orchestration model, e.g., a BPMN-based model, into an imperative programming language (such as python).

Regarding (ii) and (iii), the RPST connects graph-based process modeling languages such as BPMN or EPCs to the internal implementation of process engines. Process engines like most compilers or virtual machines (e.g., Java, GCC, Python) internally rely on abstract syntax trees (AST)s. A RPST is an AST that is geared toward the rather minimal grammar workflow graphs often represent, i.e., many branches, no assignments, and simple conditions.

The basic idea is that RPSTs allow to decompose a graph-based model into its logical blocks (cmp. structural sound Petri nets) with one single starting/entry

---

[3] https://www.win.tue.nl/woflan/.

[4] https://cpntools.org/.

[5] https://cpnide.org/.

[6] https://yawlfoundation.github.io/.

point and one single end/exit point (called SESE fragments). The leaves of the tree are always tasks, and branches represent logical constructs such as XOR, OR, or PARALLEL. A similar idea has been followed by [199] with respect to applying graph reduction techniques on process orchestration models for verification. The reduction rules also operate along the basic building blocks of the orchestration model.

Building the RPST for a given process orchestration model is based on a decomposition of the model into basic building blocks. This requires that the model is *block-structured* into SESE-fragments with a unique split node and a unique join node. Moreover, blocks might be nested, but must not overlap. For details on the decomposition algorithms, we refer to [199, 218]. Based on the decomposition, the RPST can be built.

Figure 6.4 illustrates the decomposition of (a) a given BPMN-based process orchestration model (top) into the (b) corresponding RPST (bottom, left) and (c) the corresponding CPEE tree (cf. Sect. 6.2.3). We can see that the process orchestration model consists of a sequence, which consists of a parallel branching block, a task, and an alternative branching. Note that the parallel branching and task C OR task C and the alternative branching form a sequence again. Here the result of the decomposition is not unique, i.e., two options exist. We opted for putting the task and the alternative branching into the sequence. The RPST contains the building blocks and represents their nesting by its hierarchical structuring. Moreover, it comprises the edges of the BPMN model as leaf nodes.

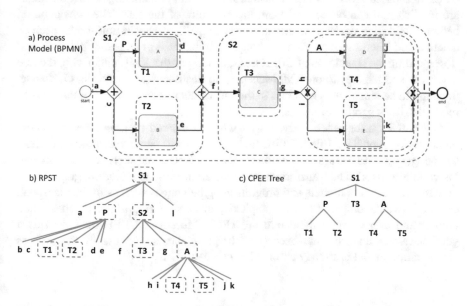

Fig. 6.4 (a) BPMN-based process orchestration model with decomposition (using SAP Signavio®); (b) corresponding RPST (example); (c) corresponding CPEE tree

The applications of the RPST are manifold. The IBM WebSphere Business Process Suite [111], for example, supports different languages such as BPEL and BPMN. All formats are transformed to an RPST. The RPST is used for control-flow analysis (different branches of the tree can be analyzed in parallel) and refactoring (find identical branches). The cloud process execution engine (CPEE)[7] utilizes an XML representation of the RPST as the native format of its BPMN modeler, i.e., when a BPMN process orchestration model is instantiated, the RPST is translated into executable code, compiled, and executed on a target machine. Further applications comprise efficient difference and merge algorithms and, in principle, every technique known from compiler theory, such as data-flow analysis or code optimization.

6.2.3   CPEE Trees

Cloud process execution engine (CPEE) trees are a RPST inspired implementation for storing process models and constitute the process orchestration model employed by the corresponding process engine. For a detailed introduction of its architecture, interfaces, and application as manufacturing orchestration engine, see [138].

CPEE trees are XML based comprising a small set of elements and their potential children (for a description, see XML NS http://cpee.org/ns/description/1.0). The CPEE tree-based process orchestration models do not contain edges, i.e., the edges are implicit and can be derived from the structure of the tree. The consideration behind this design decision is that adaptations of the orchestration model such as deletion and insertion of nodes do not require adjustment of edges.

Regarding the soundness of CPEE trees, as long as the XML underlying the tree is correct and adheres to an XML schema, no deadlocks are possible. Of course, there might be hidden dependencies in the individual implementation of task, which might deadlock parallel branches.

CPEE trees offer several advantages when compared to graph-based process orchestration models. At first, CPEE trees are easier to parse than process orchestration graphs. As mentioned before, model adaptations such as deletion and insertion are trivial. The transformation to different formats including graph-based process orchestration models and programming languages such as python is trivial, especially when compared to the complexity of parsing graph-based orchestration models and transforming them into an RPST. Moreover, CPEE trees provide a good basis for analysis and execution. In particular, soundness of the process orchestration model is already enforced w.r.t. deadlocks.

---

[7] cpee.org.

CPEE trees support all of the common *workflow patterns*.[8] The workflow patterns describe common control structures in process orchestrations. In detail, CPEE trees support the following elements, arranged in a hierarchical tree structure:

- **ROOT** `<description xmlns="http://cpee.org/ns/description/1.0"/>`
- **task** `<call id="a1" endpoint="..."/>`
  A **task** describes process tasks/activities and its call to functionality (cf. task design in Sect. 6.4). A task has input arguments and potentially modifies the instance context (data). A task might delegate work to humans, hardware, or arbitrary software as long as they accept the input and generate the expected output. This element can have no children.
- **parallel** `<parallel wait="-1" cancel="last"/>`
  The children of this element will be evaluated. The result of this evaluation determines the number of parallel branches. The mode determines the join semantic: -1 means that all parallel branches have to be finished. Any number bigger than 0 means that after this number of branches (or all), all remaining branches will be canceled. The cancel attribute further refines the join semantic: if wait is 1 and cancel is last, then after one branch ended, all other branches are canceled, no matter at which task they currently are. If wait is 1 and cancel is first, after the first task of any branch finishes, all other branches are canceled, and the original branch continues normally. This is the equivalent of an event-based gateway.
- **loop** `<loop mode="pre_test" condition="..."/>`
  The children of this element will be repeated over and over. The mode determines if the condition is evaluated before or after the first iteration. The loop continues until the condition is false.
- **escape** `<escape/>`
  Escape realizes a jump out of the loop if execution is inside a loop, even if the loop is not the parent. If no ancestor is a loop, the escape is ignored.
- **choose** `<choose mode="exclusive"/>`
  For choose, only the following two children are allowed, i.e., `exclusive` and `inclusive`. The mode allows for differentiation between exclusive and inclusive or. Important note: the order of the children determines the order of the evaluation.
- **alternative** `<alternative condition=""/>`
  If the condition evaluates to true, an alternatives' children are traversed.
- **otherwise** `<otherwise condition=""/>`
  If no alternative has been found, the children of the otherwise element are traversed. If no otherwise can be found, an empty otherwise is assumed. The otherwise does not have to be the last child of choose to work properly.
- **script task** `<manipulate id="a2" label="...">...</manipulate>`

---

[8] http://www.workflowpatterns.com/.

A script task can hold arbitrary code. It is up to execution to make use of this code (cf. task design in Sect. 6.4). The code may modify instance context (data).

- **terminate** `<terminate/>`
  Terminate immediately terminates execution if encountered. Is not intended to have any children.

- **stop** `<stop id="a2"/>`
  Stop is intended to pause the execution of an instance. The difference between terminate and stop is that termination is final, i.e., an instance is finished after execution. A stopped instance might continue executing at exactly the position it stopped. Is not intended to have children.

Note that only elements where a potential execution can stop have an id, i.e., task, script task, and stop. All other elements cannot be interrupted during execution.

CPEE trees are ordered trees, i.e., the order of elements in each node is important. CPEE trees are traversed in depth-first order (see exception: parallel branch) and pre-order. For the example tree depicted in Fig. 6.5, the traversal order results in ABCDEF.

Leaves are task, script, terminate, stop, and escape. If any other element is a leaf, it can be ignored. Leaves have no other elements as children. Branches comprise:

- **Choose**: Alternative and Otherwise are allowed children.
- **Alternative**: All elements are allowed children.
- **Otherwise**: All elements are allowed children.
- **Parallel**: All elements are allowed children. For standard BPMN syntax, only parallel branches are used.
- **Parallel Branch**: All elements are allowed children.

Figure 6.6 shows a CPEE tree sequence in its XML representation (left side) and the graphical, BPMN-based representation (right side). The "lines" of the XML code reflect the nodes in the CPEE tree and are denoted as A, B, C, and D. Moreover, the figure shows how the XML representation maps to the BPMN-based representation, i.e., task B to task `Task1`. The depth-first, pre-order traversal of the nodes in the tree results in the following order of process tasks ABCD where the traversal respects that the order of elements B, C, and D is important and influences the execution.

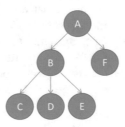

Fig. 6.5 Example tree

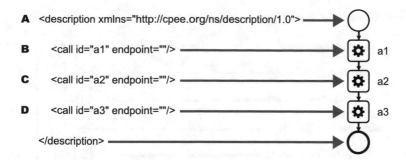

Fig. 6.6 Sequence-CPEE tree: XML representation (left side) and graphical representation (right side)

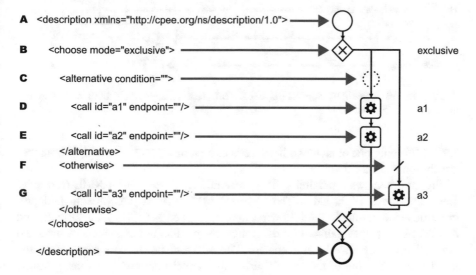

Fig. 6.7 Exclusive Split/XOR Split-CPEE tree: XML representation (left side) and graphical representation (right side)

Figure 6.7 depicts an exclusive split/XOR split represented as CPEE tree in XML (left side) and graph-based (right side). The traversal of the tree results in the following potential orders of task executions, i.e., ABCDE and ABCFG, depending on which condition evaluates to TRUE. Note that **otherwise** denotes the default path.

Figure 6.8 shows an inclusive split/OR split represented as CPEE tree in XML (left side) and graph-based (right side). The semantics of the OR split is challenging and has been subject to research (cf., e.g., [54]). Basically, an OR split represents a mixture of an XOR split and an AND split, i.e., either one of the branches is chosen and executed during runtime or both, depending on the conditions. For the traversal of the example CPEE tree, the following task orders result, i.e., ABCD, ABCEF,

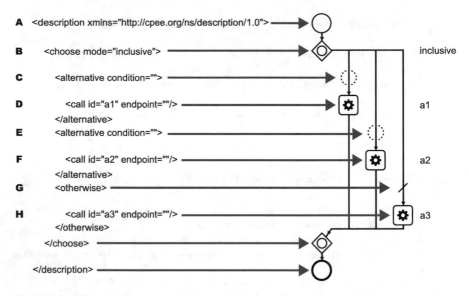

A   <description xmlns="http://cpee.org/ns/description/1.0">

B   <choose mode="inclusive">   inclusive

C   <alternative condition="">

D   <call id="a1" endpoint=""/>   a1
             </alternative>
E   <alternative condition="">

F   <call id="a2" endpoint=""/>   a2
             </alternative>
G   <otherwise>

H   <call id="a3" endpoint=""/>   a3
             </otherwise>
          </choose>

       </description>

Fig. 6.8 Inclusive Split/OR Split-CPEE tree: XML representation (left side) and graphical representation (right side)

ABCEGH if only one branch or otherwise is chosen or ABCDEF if multiple branches are chosen and executed.

Figure 6.9 shows a parallel split represented as CPEE tree in XML (left side) and graph-based (right side). The traversal in depth-first plus breadth and pre-order traversal results in the following task order, i.e., ABCFDEG, ABCFDGE, and ABCFGDE. Note that wait=−1 holds. Hence, the parallel branches are synchronized after all branches have been executed. The different task orders result from the interleaved execution of the task in different parallel branches (such tasks can be executed in arbitrary order).

In Fig. 6.10, we can see a loop structure represented by CPEE trees featuring a pre-test strategy, i.e., the loop condition is tested each time before executing the tasks in the loop body. The traversal order for this example results in A(BCDE)∗B, i.e., the condition from B is tested before each CDE. For three iterations, for example, the task order turns out as ABCDEBCDEBCDEB.

By contrast to the pre-test loop structure shown in Figs. 6.10, 6.11 depicts a loop structure with post-test evaluation strategy for the loop condition. The traversal strategy, consequently, yields task order A(CDEB)+ as the condition from B is tested after each CDE.

More control flow patterns such as local synchronizing merge and general synchronizing merge can be expressed based on CPEE trees and are described in [139].

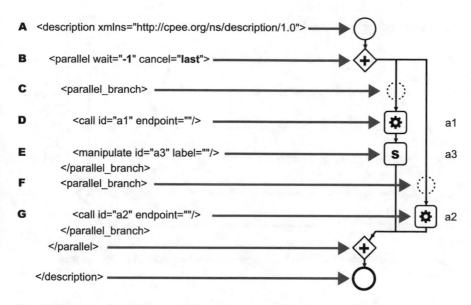

Fig. 6.9 Parallel split-CPEE tree: XML representation (left side) and graphical representation (right side)

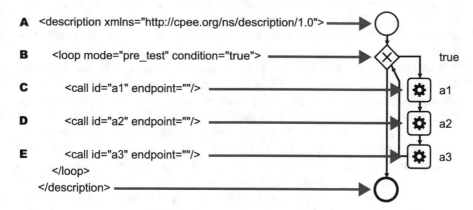

Fig. 6.10 Pre-test loop-CPEE tree: XML representation (left side) and graphical representation (right side)

The following considerations will be based on CPEE trees as they are supported by a fully open-source process engine cpee.org such that every concept described in this book can be directly tried out in a hands-on manner.

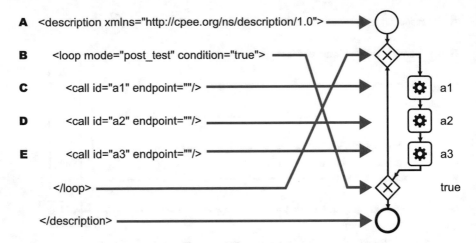

A <description xmlns="http://cpee.org/ns/description/1.0">

B   <loop mode="post_test" condition="true">

C   <call id="a1" endpoint=""/>

D   <call id="a2" endpoint=""/>

E   <call id="a3" endpoint=""/>

   </loop>

  </description>

Fig. 6.11 Post-test loop-CPEE tree: XML representation (left side) and graphical representation (right side)

6.3   Data Flow

At this point, we have discussed control flow modeling and verification. In the following, we will focus on data flow aspects, as data flow constitutes a crucial perspective on processes and is a major interoperability aspect in process orchestration.

Consider, for example, the simple BPMN-based process orchestration model depicted in Fig. 6.12. We can see that task A writes on a *data object* d, which is subsequently read by task B. The write access of A on d is expressed by a *message flow* (dashed edge) from the task to the data object and the read access from B on d by a message flow from the data object to the task, i.e., the direction of the message flow indicates the access type (write/read). Doing so, we can establish a data exchange between two functional units, i.e., process tasks, in a process-oriented way, i.e., along a well-defined control flow (in this case A before B). The order is important as B cannot be executed without A providing data object d if d constitutes a mandatory input for B. Here we can see that tasks are not just "boxes" but are functional units that might invoke services or application programs that need to be supplied with input parameters (and might provide output parameters themselves).

In CPEE trees, data flow is realized over the *process context*, i.e., all input to a task must come from the process context and output from a task can be stored in the process context. The process context consists of a list of variables with a name and a value. For CPEE trees, the values comprise the types String, Integer, Float, and JSON. Everything else will be represented as an IETF RFC 2397 data-url.

Consider the example depicted in Fig. 6.13. One data element named `result` exists. The data element has the string value `Timeout: 12`. `Task 1` is a task that is implemented through the endpoint `timeout`. `Task 1` is implemented through

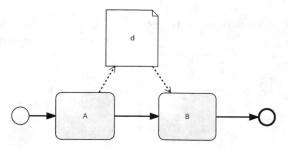

Fig. 6.12 Process orchestration example with data flow, modeled in BPMN (using SAP Signavio®)

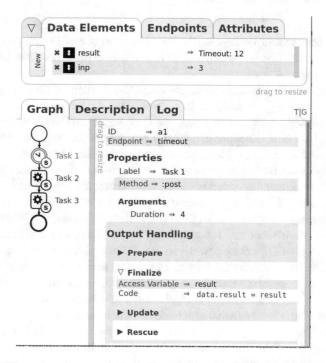

Fig. 6.13 CPEE tree-based process orchestration model (example) with data flow

a REST service where the call method is `post`. The static argument is 4. For a process to be dynamic, i.e., read data in one task and pass it as an argument to the next task, it is necessary to use data elements as argument values and write data elements when a task returns data. For example, to pass the data element `inp` as an argument, `Duration` is set to `!data.inp` (formally `Duration` $\implies$ `!data.inp`). Each argument value that starts with a `!` can access all data elements, all endpoints, and all arguments with `data.name`, `endpoints.name`, and `arguments.name`. The output of the task/event is handled through a code snippet in `Finalize` as follows: Everything that is returned is stored in `result`.

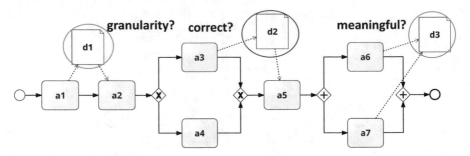

Fig. 6.14 Selected data flow correctness problems based on an example BPMN-based process orchestration model (using SAP Signavio®)

Everything that should be kept in the process context can be assigned to a data element, i.e. `data.name = result`. If result is a json, keys can be accessed, i.e.: `data.name = result["key"]`.

In contrast to other process management systems such as Camunda[9] (BPMN-based, using data objects and message flows) and AristaFlow[10] (based on well-structured marking nets [177], using data elements and read/write edges), in CPEE trees, data flow is neither graphically represented nor represented by special elements. Arguments describe input to the implementation. Output handling dynamically filters the received data and moves it to the process context (data elements).

Figure 6.14 illustrates selected data flow correctness problems that might occur when using semantically higher orchestration modeling languages. The first problem concerns the granularity of data modeling (blue circle). When modeling BPMN-based orchestrations, for example, data objects can be defined at any granularity level, i.e., a data object can be defined at granularity `complaint` and at granularity `customer id` (cf. Fig. 5.3). Obviously, the granularity level with `customer complaint` is too coarse for implementation and execution as `customer complaint` might comprise several data elements that would be at the right granularity level to serve as input/output parameters, e.g., `customer id`. Hence, either the modeling of data objects must follow strict guidelines with respect to granularity or when translating the BPMN models into (another) executable language, re-modeling of the data objects becomes necessary.

Another problem concerns ensuring that (mandatory) input data is sufficiently provided at the time it is required. For the process model depicted in Fig. 6.14, the correct provision of d2 for process task a5 is not guaranteed (red circle) because d2 is written by only a3 and if the other branch of the alternative branching is chosen during runtime, d2 will not be written. As a consequence, a5 will not be supplied,

---

[9] https://camunda.com/.

[10] https://www.aristaflow.com/.

causing failure of invoking associated services and blocking of the process instance. Hence, for data objects/elements written by tasks in alternative branches, it has to be ensured that the data element will be written for every branch of the alternative branching.

Finally, for write accesses from tasks in different parallel branches (orange circle), overwriting of already written data objects might occur. Assume that, for example, $a6$ writes $d3$ first followed by a write access by $a7$; then, the value written by $a6$ will be overwritten before any other task might read and process this value as input. This data flow modeling does not necessarily result in errors or blocking of the process such as the missing input data problem, but still might not be desired and hence should be avoided.

How do control and data flow aspects of process orchestrations support and further interoperability and integration? Based on the control flow, the tasks of a process orchestration can be put into relation to each other, i.e., following a well-defined process logic. However, without considering their functional aspect and the data flow, the interoperability and integration power is relatively low. Then, the orchestration rather provides an overview of the intended interoperability and integration in a model-based manner. With defining the data flow, interoperability between the process tasks exchanging the data in the specified order is realized. In the next section, the functional aspect and, connected with this, the integration of services and application programs as well as human actors are discussed.

6.4 Task Design: Application and Service Integration

Process tasks (also called *activities* or *tasks* for short in the following) constitute logical steps in a process orchestration model. So far, they have been merely boxes with a label, possibly reading and writing data. The functionality behind the tasks still has to be defined. It has to be, for example, defined how the input data is processed and how the output data is produced. Task functionality covers a broad range, i.e., simple scripts, invocation of services and application programs, invocation of physical devices such as machines or robot, and invocation of human interaction, e.g., performing a surgery or washing a patient. Basically, we can distinguish between tasks for which services, application programs, or machines are automatically invoked by the process management system/process engine and no process participant is involved (*fully automated*) and tasks for which one or more work items are assigned to human actors, possibly supported by application programs, services, or machines (*interactive*). In this context, *robotic process automation* aims at automating mostly simple and repetitive interactive tasks by putting a (software) robot on top of the user interface, mimicking the user interactions [8].

Tasks communicate with functionalities, e.g., built-in or Web services that implement them. Tasks send input (optional) and receive output that can be merged

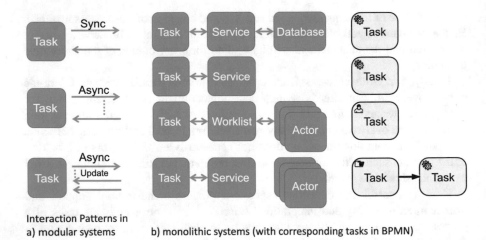

Interaction Patterns in
a) modular systems   b) monolithic systems (with corresponding tasks in BPMN)

Fig. 6.15 Interaction patterns between tasks and their implementations for (**a**) modular and (**b**) monolithic systems

with the process context or process data respectively. Figure 6.15a depicts the basic interaction patterns between tasks and their implementations:

- **Sync** answers a request immediately. It is not important for the implementations to know details about the tasks. Sync is suited for requests where the implementation can return data immediately. A process can only be stopped upon return.
- **Async** answers a request later. An implementation has to know the instance and the task id, in order to successfully address the task upon return. Async is suited for long-running requests, which can take months or years. A process engine can cancel such a task if it is, for example, stopping. The explanation is as follows: the implementation actively returns data. Thus, it can receive information about whether data is no longer needed and react accordingly.
- **Async Update** answers a request multiple times and can be understood as a special form of Async. Async Update is suited for long-running requests, which can take months or years. It is used for informing the process engine about progress or sending partial results.

There is a difference between interaction patterns for modular systems and monolithic systems (cf. Fig. 6.15). For monolithic process engines, worklists or database query functionality might be built into the engine. For modular process engines such as cpee.org, everything is implemented as external services.

For monolithic systems as shown in Fig. 6.15b, the following variants exist (from top to down):

- Engine communicates with an external service that, in turn, implements database access.
- Engine communicates with an external service that receives input and generates output.

- Engine communicates with a special external service that implements a UI for actors to interact with a process task.
- Engine communicates with an external service that passively tracks the work done by humans.

In Camunda, for example, implementations are external services that utilize a library/API in the following ways:

- Java through `org.camunda.bpm.client.ExternalTaskClient`
- NodeJS `ycamunda-external-task-client-js`
- Python `camunda-external-task-client-python3`

Each implementation utilizes a Camunda/community provided API. The features of the API control all interactions with the engine.

By contrast, cpee.org is an example for a modular engine. It utilizes plain HTTP with special HTTP headers instead of a custom API. cpee.org is fully language agnostic; all programming languages with support for HTTP can be used. Headers sent with each HTTP call to an implementation are:

- CPEE-BASE—base location of the engine where the instance is running on (e.g., `cpee.org/flow/engine/`)
- CPEE-INSTANCE—instance number (e.g., 123)
- CPEE-INSTANCE-URL—URL pointing to the instance (e.g., `cpee.org/flow/engine/123`)
- CPEE-INSTANCE-UUID—unique identifier of the instance
- CPEE-CALLBACK—URL to send any information to, should the implementation decide to answer asynchronously
- CPEE-CALLBACK-ID—unique identifier for the answer
- CPEE-ACTIVITY—id of the task calling the implementation (e.g., a1)
- CPEE-LABEL—label of the task calling the implementation (e.g., Query Production Schedule)

Each task implementation for CPEE can utilize the following HTTP headers in their response (cf. Fig. 6.15a):

- **Sync**

  - CPEE-SALVAGE response header: implementation signals it internally failed and wants to retry.
  - CPEE-INSTANTIATION response header: the implementation creates a sub-process.
  - CPEE-EVENT: tells the engine to send a custom event; used, e.g., by worklists to communicate that a user took or gave back a task.

- **Async**

  - CPEE-CALLBACK true response header and value: implementation signals that it wants to send data later, to the provided CPEE-CALLBACK request header.
  - All the headers above.

- **Async Update**

  - CPEE-UPDATE true response header and value: Implementation signals that
    it wants to send more data after this response.
  - CPEE-UPDATE-STATUS: sets the engine status with the response.
  - All the headers above.

Tasks have associated attributes, and their definition constitutes a vital part of
the task design. The ID uniquely identifies the task in a process. The endpoint
provides the link to the functionality that implements the task. We will spend more
words on endpoints, i.e., on method & arguments, and their significance for
interoperability in the next paragraph. The label describes the task. The output
handling has been discussed in Sect. 6.3 on data flow. From the point of view of
the process model, a task has an external implementation, which is a black box. It is
passed some input (arguments) and returns some output. The output is processed
by using code snippets stored in output handling.

As endpoints are links to the implementation of a task, they are the basic
instrument for application integration and hence interoperability in process orchestrations. Each task has to point to at least one endpoint that implements it. Endpoints
can be addressed through a variety of different protocols, such as SOAP, REST,
and OPC-UA. Standard endpoints for CPEE trees are assumed to point to REST
services. They have a method, i.e., GET, POST, PUT, and DELETE. Moreover,
they have 0..*n* arguments. Arguments are always name/value pairs. The same name
may occur more than once. By default, all endpoints are considered to be automatic
tasks. If special annotations for a REST service exist, the visual representation of the
task changes to represent its purpose. Examples comprise Sub-process, Send
message, Receive message, and Wait. Nonetheless, even the creation of a
sub-process is implemented as a REST service with specific parameters. i.e., the
path to the process model, which represents the sub-process and data elements
passed to the sub-process upon creation, denoted by the BPMN start event with
envelope.

Figure 6.16 shows the design of Task 1 in a simple process orchestration
model. Its id is a1, and its label is Task 1. The endpoint is timeout with method
POST and argument "Duration." The URL for the endpoint can be accessed in tab
Endpoints. The output of Task1 is written into the process context, i.e., data
element result.

Task execution undergoes a life cycle, typically including task or activity
states *Activated, Started, Running, Skipped, Suspended, Completed,* and *Failed,*
with well-defined transitions between these states following a life cycle model.
Typically, if all preconditions for the execution of a task are fulfilled according
to the formal execution semantics of the underlying process meta model, the task
becomes activated. If it is selected for execution, the task is started and becomes
running during execution. If execution is finished successfully, the task is completed,
otherwise failed. For CPEE trees, the task life cycle model can be found in [138].
Here, we can find additional states for syncing before and after the task if some

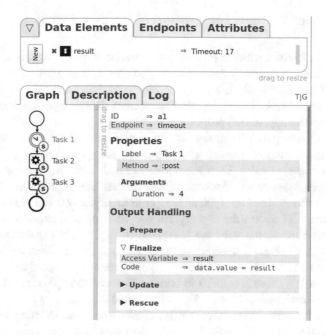

Fig. 6.16 Task design in CPEE (example)

constraints on the task execution are imposed. Other task or activity life cycle models include the one of eXtensible Event Stream (XES).[11]

Significance of Task Design for Interoperability and Application Integration
The control flow, data flow, and task design in a process orchestration enable the process-oriented integration of multiple applications and services as well as the data exchange between them. In detail, it works as follows: at the process orchestration level—which is controlled by the process engine—a task is enabled according to the formal execution semantics of the process meta model. Once it is enabled and started, the task is provided with the mandatory input data from the process context. Then the task invokes the assigned application program or service using the defined endpoint. The task passes its input data from the process context to the (external) application program or service. The application program or service receives the input data, performs its functionality, and passes the mandatory output data back to the task. The task receives the output data from the application program or service and writes it back to the process context. This is done for several tasks along the process logic and builds the integrated execution and data exchange of several application programs and services.

---

[11] https://xes-standard.org/.

6.5 Worklist Design: Integration of Human Work

Human actors interact with the process orchestration through *worklists*, i.e., lists of work items that are currently due for a specific person. The work items are not just information but include all data and functionalities defined for the associated task (see data flow and task design), i.e., process context data as input and the invocation of the appropriate application program or service.

Connected with worklist design is the *organizational aspect* of the process, i.e., the authorization of human actors to work on specific tasks. Authorization is defined via *access rules*. They are defined at task level and refer to an *organization model (organigram)*. An organigram reflects the organization structure of a company or organization. Typically, it defines *organizational units*, *roles*, and *actors*. Figure 6.17 shows the organigram for the insurance process orchestration example described in the use case presented in Fig. 6.1. It consists of organizational units `Insurance Company`, `Complaint Dept.`, and `Accounting`, where `Complaint Dept.` and `Accounting` are subordinated to `Insurance Company`. Role[12] `Clerk` belongs to organization unit `Complaint Dept.`, and two actors are assigned to `Clerk`, i.e., `Smith` and `Jones`.

Based on the organigram, access rules can be specified, defining which actors are authorized to work on a task. An established way to define access rules is *role-*

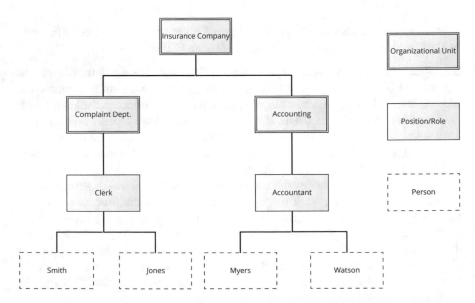

Fig. 6.17 Organigram for insurance process orchestration example (using SAP Signavio®)

---

[12] In the following, we will use the concept of roles. Positions can be also used to describe organizational structures.

based access control (RBAC) [126]. Defining access rules at role level leads to an abstraction from assigning access rules directly to actors who might change due to, for example, leaving the company. This means that authorization is defined based on roles, and during runtime, the roles are resolved to actors that are currently present in the organizational model. An example for a task `task` based on the example organigram would be:

$$\texttt{access\_rule (task)} \leftarrow \texttt{Role="Clerk"}$$

For this access rule, actors `Smith` and `Jones` qualify and would be offered to work on task `task` during runtime.

Note that authorization can also comprise additional rules defining, for example, separation of duties (two tasks are to be executed by different actors for a given process instance) or binding of duties (two tasks are to be executed by the same person for a given process instance). Such authorization rules are defined on top of the rules handling the access of actors to tasks.

Different ways of modeling and visualizing organizational information for process orchestration models exist. Figure 6.18 shows an alternative way of visualizing organizational models as OrbitFlowers [124]. Organizational units and roles are depicted as circles (organizational units, blue; roles, purple) and connected via lines in order to express that a role belongs to an organizational unit. The size of

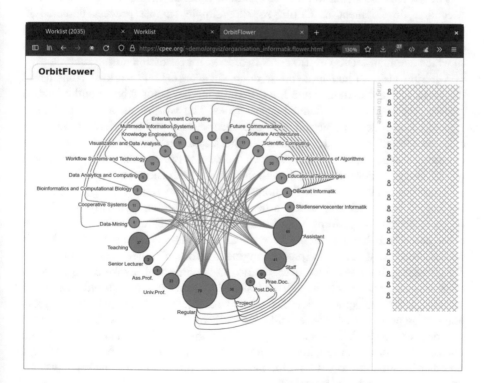

Fig. 6.18 Organigram for higher education institution visualized as OrbitFlower

the circles represents the number of actors that belong to an organizational unit or have a certain role. When selecting an organizational unit or role, on the right-hand side, the list of associated actors is displayed. In the example, organizational unit Workflow Systems and Technology has been selected. The role with the most associated actors is Regular, followed by Assistant.

Organizational information available as organizational model or organigram can be used to define access rules for the tasks. In BPMN, for example, access rules are modeled and assigned to tasks based on *pools* and *lanes*. A task is assigned a role or organizational unit if it is placed within the corresponding lane. This way, on the one hand, the assignment of tasks to roles and organizational units can be seen right away. On the other hand, the assignment of more complex access rules connecting multiple roles and organizational units by logical operators such as AND or OR becomes difficult. Take the example depicted in Fig. 6.19. For a simplified version of the running customer complaint process, we can see the two pools, Customer and Insurance Company and, within the latter, two lanes representing the roles Clerk and Accountant as captured in the associated organigram (cf. Fig. 6.17). For task inform customer, for example, the access rule expressed by the pools and lanes is that the task can be performed by an actor having role Clerk and belonging to the organizational unit Insurance Company.

For access rule definition and assignment to tasks in the context of process execution development in CPEE, see the simple sample process depicted in Fig. 6.20. At task design level, the corresponding model is assigned via the given endpoint, and the access rule is defined as Role="Assistant." This determines to which actors task OK OR NOT OK is offered for execution during runtime.

Offering tasks to human actors is done via *worklists*. A worklist contains all the tasks that are currently due for a certain human actor who is authorized to perform the tasks via the defined access rules. The worklist of a human actor is typically embedded into her/his user interface. A task can be offered to multiple actors at a time, i.e., to all actors that are authorized to perform it. The process engine determines which tasks are due, resolves their access rules over the organizational model, and provides the information to the service with endpoint "worklists."

Then the control shifts to the human actors. If no other strategy is defined, the human actor that first selects a task from the worklist (typically by clicking on it) is the one to perform it, i.e., the task is removed from the worklists of all other authorized human actors. As soon as a human actor selects the task, this information is sent back to the process engine to inform all other worklists to remove the corresponding entry. Moreover, the process engine will invoke the application program or service associated with the task and pass on the input data elements to the worklist. From the point of view of the human actor, in her/his user interface, these application programs or services will potentially open, and the mandatory input data will be provided to the human actors to perform the task. The data elements should contain all information required by actors to work on the task. The actors will get no other information to work on the task (although they can use backend systems that are not known to the process engine).

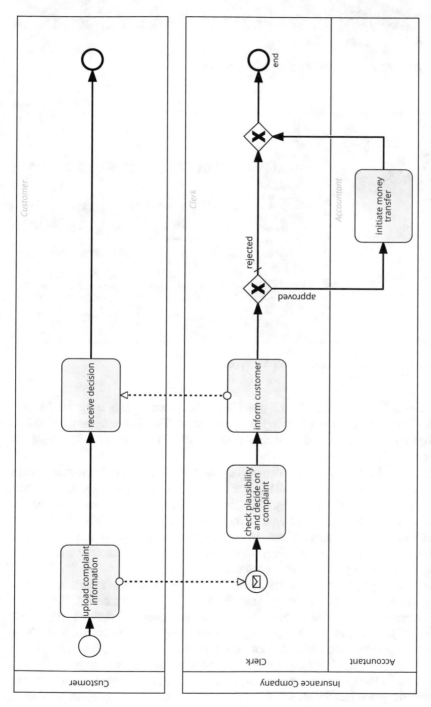

Fig. 6.19 Pools and lanes for simplified customer complaint process (using SAP Signavio®)

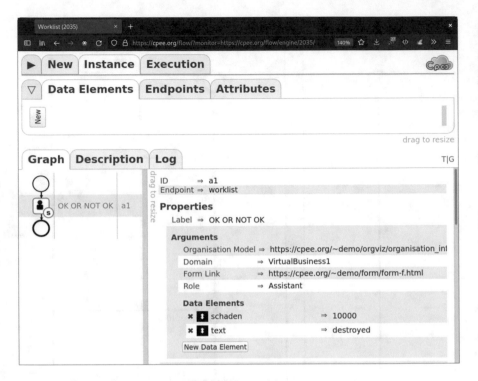

Fig. 6.20 Worklist specification in task design (example)

In Fig. 6.20, the worklist form is provided to the corresponding endpoint, i.e., link to an HTML form to be shown to the human actor. The data elements and values to be passed on are `schaden` with a value of 10.000 and `text` with a value of `destroyed`.

Figures 6.21, 6.22 and 6.23 depict the interaction of human actor `manglej6` with the worklist. In Fig. 6.21a, the human actor logs into the domain `VirtualBusiness1` (see Fig. 6.20). Figure 6.21b shows the worklist for this actor. There are three tasks offered at the moment that are part of three different process instances, i.e., task `OK OR NOT OK` is part of process instances 2035 and 2036; hence, two items are offered in the worklist. There is another task `Check Compliance` for process instance 2037.

Actor `manglej6` can now choose which of the three tasks to select. Assume that task `OK OR NOT OK` for process instance 2036 is selected (cf. Fig. 6.22c). The corresponding HTML form with the data elements (all defined in the task design) is provided by the process engine and displayed to the human actor. Note that the data values are embedded into the text of the form, e.g., the value of data element `schaden` of 10.000 is embedded in the first sentence `The overall cost ....`. The human actor can now review the case for the given instance and perform the work, i.e., decide whether or not it is `OK`. In the example, `OK` is selected.

a)

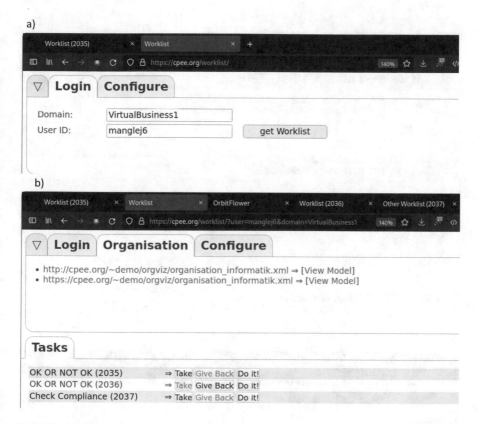

Fig. 6.21   CPEE: (a) login and (b) worklist

After clicking on Submit, the information is sent back to the process engine, i.e., output data element bla is provided with value ok (cf. Fig. 6.23d). Moreover, as we can see in Fig. 6.23, task OK OR NOT OK is completed.

For both modular monolithic process engines/systems, the transition between the different task/activity life cycle states works as follows: once the task can be activated, it is put into the worklists. If it is selected, it is started and becomes running during its execution. If it is successfully finished, it is completed, and the control goes back to the process engine. These shifts of control between process engine, worklist, and human actor can be implemented by different strategies, i.e., from classical pull where the worklists ask the process engine whether new tasks are available to classical push where the process engine pushes the information on newly available tasks to all worklists. In between is the strategy of a time-driven push, balancing the risks of outdated worklists and unnecessary communication.

Also worklists undergo a life cycle reflecting the different interactions between the worklist and the process engine, e.g., *add* or human actor respectively, e.g., *take* and *give back*. The detailed CPEE worklist life cycle model can be found in [138]. Note that there is also a state *assign* in which different assignment strategies of tasks to human actors can be implemented such as round-robin and lowest workload.

c)

Fig. 6.22 CPEE: (**c**) Selection of tasks

d)

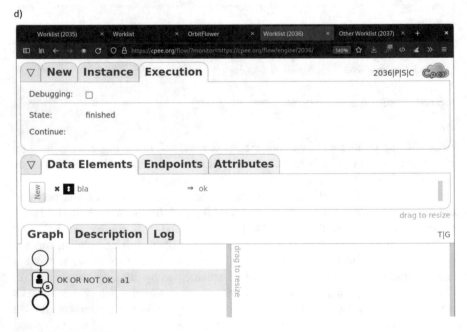

Fig. 6.23 CPEE: (**d**) results in process engine

Significance of Worklist Design for Interoperability and Integration of Human Actors The main interoperability aspect of worklists in process orchestrations is to integrate human work with processes, services, and physical devices. The process orchestration defines how the human work is integrated into the process orchestration context, i.e., when and how this human work is required for fulfilling the goals of the process orchestration. The human actors are supported by worklists in presenting the tasks that are currently due, together with the necessary data elements and application program/service to perform the tasks. Output data created by human work is "taken back" via the worklist and seamlessly integrated into the process context.

6.6 Correlation

Correlation is an important principle to realize application and service interoperability and integration for process orchestrations (cf. Sect. 6.4) and to realize process choreographies (cf. Sect. 8).

Figure 6.24 depicts the mechanism and components of correlation in process orchestrations. From the point of view of the process engine, two patterns are realized based on correlation. The first pattern describes the process engine asking an external service for some results. The second pattern describes the process engine reacting on some external event. This event can trigger a new process instance to be started (e.g., for process P2, indicated by an incoming arrow to message start event ✉) or the process engine waits for some external message (indicated by an incoming arrow to a task, e.g., task T1 in process P1 and task T2 in process P2). With external sources the following challenges arise:

- External source may be unknown.
- External source may send the message long before an instance requires the value.
- External source may send the value long after an instance requires the value.
- The contents of a message contain the key to decide what to do.

A correlator has to be able to receive messages from arbitrary sources and to analyze the contents of the message. A message might be a mail received via IMAP, a Word document, or Excel sheet received via HTML Form upload, a CAD file, or, more generically, any file format submitted through any means/protocol. Moreover, the correlator has to be able to *forward* the message to a potential instance that is waiting for the message, to *store* the message for later use, or to create a new instance of a process with the message as input (*instantiate*). For these tasks, the correlator requires a set of rules to analyze incoming messages with respect to their type, e.g., email; where to find the required information in the message, e.g., that the subject contains the required ticket number; and what to do with the message, i.e., forward or instantiate.

In order to specify the rules, a correlator has to support a rule language to describe how to extract correlation information. One example is a Word file with heading "Customer Contract" on page 1 that contains the signature of a particular

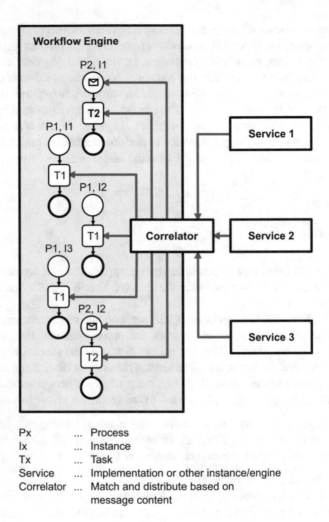

Fig. 6.24 Correlation in process orchestrations

person at the end of page 7 as well as a ticket number in the form #\w{12} on page 2. Another example is an Excel sheet with three worksheets where on the first worksheet, cell A1 contains the identifier of the customer.

The correlation can have two targets, i.e., process instantiation or tasks waiting for a message. The correlator identifies the targets in the following ways: Processes that are to be instantiated have to contain correlation rules when to do so, for example, a Word file with heading "Customer Contract" on page 1 that contains the signature of a particular person at the end of page 7 as well as a ticket number in the form #\w{12} on page 2 (matching the first example for the correlation rule specified above). The rule is generic, i.e., any match leads to an instantiation. The message creates an instance and at the same time serves as input to the resulting process instance (see process P2 in Fig. 6.24). The correlator has to analyze each process model to extract the corresponding correlation rules. Instances that require a certain message, but do not have any direct means to contact a source, have to make a correlation request to get the required information from the correlator, for example, *"I need a Word file with heading "Customer* Contract*" on page 1 that contains the signature of* John Boss *at the end of page 7 and a ticket number in the form #QWER12tzui34 on page 2.* The request is special as only messages matching this exact request are of interest. The correlator can store a list of requests on the fly and delete entries whenever a request has been fulfilled.

When a message is received, the correlator checks for matching correlation rules to instantiate a process. If such a message is found, the message is dropped after instantiation. If a matching correlation request exists, the correlator forwards the message. What happens to the message after the forward is specified in the corresponding *data retention* policy? If there is no policy, the message is dropped after forward. Possible data retention policies are:

- Store indefinitely: other requests can be answered.
- Store for a limited time: other requests can be answered.
- Store with additional request rules: additional parameters have to be fulfilled in order to reuse the message to fulfill request, for example, a requestor has to submit a code to get the info.
- Queue vs. Slot:
  - Slot: messages can replace other existing messages; only the newest message fitting a correlation request is stored.
  - Queue: all messages are stored; the newest message fitting a correlation request is delivered.

Data retention is also applied if no matches exist.

Significance of Correlation for Interoperability and Application Integration
Correlation is a core mechanism to realize interoperability and integration for process orchestrations, i.e., to realize the invocation of external services and application programs via message exchanges to instantiate processes and fulfill message requests of process tasks. Correlation as a principle contributes to the following requirements that are central to interoperability and process orchestrations:

- *Security:* correlators connect external systems to internal process instances without exposing the internal structure.
- *Loose coupling:* external systems have a single point where to send information.
- *Policy enforcing:* how to deal with message retention, contributes to loose coupling, and maintainability.
- *Compliance checking:* incoming data can be checked before it enters internal infrastructure
- *Maintainability:* single place to deal with incoming messages. No need to implement anything in the process engine.

The alternative would be much more complicated and relying on tightly coupled systems. The external services (cf. Fig. 6.24) can also be other process engines or BPM systems. Hence, correlation is also imperative for realizing process choreographies (cf. Sect. 8).

6.7   Case Study: Manufacturing Orchestration

We follow up on the case study in manufacturing presented in Sect. 5.5 and present how we can go from conceptual design of a manufacturing process orchestration to its execution design. Figure 6.25 depicts the conceptual design phase user interface

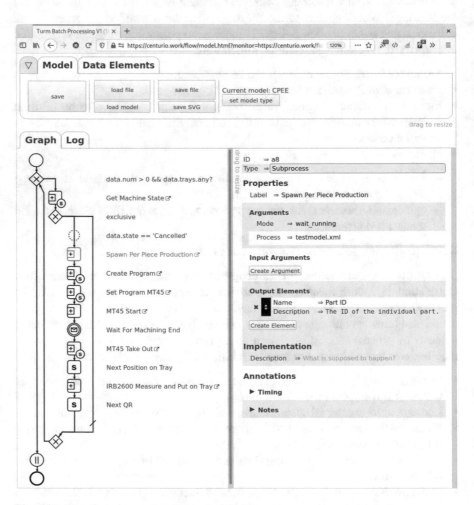

Fig. 6.25 Manufacturing process: conceptual design

in the CPEE. The user is supported in eliciting and engineering the requirements of
the process orchestration during the conceptual design based on:

- Textual description of input and output of tasks.
- Limited set of task types.
- Specification of the control flow
- Batch view vs. product view vs. machine view
- Production vs. production (sensor) data collection

Based on the conceptual design, the following execution gaps have to be bridged
in order to arrive at an executable process orchestration model (cf. Fig. 6.26):

- For the tasks, we have to hook up functionalities and define how to pass
  parameters between them.
- Handle response (finalize)
- Handle partial response (update)
- Handle problems (rescue)
- Annotate for runtime compliance checking
- Handle the collection of complementary sensor data, processing and automatic
  visualization (data stream handling)
- Step by step testing and evolution

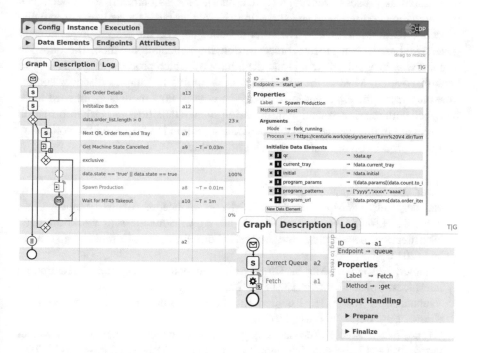

Fig. 6.26 Manufacturing process: execution design

6.8   Conclusion and Lessons Learned

The design of executable process orchestrations as means to foster the interoperability between tasks, services, and human work necessitates (i) a formal execution semantics of the used process meta model; (ii) correctly specified data flow; (iii) task design with invocation of applications, services, machines, and human actors; and (iv) correlation. In this chapter, we illustrated (i) for Workflow Nets, RPST, and CPEE Trees. Concepts and methods for (ii) and (iii) were mainly introduced based on CPEE Nets and the CPEE engine but can be seen as representative for the general question of how to establish interoperability between process tasks and their functionality. One basic concept for process-induced interoperability is the correlator mechanism, which is generic and can be applied in process orchestrations and process choreographies (cf. Chap. 8). Overall, process orchestration constitutes a powerful mechanism to establish interoperability between systems, services, and human work in a process-oriented way. This thought is furthered by discussing enterprise application integration in Chap. 7.

Chapters 5 and 6 realize a model-driven way of developing process orchestration, i.e., following a top-down approach from conceptual model to executable model and code. Especially with the advent of *process mining* [7], a bottom-up way of realizing process orchestrations has become feasible: based on process-oriented data stored as *process event logs* (conceptual), process orchestration models can be automatically discovered and serve, in principle, as basis for realizing executable process orchestration models. The latter depends on (i) if the process log is already generated based on a process orchestration implementation—then, the question remains why to again realize it—and (ii) otherwise which process perspectives have been discovered. Most of the existing process mining techniques discover control flow only from process event logs. Then, the control flow models again need to be equipped with missing execution information such as data flow and task information as discussed in this chapter. We will dedicate a section in Chap. 8 on the bottom-up design of process orchestrations and choreographies.

Further Reading

1. van der Aalst, W.M.P., van Hee, K.M., ter Hofstede, A.H.M., Sidorova, N., Verbeek, H.M.W., Voorhoeve, M., Wynn, M.T.: Soundness of workflow nets: classification, decidability, and analysis. Formal Aspects Comput. **23**(3), 333–363 (2011)
2. Mangler, J., Rinderle-Ma, S.: Cloud process execution engine: architecture and interfaces. CoRR **abs/2208.12214** (2022)
3. Vanhatalo, J., Völzer, H., Koehler, J.: The refined process structure tree. Data Knowl. Eng. **68**(9), 793–818 (2009)
4. Weske, M.: Business Process Management – Concepts, Languages, Architectures, pp. 1–417, 3rd edn. Springer, Berlin (2019). ISBN 978-3-662-59431-5

Chapter 7
Integration Patterns and Processes

7.1 Motivation and Goals

In previous chapters (cf. Chaps. 4–6), we saw how orchestration of applications, services, and processes can be achieved through interoperable or tightly integrated systems. However, in practice, not all systems or system components are tightly integrated and thus interoperable. In fact, the emergence of business, technological, and social trends led to a growing number of distributed, loosely coupled, and often non-interoperable cloud, hybrid (i. e., combination of on-premise and cloud), and mobile applications [188]. While an orchestration runs business process or combines applications into one or several processes, integration enables orchestration across non-interoperable components.

The challenges of integrating loosely coupled, federated systems and components are not limited to performance and security (e. g., when communicating over public networks) but especially the combination and integration of non-interoperable parts. To integrate such applications and address the challenges, solid and reliable foundations are required. Such foundations can be found in the enterprise integration patterns [107] and their recent extensions [106, 187, 188, 191, 193, 195], which were inspired by the pattern authors in [231]. Integration patterns are informal descriptions and rather meant to be a catalog of best practices or a checklist (cf. [231]), when building integration systems. However, since the currently informal pattern descriptions intentionally leave room for interpretation for their usage in the context of executable integration processes (e. g., when used as building blocks of such systems), and thus making their practical cumbersome, formal definitions are required to give them precise semantics and to make them meaningful (e. g., when working in practical integration projects).

In this chapter (cf. Fig. 7.1), we introduce basic integration concepts in the form of patterns as well as a background on suitable formalisms to define the patterns in Sect. 7.2. The integration patterns are introduced and formally defined as fundamental layer to tackle application integration in Sect. 7.3. The chapter also

© Springer Nature Switzerland AG 2024
S. Rinderle-Ma et al., *Fundamentals of Information Systems Interoperability*,
https://doi.org/10.1007/978-3-031-48322-6_7

Levels .../ Tasks ↓	Syntactical	Semantic	Organizational
Exchange	Exchange formats, e.g., XML, relational databases, JSON, BSON, YAML, MessagePack; query languages: XPath, XQuery, SQL; transformation languages, e.g., XSLT	Schema matching and mapping; ontologies;	Message exchange; correlation
Integrate	SQL/XML standard; native XML databases; REST and GraphQL	Edge table, shredding; XML schema and RNG; schema and data integration; service integration	Correlation and choreography
Orchestrate	BPMN, Petri Nets, Workflow Nets, RPST, CPEE Trees, Colored Petri Nets	Verification, task and worklist design; service invocation; correlation; integration patterns and processes	Choreography

Fig. 7.1 Interoperability perspectives I: Chap. 7

spans the bridge between service interoperability (cf. Chap. 4) and process-oriented service integration based on patterns like the "correlator" (cf. Sect. 6.6). We recall the idea of a correlator, which is to collect messages (i. e., exchanged data via network) from services and reliably relay them to the services that need them. Moreover, it is shown how the patterns can be composed to integration processes that need to be formalized and implemented to come into effect in practical scenarios in Sect. 7.4. The chapter also presents a hybrid integration and an Internet of things scenario as case studies in Sect. 7.5.

7.2 Basic Integration Concepts and Formalisms

In this section, we first give a background on basic integration concepts as integration patterns and processes. Then, we extend our knowledge of Petri Nets (cf. Sect. 5.4) with data by formalisms like Coloured Petri Nets (CPNs), database transactions by Database Nets (DB-nets), and time by Timed-arc Petri Nets (TAPNs), with which those patterns can be sufficiently defined for the purpose of expressing and reasoning over their semantics. The background on CPNs will be picked up again later in the context of process choreographies in Chap. 8.

7.2.1   Integration Patterns and Processes

So far, an interoperability notion of applications and processes has been introduced by means of services and their orchestration. We recall that interoperability requires two (or more) systems to work together unchanged, even though they were not designed for that (cf. Bobby Wolf[1]). Consequently, integrating interoperable systems is trivial, but requires common, vendor-independent standards (e. g., governance, enforcement) and technology (e. g., WS-I, WSDL, SOAP, WS-RM). In case that does not work (e. g., due to deviating standards) or might not be given (e. g., missing design), more direct means of combining the systems is required, called integration. While the term "integration" refers to re-establishing or completion of a union of differentiated entities in the sense of inclusion or incorporation into a bigger whole, one could more practically say that custom logic (possibly including source code) is required to connect two (or more) systems.

7.2.1.1   Integration Patterns

In an attempt to structure common building blocks when integrating systems, Hohpe and Woolf [107] collected the state-of-the-art foundations of EAI and its system implementations as collection of EIPs in 2004. These patterns ground EAI on a message-oriented integration style with the characteristics of decoupling senders from receivers and solving the connection and variety problems for textual message formats. More precisely, the message-oriented foundations are based on the *Pipes-and-Filters* architecture style [45, 150, 162] (also known as dataflow), which became an architecture style for the processing and exchange of data [45] and later an integration pattern [107]. The enterprise integration pattern catalog combines Hohpe's and Woolf's previous, independent work on "enterprise integration patterns" [105] and "patterns of system integration with enterprise messaging" [224], respectively, and actually denotes a pattern language[2] (i. e., a matrix of connected patterns [227]), which shall help a user during the decision process, when designing and building an integration system, as recently stated by the EIP authors [231]. Thereby, the pattern descriptions provide a practical but structured documentation of expert knowledge according to a pattern format (e. g., name, problem/driving question, forces, solution, related patterns) that can be comprehensible for non-experts.

The messaging patterns from 2004 cover basic integration aspects like *Message Construction*, *Message Endpoints*, *Message Channels*, *Message Routing*, *Message Transformation*, and *System Management*. A decade after their first description, the pattern author's acknowledged that important aspects are missing [231], which led

---

[1] https://www.ibm.com/developerworks/community/blogs/woolf/entry/interoperability_vs_integration?lang=en.

[2] We use the terms *pattern catalog* and *pattern language* synonymously, despite their subtle differences.

Fig. 7.2 Overview of application integration patterns (from [107, 187, 188, 191, 193, 195]); **bold** patterns defined and realized subsequently

to recent additions—found in current integration systems (cf. [188])—of *Integration Adapters* [187], *Exception Handling* (incl. fault tolerance) [193, 195], *Storage* and *Security* [188, 191], as well as extensions of message transformation and system management [188, 191]. Together, the extended integration patterns are depicted in Fig. 7.2. The pipes-and-filters style allows for the use of direct communication as well as *message queuing* [107] for the wiring of the communication and integration architecture. They are categorized according to the EAI system domain aspects, for which they provide an abstraction, by chronologically following the flow of a message, and are briefly introduced and described subsequently.

Message Construction   The messaging patterns are grounded in the *messaging* integration style (e. g., in contrast to *shared database*) [107, 198], and thus the basic EAI domain aspect is a *Message*. This category describes the different types of messages, which are usually required by an integration solution. A message is described as packets of data, which are exchanged via pipes (i. e., *Message Channels*) and processed by filters (i. e., *Message Routing*, *Message Transformation*). The message types range from a simple *Command Message* without usable information, over an *Event Message* with limited formats and data, to a *Document Message* with arbitrary, textual formats. A message can contain additional information like a *Return Address* and a *Correlation Identifier* (e. g., to identify the sender, the request in an asynchronous communication, respectively) or a *Message Sequence* (e. g., to decompose large messages to smaller chunks), which might be required during the message processing.

Message Endpoints   The message exchange usually happens between abstract participants, called *Endpoints*. Endpoints abstract from different kinds of applications (e. g., business, cloud, mobile, social), services (e. g., SOA, EDA), and devices (e. g., mobile, sensor). The endpoints are connected to the communication channels and thus act as *sender* or *receiver* of messages. Notably, although the integration patterns in [107] are asynchronous and stateless by description, practical realizations of patterns like *Idempotent Receiver* require a persistent state. With that, an idempotent receiver can identify and handle duplicate messages.

Message Channels   The Message Channels facilitate the exchange of messages between one-to-many senders and one-to-many receivers (e. g., *Point-to-Point Channel*, *Publish-Subscribe Channel*). These channels transport messages of certain format (e. g., *Datatype Channel*), guarantee certain service qualities (e. g., best effort or at least once delivery [81, 187]), and deal with delivery failures (e. g., *Dead Letter Channel*, *Invalid Message Channel*). In addition, even more abstract concepts like *Messaging Bridge* (i. e., connecting multiple messaging systems) or meta-concepts like *Message Bus* (i. e., denoting a *Message-oriented Middleware* [26, 56]) are part of this category.

Message Routing   The routing patterns describe different ways to determine the recipient(s) of a message. The sender does not need to know the actual receiver, which essentially denotes the aspect of *decoupling* allowed by the patterns. Besides simple structural routing from pipe to filter, the routing requires access to the message's data (e. g., *Content-based Router* , *Recipient List*) or even changes the message for a correct routing (e. g., by decomposing one message into several messages using a *Splitter* , or combining several, related messages to one with an *Aggregator*).

Message Transformation   The *variety* and potential incompatibility of the textual formats of heterogeneous endpoints require message transformations from the senders' formats into formats understood by the recipients of a message. The transformation patterns provide a solution to this second decoupling aspect, allowing the endpoints to remain unchanged. Within the integration system, the message processing patterns require a standardized access to the data (i. e., common message format) in the form of a "lingua franca," which is provided by the *Canonical Data Model*, thus solving the variety problem for textual message formats. The solutions contain changes to the data (e. g., *Content Filter*, *Content Enricher*), contextualization of the data (e. g., *Envelope Wrapper*), as well as transport of references with a claim to stored messages that can be materialized using the claim (e. g., *Claim Check*).

Recent extensions differentiate transformations in terms of data representation (e. g., Encoder, Compress), data structure (e. g., Message Mapper), and custom extensions or user-defined functions (e. g., Script).

System Management Loose coupling and distributed applications are more difficult to administrate than a monolithic system. Therefore, a basic set of *System Management* patterns allows for the monitoring (e. g., *Control Bus*, *Wire Tap*, *Detour*), tracing (e. g., *Message History*), and testing of the system (e. g., *Test Message*).

Especially when operating integration systems in (public) cloud setups, additional patterns for observability (e. g., *Message Interceptor*), alerting (e. g., *Raise Indicator*), and workload management (e. g., *Scheduler*) have been identified.

Integration Adapters Participants communicate with each other by using message endpoints. When an integration middleware mediates between participants, integration adapters play an important role to involve other integration concepts. For example, integration adapters help to implement more fault-tolerant communication (e. g., *Timed Redelivery*) and bridge between communication styles (e. g., *Synch / Asynch Bridge*) and on a protocol level (e. g., *Protocol Switch*). Integration adapters are fundamental to ensure service qualities beyond fire-and-forget (*Best-Effort*) like *At-Least Once* and *Exactly-Once* with improved endpoints like *Commutative Endpoint*. Thereby, they can become integration sub-processes themselves (e. g., *Adapter Flow*).

Exception Handling When routing and transforming message, exceptional situations might occur. The integration patterns allow for fault-tolerant request handling (e. g., *Circuit Breaker*, *Failover Request Handler*), routing with compensations (e. g., *Failover Router*, *Compensation Sphere*), and preventive processing (e. g., *Message Validator*, *Message Cancellation*, *Catch*).

Storage Not only for service qualities like guaranteed and exactly only delivery, which practically requires an persistent idempotent receiver, the storage of certain data/variables is a recurring solution in current systems to realize a variety of use cases (e. g., a *Store Accessor* is flexibly used to preserve and document messages sent to an endpoint). Some of the stores are used for secure message exchange on a protocol and message level.

Security Not only in hybrid and cloud integration cases is security a major concern: Confidentiality (e. g., *Encryptor*), integrity/authenticity/availability (e. g., *Signer*,

Verifier, *Redundant Store*), and authorization (e. g., *Principle Propagation*) are relevant.

7.2.1.2   Integration Processes

Most of the single integration patterns denote atomic building blocks to compose more complex integration logic. Other patterns like *Request-Reply* or *Composed Message Processor* are compositions of the atomic patterns [107]. The atomic and composed patterns can be wired by direct communication links and Message Channels to *integration scenarios* in a pipes-and-filter style, also called *pattern compositions*.

For example, the two composed pattern examples in Example 7.1 (i. e., Request-Reply, Composed Message Processor) illustrate the capabilities of describing integration scenarios on a process level in *Business Process Model and Notation* (BPMN) [95]. The patterns [185] and their compositions [184] are represented by BPMN *Collaboration Diagrams*, which allow for a more detailed description of the control and data flows and other (novel) EAI concepts like those developed in this work like integration adapters [187] and exception handling [194, 196].

Example 7.1 The synchronous communication between two endpoints can be realized by the Request-Reply pattern, shown in Fig. 7.3. A requesting participant constructs a request message *Request*, which is transported by a Message Channel *Request channel* to a responding participant, returning the corresponding *Response* message to the request via the reply channel. The requesting participant does not need to wait for the reply, before continuing the processing. While the Request-Reply pattern describes the (a)synchronous interaction of endpoints, by combining messages and channels, Fig. 7.3b shows a more complex composition of atomic patterns representing a Composed Message Processor pattern. This message processor splits an incoming message *msg* into its parts and routes them individually to subsequent processors. Since the concept of an arbitrary filter (e. g., user-defined

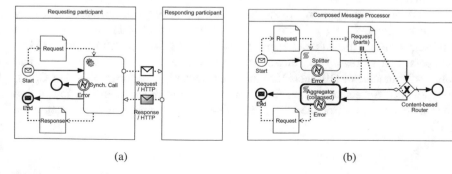

(a)   (b)

Fig. 7.3 Pattern composition in BPMN (Notation from [184] using SAP Signavio®). (**a**) Request-Reply. (**b**) Composed Message Processor

function) does not exist in the original EIPs, these processors are indicated by unnamed filters. After the processing, the resulting and related message parts are aggregated according to an aggregation strategy and based on a completion condition (not shown). □

Thereby, the Request-Reply pattern is denoted by Fig. 7.3a, by a *Requesting participant* and a *Responding participant*. While the control flow is equally denoted by BPMN *Sequence Flows*, the data flow uses a combination of BPMN *Message Flow* and *Data Object* with *Data Association* elements that are grounded in BPMN data definitions unlike in the EIP icon notation. The synchronous behavior is given by a BPMN *Service Task*, called *Synch. Call*, which receives the request and forwards it to the receiver. The response message is returned, and any errors are handled by a BPMN *Intermediate Error Event*. Similarly, the Composed Message Processor in Fig. 7.3b allows for superior concepts compared to the EIP icon notation like annotations for multiple messages forwarded by the Splitter, conditional and default Sequence Flows, and different BPMN *Activity* types like the BPMN *Script Task*. Furthermore, the Aggregator is a complex pattern that can be abstracted as BPMN *Call Activity*, denoting that more complex logic is linked.

Despite the rich and seemingly suitable syntax of the BPMN-based approach, the BPMN execution semantics differ from those of the patterns (e. g., in terms of message processing [184] and representation of integration adapters [187]). For further details, we refer to our previous work on modeling EIPs [184, 187, 194, 196]. Hence, in this work, the BPMN diagrams are used to illustrate certain integration scenarios and their aspects, but cannot be seen as a sound and complete integration modeling language, and thus left for future work.

7.2.2   Formal Specification

Petri nets provide built-in structural correctness criteria and allow for checking the behavioral correctness of process models (cf. Sect. 5.4), which makes them a good fit for formally defining integration logic in the form of patterns and their compositions as integration processes. However, integration scenarios not only require correctness on (i) control flow level (cf. Sect. 7.2.1.1) but also (ii) data representation and format that are given by Coloured Petri Nets (short CPNs) [115]; (iii) persistent storage; (iv) transactional data create, retrieve, update, delete and rollback semantics of DB-nets [155] that were recently developed on top of CPNs; and (v) time. Subsequently, we discuss formalization requirements of integration patterns before we introduce CPNs and DB-nets by example of basic integration concepts.

7.2.2.1   Formalization Requirements

The first requirement is a formal representation and analysis capabilities on the control flow *Control flow*, which is inherently covered by any PN approach and thus in CPN. However, there are two particularities in the routing patterns that we capture in requirement *Msg. channel priority, order*: (a) the ordered evaluation of Msg. channel conditions or prioritized evaluation of guards of sibling PN transitions, required for the content-based router pattern, and (b) the enablement or firing of a PN transition according to a ratio for the realization of a Load Balancer. In both cases, neither execution priorities nor ratios are trivially in CPN.

Furthermore, there are patterns in the catalogs with data and message format aspects, which require an expressive CPN token representation (e. g., for encodings, security, complex message protocols), for which we add as a second requirement *data, format* that has to allow for the formal analysis of the data. Although CPNs have to be severely restricted (e. g., finite color domains, pre-defined number of elements) for that, we require a formalism that promises a relational representation that can be formally analyzed.

We capture the patterns with time-related requirements as *time*: First, (a) a timeout is required that allows for the numerical representation of fixed, relative time (no global time). An expiry date (b) must be defined, denoting a discrete point in time according to a global time (i. e., based on existing message content). Moreover, the specification of a delay (c) is required that is a numerical, fixed value time to wait or pause until continued (e. g., also often used in a redelivery policy). Finally, patterns like the Throttler require (d) message/time ratio processing, which specifies the number of messages that are sent during a period of time. Consequently, a quantified, fixed time delay or duration semantics is required.

The patterns with resources *(external) resources* require (a) create, retrieve, update, and delete (*CRUD*) access to external services or resources and (b) *transaction* semantics on a pattern level. Similarly, exception semantics are present in patterns as *exceptions*, which require *compensations* and other post-error actions. Consequently, a PN definition that allows for reasoning over these timing and structured (persistent) data access is required.

7.2.2.2   Coloured Petri Nets

We recall from Sect. 5.4 that a Petri Net processes resources called tokens. Places hold these resources, and transitions process them. A flow relation or arcs connects places with transitions and vice versa. In Coloured Petri Nets (CPNs) [115], the tokens are typed by a color and represented by a variable-free expression. Similarly, places are typed as well and are restricted to hold tokens of the same color. Arc inscriptions specify the type of tokens that are consumed or produced by a transition.

For a formal definition of a CPN, we first need to understand *multisets*, which is a set that can contain an element more than once. More formally, for a set C, the multiset M is a function $M : C \rightarrow \mathbb{N}$, assigning each element of C its number of occurrences in M. C_{MS} denotes the set of all multisets over a set C. For example, $[a, c, d, c]$ is a multiset of a set $C = \{a, b, c, d\}$ with occurrences of one "a", two "c", and one "d" elements.

Definition 7.1 (Coloured Petri Net) A Coloured Petri Net is a tuple $CPN = (\Sigma, P, T, F, N, C, G, E, I)$, where:

- Σ is a finite set of types (color sets),
- P and T are finite disjoint sets of places and transitions,
- $F \subseteq P \times T \cup T \times P$ is the flow relation between places and transitions,
- C is a color function $C : P \to \Sigma$, assigning each place a color / type,
- G is a guard function from T into expressions, s.t. $\forall t \in T : Type(G(t)) = Boolean \wedge Type(Var(G(t))) \subseteq \Sigma$,
- E is an arc expression function from F into expressions, s.t. $\forall a \in F : Type(E(a)) = C(p(a))_{MS} \wedge Type(Var(E(a))) \subseteq \Sigma$, with $p(a)$ denoting the place of arc a, and
- I is and initialization function from P into variable-free expressions, s.t. $\forall p \in P : Type(I(p)) = C(p)_{MS}$.   □

Notably, the guards evaluate to *true* or *false*, and the types of the used variables $Var(G(t))$ are included in the given color set Σ. The arc expressions must evaluate to the same color/type as adjacent places p, and the types of the used variables are included in the given color set σ. Finally, each token/expression on p is a multiset over the color of p.

CPN Execution Semantics (intuition) A CPN is executed by state transitions of the typed tokens. The state of a CPN is defined by a *marking*, a function M from P into variable-free expressions, s.t. $\forall p \in P : Type(M(p)) = C(p)_{MS}$, which assigns to every place a possibly empty multiset of expressions (i. e., values). Those expressions are called *tokens* on the corresponding places, and they must have the same type color as the place. The initial marking of a CPN is given by the initialization function I in Definition 7.1.

The state of a CPN progresses through firing transitions. To fire a transition $t \in T$, a *binding* of all variables related to t is needed (i. e., variables in labels of arcs connecting to and the guard of t). The binding of t assigns a type-correct color to every variable of t, and the guard of t must evaluate to true. The arc expression $E(p, t)$ of a transition t and one of its antecedent places p evaluates under binding b to $E(p, t)\langle b \rangle$. For a binding b, a transition t is *enabled* to fire, if for all antecedent places p of t, with $(p, t) \in F$ the number of tokens required by the corresponding arc label is present on the antecedent place under binding $b : E(p, t)\langle b \rangle \leq M(p)$. Through firing a transition t with binding b in a marking M_1, a new marking M_2 is reached:

$$\forall p \in P : M_2(p) = M_1(p) - E(p, t)\langle b \rangle + E(t, p)\langle b \rangle,$$

which removes the tokens of the antecedent places and produces new tokens on the succeeding places.

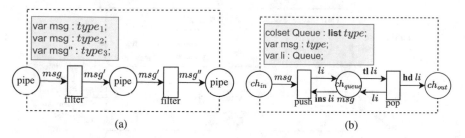

Fig. 7.4 Basic integration patterns in CPN. (**a**) Pipes and Filters. (**b**) Point-to-Point Channel (ordered)

In Example 7.2, we illustrate the representation of two basic integration patterns in CPN, for which we use the notation of CPN tools.[3]

Example 7.2 (Basic Integration Patterns in CPN)
The pipes and filters pattern is specified as a sequence of (filter) steps that are triggered through an event/the arrival of a message. Figure 7.4a depicts pipes as CPN place and filters as CPN transitions that are connected through arcs. When a token/message emph*msg* arrives in one of the *pipe* places, the subsequent *filter* transition fires by removing the message from the preceding place, filtering/changing the message according to a specified procedure, and putting an altered message (i. e., msg', msg'') to the succeeding place.

The Point-to-Point (p2p) channel, shown in Fig. 7.4b, is a unidirectional communication from sender to receiver that takes the message. Since, the *pipe* places in the previous example already denote simple, unordered p2p-channels, this example show a p2p-channel with ordered message delivery. The *push* transition fires by consuming message msg from ch_{in} and adds it as last element to the list li on place ch_{queue} with **ins** li msg. Similarly, transition *pop* fires by removing the first element msg from the list on place ch_{queue} with **hd** li and putting it one place ch_{out}. The remaining list is put back to ch_{queue} with **tl** li.   □

7.2.2.3   DB-nets

When facing the problem of formalizing multi-perspective models that suitably account for the dynamics of a system (i. e., the process perspective) and how it interacts with data (i. e., the data perspective), several design choices can be made. In the Petri net tradition, the vast majority of formal models striving for this integration approaches the problem by enriching execution threads (i. e., tokens) with complex data. Notable examples within this tradition are data nets [125] and ν-nets [197], Petri nets with nested terms [213], nested relations [102], and XML documents [18].

---

[3] https://cpnide.org/.

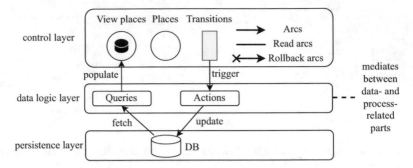

Fig. 7.5 The conceptual components of DB-nets (adapted from [155])

While all of the approaches treat data subsidiary to the control-flow dimension, the EIPs require data elements attached to tokens being connected to each other by explicitly represented global data models. Consequently, they do not allow for reasoning on persistent, relational data such as tree or graph structured message formats [186].

With a good understanding of CPNs and their data representation through typed tokens, we now look into the framework of DB-nets [155], which conceptually extends CPNs by persistent relational data and allows for reasoning over it. Figure 7.5 shows the underlying conceptual model of DB-nets that consists of three layers. On the one hand, a DB-net separately represents *persistence* storage (constituted by a full-fledged relational database with constraints) and *control* (captured as a CPN with additional, specific constructs). On the other hand, it explicitly handles their interplay through a *data logic* intermediate layer, which provides the control layer with queries and database operations (such as `trigger`, `update`, `fetch`, `populate`). Updates are transactional, that is, are only committed if the resulting instance of the persistence layer satisfies the database constraints. The control layer is informed about the outcome of an update and can consequently compensate in case of a rollback. Since DB-nets are based on CPNs, it is possible to lift existing simulation techniques from CPNs to DB-nets [155].

Definition 7.2 ([155]) A *DB-net* is a tuple $\langle \mathfrak{D}, \mathcal{P}, \mathcal{L}, \mathcal{N} \rangle$, where:

- $\mathfrak{D}$ is a type domain—a finite set of data types, each of the form $D = \langle \Delta_D, \Gamma_D \rangle$, where Δ_D is the value domain of D and Γ_D is a set of domain-specific (rigid) predicates.
- $\mathcal{P}$ is a $\mathfrak{D}$-typed **persistence layer**, i.e., a pair $\langle \mathcal{R}, E \rangle$, where $\mathcal{R}$ is a $\mathfrak{D}$-typed database schema and E is a finite set of first-order FO($\mathfrak{D}$) constraints over $\mathcal{R}$. [4]
- $\mathcal{L}$ is a $\mathfrak{D}$-typed **data logic layer** over $\mathcal{P}$, i.e., a pair $\langle Q, A \rangle$, where Q is a finite set of FO($\mathfrak{D}$) queries over $\mathcal{P}$ and A is a finite set of actions over $\mathcal{P}$. Each action

---

[4] These constraints capture typical database constraints such as key and foreign key dependencies.

in A is parameterized and uses its parameters to express a series of insertions and deletions over $\mathcal{P}$.

- $\mathcal{N}$ is a $\mathfrak{D}$-typed **control layer** $\mathcal{L}$, i.e., a tuple $(P, T, F_{in}, F_{out}, \texttt{color}, \texttt{query}, \texttt{guard}, \texttt{act})$, where:

  - $P = P_c \uplus P_v$ is a finite set of places partitioned into control places P_c and so-called view places P_v,
  - T is a finite set of transitions,
  - F_{in} is an input flow from P to T
  - F_{out} and F_{rb} are, respectively, an output and rollback flow from T to P_c
  - $\texttt{color}$ is a color assignment over P (mapping P to a cartesian product of data types),
  - $\texttt{query}$ is a query assignment from P_v to Q (mapping the results of Q as tokens of P_v),
  - $\texttt{guard}$ is a transition guard assignment over T (mapping each transition to a formula over its input inscriptions), and
  - $\texttt{act}$ is an action assignment from T to A (mapping some transitions to actions triggering updates over the persistence layer). $\qquad\Box$

Input and output/rollback flows contain inscriptions that match the components of colored tokens present in the input and output/rollback places of a transition. Such inscriptions consist of tuples of (typed) variables, which then can be mentioned in the transition guard as well as in the action assignment (to bind the updates induced by the action to the values chosen to match the inscriptions), and also, in case of the output flow, the inscriptions may contain rigid predicates. Specifically, given a transition t, we denote by $InVars(t)$ the set of variables mentioned in its input flows, by $OutVars(t)$ the set of variables mentioned in its output flows, and by $Vars(t) = InVars(t) \cup OutVars(t)$ the set of variables occurring in the action assignment of t (if any). Fresh variables $FreshVars(t) = OutVars(t) \setminus InVars(t)$ denote those output variables that do not match any corresponding input variables and are consequently interpreted as external inputs. While input inscriptions are used to match tokens from the input places to $InVars(t)$, the output expressions that involve rigid predicates operate over $OutVars(t)$. In case of numerical types, these expressions can be used to compare values or to arithmetically operate over them. We call *plain* a DB-net that employs matching output inscriptions only (i.e., does not use expressions).

Intuitively, each view place is used to expose a portion of the persistence layer in the control layer, so that each token represents one of the answers produced by the query attached to the place. Such tokens are not directly consumed but only read by transitions, so as to match the input inscriptions with query answers. A transition in the control layer may bind its input inscriptions to the parameters of data logic action attached to the transition itself, thus providing a mechanism to trigger a database update upon transition firing (and consequently indirectly change also the content of view places). If the induced update commits correctly, the transition emits tokens through its output arcs, whereas if the update rolls back, the transition emits tokens through its rollback arcs.

The terms message and (DB-net, CPN) token will be used synonymously hereinafter.

Db-net Execution Semantics We briefly recall the execution semantics of DB-nets. A state of a DB-net captures at once a state of the persistence layer (i. e., an instance of the database) and that of the control layer (i. e., a net marking, where the content of view places must be compatible with that of the database instance). More technically, in each moment (called *snapshot*), the persistence layer is associated with a database instance I, and the control layer is associated with a marking m aligned with I via query (for what concerns the content of view places). The corresponding snapshot is then simply the pair $\langle I, m \rangle$. Tokens in m have to carry data compatible with the color of the places, and the marking of a view place P_v must correspond to the associated queries over the underlying database instance.

Similar to CPNs, the firing of a transition t in a snapshot is defined by a binding that maps the value domains of the different layers, if several properties are guaranteed, e. g., the guard attached to t is satisfied. More specifically, we have the following.

Definition 7.3 (Transition Enablement [155]) Let B be a DB-net$\langle \mathfrak{D}, \mathcal{P}, \mathcal{L}, \mathcal{N}, \rangle$ and t a transition in $\mathcal{N}$. Let σ be a binding for t, i. e., a substitution $\sigma : Vars(t) \rightarrow \Delta_{\mathfrak{D}}$.[5] A transition $t \in T$ is *enabled* in a B-snapshot $\langle I, m \rangle$ with binding σ, if:

- For every place $p \in \mathcal{P}$, $m(p)$ provides enough tokens matching those required by inscription $w = F_{in}(\langle p, t \rangle)$, once w is grounded by σ, i. e., $\sigma(w) \subseteq m(p)$;
- the guard $\mathtt{guard}(t)\sigma$ evaluates to true;
- σ is injective over *FreshVars*(t), thus guaranteeing that fresh variables are assigned to pairwise distinct values of σ, and for every fresh variable $v \in$ *FreshVars*(t), $\sigma(v) \notin (Adom_{\mathtt{type}(v)}(I) \cup Adom_{\mathtt{type}(v)}(m))$.[6] $\square$

Firing an enabled transition has the following effects:

1. all matching tokens in control places P_c are consumed;
2. the action instance $\mathtt{action}$—induced by the firing—is applied on the current database instance in an atomic transaction (and rolled back, if not successful);
3. accordingly, tokens on output places F_{out} or rollback places F_{rb} (i. e., those connected via rollback flow) are produced.

Technically, we have the following.

Definition 7.4 (Transition Firing [155]) Let B be a DB-net$\langle \mathfrak{D}, \mathcal{P}, \mathcal{L}, \mathcal{N} \rangle$ and $s_1 = \langle I_1, m_1 \rangle, s_2 = \langle I_2, m_2 \rangle$ be two B-snapshots. Fix a transition t of $\mathcal{N}$ and a binding σ such that t is enabled in s_1 with σ (cf. Definition 7.3). Let $I_3 = apply(action_\sigma(t), I_1)$ be the database instance resulting from the application of the action attached to t on database instance I_1 with binding σ for the action parameters.

---

[5] We assume σ to be naturally extended to arc inscriptions. In case when an arc inscription contains an expression, σ will be applied to its variables.

[6] $Adom_D(X)$ is the set of values of type D explicitly contained in X.

For a control place p, let $w_{in}(p, t) = F_{in}(\langle p, t \rangle)$, and $w_{out}(p, t) = F_{out}(\langle p, t \rangle)$ if I_3 is compliant with $\mathcal{P}$, or $w_{out}(p, t) = F_{rb}(\langle p, t \rangle)$ otherwise. We say that t *fires* in s_1 with binding σ producing s_2, written $s_1[t, \sigma\rangle s_2$, if:

- if I_3 is compliant with $\mathcal{P}$, then $I_2 = I_3$, otherwise $I_2 = I_1$;
- for each control place p, m_2 corresponds to m_1 with the following changes: $\sigma(w_{in}(p, t))$ tokens are removed from p, and $\sigma(w_{out}(p, t))$ are added to p. In formulae: $m_2(p_c) = (m_1(p_c) - \sigma(w_{in}(p, t))) + \sigma(w_{out}(p, t))$. $\qquad\square$

All in all, the complete execution semantics of a DB-net is captured by a possibly infinite-state transition system where each transition represents the firing of an enabled transition in the control layer of the net with a given binding, and each state is a snapshot. The infinity comes from the presence of external inputs and the fact that domains/colors may have an infinite domain. It is important to notice that the resulting transition system may be infinite even if the control layer is bounded in the classical Petri net sense.

Example 7.3 Figure 7.6 defines the semantics of a commonly used stateful Aggregator pattern [107]. The Aggregator collects messages in a persistent storage that is accessed via a special view place ch_p and then aggregates them based either on the completion condition (e. g., sequence status is *complete*, modeled via *Aggregate* transition) or on timeout of 30 time units (e. g., sequence status is *expired*, modeled

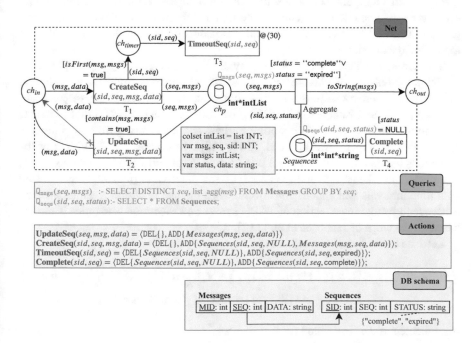

Fig. 7.6 Aggregator pattern variant as a timed DB-net. The graphical notation is in line with [155]

via transition *T3*). To collect messages and assign them to correct sequences, the net correlates every incoming *msg* token to those in place ch_p, which, in turn, stores pairs of sequences and lists of messages that have already been collected. If the message is the first in a sequence, new entries, one containing information about the message and another containing data about the referenced sequence, are added to tables called *Messages* and *Sequences*, respectively. This is achieved by firing transition *T1* and executing action *CreateSeq* attached to it. Otherwise, a message is inserted into *Messages* by firing *T2* and executing *UpdateSeq*. However, the update by *UpdateSeq* fails, if a message is already in the database or a referenced sequence has already been aggregated due to a timeout (i. e., status is *expired*). In this case, the net switches to an alternative rollback flow (a directed arc from *T2* to ch_{in}) and puts the message back to the message channel ch_{in}. The sequence completion logic is defined depending on a specific pattern application scenario and must always be realized in transition T_4 that executes an update that changes a given sequence state. $\square$

7.2.2.4   DB-nets with Time

We now extend the DB-net model so as to account for an explicit notion of time. In the spectrum of timed extensions to PNs, we subsequently extend the DB-net control layer $\mathcal{N}$ with a temporal semantics similar to TAPNs that achieves a suitable trade-off: it is expressive enough to capture the *time* requirements, and at the same time, it allows us to transfer the existing technical results on the verification of DB-nets to the timed extension.

The Timed-arc Petri Nets (TAPNs) by Bolognesi et al. and Hanish [41, 100] denote an extension of classical P/T nets with continuous time. Other temporal models like timed transitions add time durations for delayed firing (e. g., Ramchandani [172] and Zuberek et al. [232]) or Time petri nets (TPNs) that associate transitions with time intervals denoting earliest and latest firing time of transition after enablement (e. g., Merlin et al. [148, 149]). In contrast, in TAPNs, not the transitions but tokens carry temporal information in the form of an *age* value. While in a place, the tokens' age and the arcs between places and transitions are labeled with time intervals that enable transitions, when the age is within the interval. The subsequent, formal introduction of TAPN syntax and execution semantics is mostly based on the work of Jacobsen et al. [112].

Let I be a set of well-formed intervals

$$I \subseteq \{[a, b] \mid a, b \in \mathbb{R}, b \geq a\} \cup \{[a, b) \mid a, b \in \mathbb{R}, b > a\} \cup \{(a, b] \mid a, b \in \mathbb{R}, b > a\}$$

$$\cup \{[a, \infty) \mid a \in \mathbb{R}\} \cup \{(a, \infty) \mid a \in \mathbb{R}\}.$$

A predicate $r \in Int$ is defined for $r \in \mathbb{R}_{\geq 0}$ and $Int \in I$.

Definition 7.5 (TAPN [112]) A *TAPN* is a 5-tuple $\langle P, T, IA, OA, Inv \rangle$, where:

- P is a finite set of places;
- T is a finite set of transitions s.t. $P \cap T = \emptyset$;
- $IA \subseteq T \times \mathcal{I} \times P$ is a finite set of input arcs s.t.

$$((p, Int, t) \in IA \wedge (p, Int', t) \in IA) \implies Int = Int';$$

- $OA \subseteq T \times P$ is a finite set of output arcs;
- $Inv : P \to T^{inv}$ is a function assigning age invariants to places. $\qquad\square$

Note that multiple parallel arcs are not allowed according to [112]. The preset of a transition $t \in T$ is specified as ${}^\bullet t = \{p \in P \mid (p, Int, t) \in IA\}$, and the postset is $t^\bullet = \{p \in P \mid (t, p) \in OA\}$.

Execution Semantics The TAPN semantics for enabledness and firing require the definition of a marking M (cf. Definition 7.6), which is a function assigning a finite multiset of non-negative real numbers to each place (all such finite multisets are denoted by $\mathbb{R}_{\geq 0}$). The real numbers represent the age of tokens at a given place. Moreover, the age of every token must respect the age invariant of the place where the token is located.

Definition 7.6 (Marking [112]) Let $N = (P, T, IA, OA, Inv)$ be a TAPN. A marking M on N is a function $M : P \to \mathbb{R}_{\geq 0}$, where for every place $p \in P$ and every token $x \in M(p)$, we have $x \in Inv(p)$. The set of all markings over N is denoted by $M(N)$. $\qquad\square$

For simplicity, we use the notation (p, x) to refer to a token in the place p of age $x \in \mathbb{R}_{\geq 0}$. The multiset of a marking with n tokens located in places p_i and age x_i, for $1 \leq i \leq n$ is denoted by $M = \{(p_1, x_1), (p_2, x_2), .., (p_n, x_n)\}$. A marked TAPN is a pair (N, M_0) where N is a TAPN and M_0 is an initial marking on N where all tokens have age 0. With that, a TAPN transition is enabled as specified by Definition 7.7, when for all input arcs there is a token in the input place with an age satisfying the age guard of the respective arc. The age of the output token is 0 for all output arcs.

Definition 7.7 (Enabledness [112]) Let $N = (P, T, IA, OA, Inv)$ be a TAPN. A transition $t \in T$ is enabled in a marking M by tokens $In = \{(p, x_p) \mid p \in {}^\bullet t\} \subseteq M$ and $Out = \{(p', x_{p'}) \mid p' \in t^\bullet\}$ if there is $(p, Int, t) \in I$ with $x_p \in Int$. $\qquad\square$

On enablement, a TAPN transition fires according to Definition 7.8, which essentially denotes an immediate firing.

Definition 7.8 (Firing [112]) Let $N = (P, T, IA, OA, Inv)$ be a TAPN, M a marking on N, and $t \in T$ a transition. If t is enabled in the marking M by tokens In and Out, then it can fire and produce a marking M' defined as

$$M' = (M \setminus In) \cup Out,$$

where $\setminus$ and $\cup$ are operations on multisets. $\qquad\square$

The actual time delay is introduced by Definition 7.9.

Definition 7.9 (Time Delay [112]) Let $N = (P, T, IA, OA, Inv)$ be a TAPN and M a marking on N. A time delay $d \in \mathbb{R}_{\geq 0}$ is allowed in M, if $(x + d) \in Inv(p)$ for all $p \in P$ and all $x \in M(p)$, i.e., by delaying d time units no token violates any of the age invariants. When delaying d time units in M, we reach a marking M' defined as

$$M'(p) = \{x + d \mid \ \in M(p)\}$$

for all $p \in P$.   □

Example 7.4 Figure 7.7a illustrates the syntax and execution semantics of a basic TAPN. The tokens (*age*) in the places $p_1 - p_3$ carry an *age* information that is set to 0.0, when entering a place. Further the corresponding arcs are annotated by time intervals *Int* restricting the age of tokens available for transition firing. Initially, only transition t_1 is enabled due to the implicit default time interval $[0.0, \infty)$. That allows t_1 to fire and move the token from p_1 to the places p_4 and p_5 by resetting their age to 0.0, shown in Fig. 7.7b. The transition t_2 remains disabled for at least four time units of 1.0 due to time interval $[4.0, 5.0]$ on its second input arc, until it becomes enabled and fires.   □

A general *timed transition system* (TTS), according to [112], is a pair $T = (S, \longrightarrow)$, where S is a set of states (or processes) and $\longrightarrow \subseteq (S \times S) \cup (S \times \mathbb{R}_{\geq 0} \times S)$ is a transition relation. For discrete transitions $(s, s') \in \longrightarrow$, we write $s \longrightarrow s'$ and $s \xrightarrow{d} s'$ for delay transitions (s, d, s'), for which we write $s \Longrightarrow s'$. A TTS should satisfy all of the standard axioms (e. g., time additivity) for delay transitions from [34]. Now, a TAPN N defines a timed transition system $(\mathcal{M}(N), \longrightarrow)$, where states are markings of N, and for two markings M and M', we have $M \xrightarrow{d} M'$, if by delaying d time units in M we reach the marking M'. Thereby $\mathcal{N}_0$ and $\mathbb{R}_{\geq 0}$ denote the sets of non-negative integers and non-negative real numbers, respectively. The marking M' is reachable from marking M, if $M \Longrightarrow^* M'$, with $\Longrightarrow^*$ denoting the reflexive and transitive closure of $\Longrightarrow$.

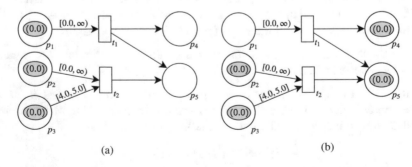

(a)   (b)

Fig. 7.7 Timed-arc Petri net example. (a) Transition t_1 enabled. (b) After firing t_1

Based on the introduced DB-nets and TAPNs, we start by explaining the intuition behind the approach and then provide the corresponding formalization. We assume that there is a global, continuous notion of time. The firing of a transition is instantaneous but can only occur in certain moments of time, while it is inhibited in others, even in presence of the required input tokens. Every *control token*, that is, token assigned to a control place, carries a (local) *age*, indicating how much time the token is spending in that control place. This means that when a token enters into a place, it is assigned an age of 0. The age then increments as the time flows, and the token stays in the same place. View places continuously access the underlying persistence layer, and consequently their (virtual) tokens do not age. Each transition is assigned to a pair of non-negative (possibly identical) rational numbers, respectively, describing the minimum and maximum age that input tokens should have when they are selected for firing the transition. Thus, such numbers identify a relative time window that expresses a delay and a deadline on the possibility of firing.

Definition 7.10 A *timed DB-net* is a tuple $\langle \mathfrak{D}, \mathcal{P}, \mathcal{L}, \mathcal{N}, \tau \rangle$ where $\langle \mathfrak{D}, \mathcal{P}, \mathcal{L}, \mathcal{N} \rangle$ is a DB-net with transitions T, and $\tau : T \rightarrow \mathbb{R}_{\geq 0}. \times (\mathbb{R}_{\geq 0}. \cup \{\infty\})$ is a *timed transition guard* mapping each transition $t \in T$ to a pair of values $\tau(t) = \langle v_1, v_2 \rangle$, such that:

* v_1 is a non-negative rational number;
* v_2 is either a non-negative rational number equal or greater than v_1, or the special constant ∞.

The default choice for τ is to map transitions to the pair $\langle 0, \infty \rangle$, which corresponds to a standard DB-net transition.

Given a transition t, we adopt the following graphical conventions:

* if $\tau(t) = \langle 0, \infty \rangle$, then no temporal label is shown for t;
* if $\tau(t)$ is of the form $\langle v, v \rangle$, we attach label "@$\langle v \rangle$" to t;
* if $\tau(t)$ is of the form $\langle v_1, v_2 \rangle$ with $v_1 \neq v_2$, we attach label "@$\langle v_1, v_2 \rangle$" to t.

Example 7.5 The Aggregator in Fig. 7.6 defines a timed transition *T3*, that can be fired precisely after 30 time units (here seconds) from the moment when a new sequence *seq* has been created. Upon firing, T_3 enables the *Aggregate* transition, by updating the sequence's status on the database to *expired* using the *TimeoutSeq* action.   □

Execution Semantics The execution semantics of timed DB-net builds on the one for standard DB-nets, extended with additional conditions on the flow of time and the temporal enablement of transitions in Definition 7.11. The management of bindings, guards, and database updates via actions is kept unaltered. What changes is that, in a snapshot, each token now comes with a corresponding age, represented as a number in $\mathbb{R}_{\geq 0}$. More formally, a marking is now a function $m : P \rightarrow \Omega_{\mathcal{D}}'^{\oplus}$, where $\Omega_{\mathcal{D}}'^{\oplus}$ consists of multisets of tuples $\langle y, o \rangle$ with $y \in \mathbb{R}_{\geq 0}$ and $o \in \Delta_{\mathfrak{D}}$.

Definition 7.11 (Transition Enablement) Let B be a timed DB-net$\langle \mathfrak{D}, \mathcal{P}, \mathcal{L}, \mathcal{N}, \tau \rangle$, and t a transition in $\mathcal{N}$ with $\tau(t) = \langle v_1, v_2 \rangle$. Let σ be a binding for t, i.e., a substitution σ : $Vars(t) \rightarrow \Delta_{\mathfrak{D}}$. A transition $t \in T$ is *enabled* in a B-snapshot $\langle I, m \rangle$ with binding σ, if:

- For every place $p \in \mathcal{P}$, $m(p)$ provides enough tokens matching those required by inscription $w = F_{in}(\langle p, t \rangle)$, once w is grounded by σ, i.e., $\sigma \subseteq m(p)$;
- the guard $\text{guard}(t)\sigma$ evaluates to true;
- for every $x_a \in InVars(t)$, $v_1 \leq \sigma(x_a) \leq v_2$, where $\tau(t) = \langle v_1, v_2 \rangle$;
- σ is injective over $FreshVars(t)$, thus guaranteeing that fresh variables are assigned to pairwise distinct values of σ, and for every fresh variable $v \in FreshVars(t)$, $\sigma(v) \notin (Adom_{\text{type}(v)}(I) \cup Adom_{\text{type}(v)}(m))$.[7]
- For each age variable $y_a \in (OutVars(t) \setminus InVars(t))$, we have that $\sigma(y_a) = 0$ (i.e., newly produced tokens get an age of 0). $\square$

As customary in several temporal extensions of Petri nets, we consider two types of evolution steps. The first type deals with *time lapses*: it indicates that a certain amount of time has elapsed with the net being quiescent, i.e., not firing any transition. This results in incrementing the age of all tokens according to the specified amount of time.

The second type deals with transition firing, which refines that of DB-nets by checking that the chosen binding selects tokens whose corresponding ages are within the delay window attached to the transition (cf. Definition 7.11). Specifically, let B be a timed DB-net $\langle \mathfrak{D}, \mathcal{P}, \mathcal{L}, \mathcal{N}, \tau \rangle$, t a transition in $\mathcal{N}$ with $\tau(t) = \langle v_1, v_2 \rangle$, and σ a binding for t. We say that t is enabled in a given B snapshot with binding σ if it is so according to DB-net enablement in Sect. 7.2.2.3 and, in addition, all the tokens selected by σ have an age that is between v_1 and v_2. Firing an enabled transition is identical to the case of standard DB-nets, with the only addition that for each produced token, its age is set to 0 (properly reconstructing the fact that it is entering into the corresponding place).

The execution semantics of a timed DB-net then follows the standard construction (using the refined notions of enablement and firing), with the addition that each snapshot may be subject to an arbitrary time lapse. This is done by imposing that every B-snapshot $\langle I, m \rangle$ is connected to every B-snapshot of the form $\langle I', m' \rangle$ where:

- $I' = I$ (i.e., the database instances are identical);
- m' is identical to m except for the ages of tokens, which all get incremented by the same, fixed amount $x \in \mathbb{Q}$ of time.

Given two B-snapshots s and s', we say that s *directly leads* to s', written $s \rightarrow s'$, if there exists a direct transition from s to s' in the transition system that captures the execution semantics of B. This means that s' results from s because of a transition firing or a certain time lapse. We extend this notion to finite execution traces $s_0 \rightarrow \ldots \rightarrow s_n$. We also write $s \overset{*}{\rightarrow} s'$ if s directly or indirectly leads to s'. If this is the case, we say that s' *reachable* from s.

---

[7] $Adom_D(X)$ is the set of values of type D explicitly contained in X.

Example 7.6 To complete the Aggregator in Fig. 7.6, when the persisted sequence in the Aggregator is complete or the sequence times out, the enabled *Aggregate* transition fires by reading the sequence number *seq* and snapshot of the sequence messages, and moving an aggregate msg' to ch_{out}. Notably, the *Aggregate* transition is invariant to which of the two causes led to the completion of the sequence.   □

7.3 Integration Pattern Realization

A pattern realization denotes a representation of a pattern as a timed DB-net (e. g., the Aggregator in Fig. 7.6). In this section, we discuss (formal) pattern realizations using timed DB-nets. Due to the high number of patterns, the formalization and corresponding in-detail description of all of them seem impractical. However, thanks to the fact that patterns can be classified into disjoint categories (see the requirement categories in Sect. 7.2.2.1), it suffices to discuss the most representative ones from each of such categories that serve as examples on how to construct the others: i. e., *control* and *data flow* only, *data flow with transacted resources*, *control flow with transacted resources and time*, *control flow with time*, and *data flow with transacted resources and time*. We call this an *instructive pattern formalization*, which strives to formalize the patterns and, at the same time, offers modeling guidelines for other patterns of the respective categories using the provided examples.

7.3.1 Control Flow: Load Balancer

To demonstrate the *control flow only* pattern, we have chosen the Load Balancer pattern (cf. Fig. 7.2). Interestingly, this pattern also covers the message channel distribution requirement (cf. Sect. 7.2.2.1) and thus can be considered as a relevant candidate of this category as well.

In a nutshell, the balancer distributes the incoming messages to a number of receivers based on a criterion that uses some probability distribution or ratio defined on the sent messages. To realize the former one could resort to stochastic PNs [24, 230] or extend the DB-net transition guards definition with an ability to sample probability values from a probability distribution (e. g., [109]). While the latter would extend the DB-net persistence layer, it is unclear whether the decidability results discussed in the previous section will still hold. Hence, we opted for the ratio criterion that, as shown in Fig. 7.8, is realized using a persistence storage and transition guards with a simple balancing scheme. Specifically, a message *msg* in channel ch_{in} leads to a lookup of the current ratio by accessing the current message counts per output channel in the database and evaluating guards assigned to one of the two transitions based on the extracted values. The ratio criterion is set up with two (generic) guards $\varphi(toCh_1, toCh_2)$ and $\neg\varphi(toCh_1, toCh_2)$, respectively, assigned to T_1 and T_2. If one of the guards holds, the corresponding

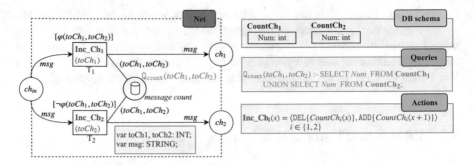

Fig. 7.8 Load balancer realization as a timed DB-net

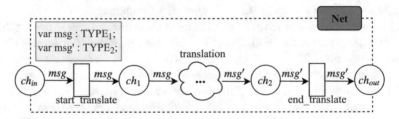

Fig. 7.9 Message translator realization as a timed DB-net

transition fires by moving the message to its output place as well as updating the table by incrementing the corresponding channel count. The latter is done by consecutively performing $Inc\_Ch_i \cdot \mathrm{del} = \{CountCh_i(x)\}$ and $Inc\_Ch_i \cdot \mathrm{add} = \{NumberCh_i(x+1)\}$ (for $i \in \{1, 2\}$).

7.3.2 Data Flow: Message Translator, Splitter

The stateless Message Translator, shown in Fig. 7.9, is the canonical example of a *data flow only* pattern (cf. [107]). The translator works on the data representation level, by transforming an incoming message of type $TYPE_1$ from ch_{in} using a subnet that starts by firing *start_translate* and finishes by firing *end_translate* and that produces a new message of type $TYPE_2$ into the receiver place ch_{out}. Note that for the representation of a subnet, we use a cloud symbol, which denotes a configurable model part in the form of a subnet. We acknowledge that some patterns like the Message Translator might have variations; however, that could also be formalized in the same way and left to the reader to do so.

The (iterative) Splitter 7.10 is an example of a non-message transformation *data flow only* pattern, which is also required for a case study scenario in Sect. 7.5. The pattern itself represents a complex routing mechanism that, given an iterable collection of input messages *it* together with two objects *pre* and *post*, is able

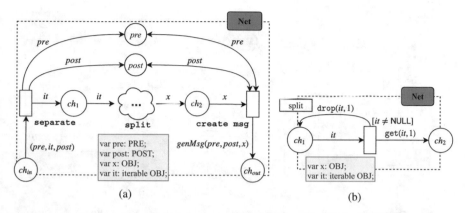

Fig. 7.10 Splitter realization and sample *split* subnet realization as a timed DB-net. (**a**) Splitter. (**b**) Example split subnet

to construct for each of its elements a new message of the form $[\langle pre \rangle]\langle it :$ $msg_i \rangle[\langle post \rangle]$ with optional *pre* and *post* parts. As shown in Fig. 7.10a, the splitter can be fully realized in CPN under certain restrictions assumed for the type of the iterable collection at hand. The entering message payloads in ch_0 are separated into its parts: *pre*, *post*, and *it*. While the first two are remembered during the processing, the iterable *it* is iteratively split into parts according to some criterion realized in the *split* subnet, which represents a custom split logic and thus is intentionally left unspecified (indicated by a cloud symbol in Fig. 7.10a).

Example 7.7 The *split* subnet can be adapted to the message format and the requirements of a specific scenario. Figure 7.10b demonstrates a possible implementation of the subnet. Here, functions *get* and *drop* are used to read and remove the n-th element of an iterable object. In our case, we alternate their applications to the *iterable* object *it* from place ch_1 in order to extract and delete its first element that is then placed into ch_2. Such a procedure is repeated until *it* is empty (i.e., it is NULL). □

Each of extracted elements from *it*, together with the information about *pre* and *post*, is then used to create a new message (by calling function *genMsg*) that is passed to the output channel ch_{out} (Fig. 7.10b).

7.3.3 Data and Control Flow: Content-Based Router

The content-based router pattern is the canonical candidate for *data and control flow* patterns. The realization of the router with conditions φ_1, φ_2 that have to be evaluated strictly in-order (cf. REQ-1(a)) is shown in Fig. 7.11a. Although the router could be realized more elegantly by using priority functions similarly to [230], we

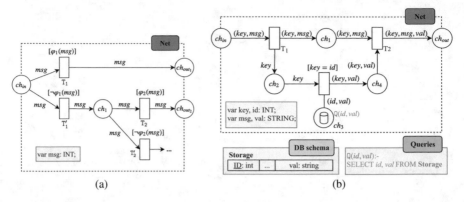

Fig. 7.11 Content-based router and content enricher realization as a timed DB-net. (**a**) Content-based Router. (**b**) Content Enricher

explicitly realized them with pair-wise negated timed DB-net transition guards. A message from incoming channel ch_{in} is first evaluated against condition φ_1. Based on the evaluation result, the message is moved either to ch_1 or ch_2. In case it has been moved to ch_2, the net proceeds with the subsequent evaluation of other conditions using the same pattern. When none of the guards can be evaluated, a non-guarded, low-priority default transition fires (not shown). This explicit realization covers the router's semantics, however, requires $(k \times 2) + 1$ transitions (i.e., condition, negation, and only one default), with the number of conditions k.

7.3.4 Data Flow with Transacted Resources: Content Enricher, Resequencer

The first pattern chosen for this category such that it includes a data flow with *transacted resources* is the Content Enricher. It requires accessing external resources (e. g., relational database) based on *data* from an incoming message. Such data are then used to enrich the content of the message. As one can see in Fig. 7.11b, the pattern uses request-reply transitions T_1 and T_2 to direct the net flow toward extracting message-relevant data from an external resource. The extraction is performed by matching a message identifier *key* with the one in the storage. While the stateless enriching part is essentially a coloured Petri net, in order to access a stateful resource in ch_3, one requires to use DB-nets so as to specify and perform queries on the external storage (cf. REQ-4(a,b)).

The stateful Resequencer is a pattern that ensures a certain order imposed on messages in (asynchronous) communication [107]. Figure 7.12 shows how the resequencer can be represented in DB-nets. The incoming message *msg* contains information about its sequence *seq* and some order information *ord* and is persisted in the database. The information about stored messages can be accessed through

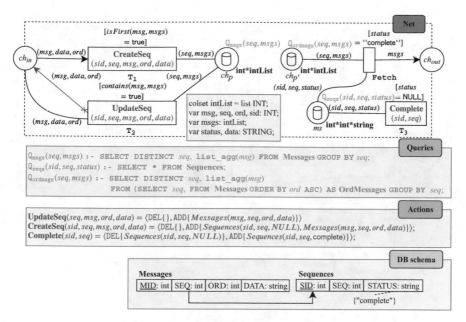

Fig. 7.12 Resquencer realization as a timed DB-net

the view place ch_p. For the first incoming message in a sequence, a corresponding sequence entry with a unique identifier value bound to sid[8] will be created in the persistent storage (sequences can be accessed in the view place ms), whereas for all subsequent messages of the same sequence, the messages are simply stored. As soon as the sequence is complete, i. e., all messages of that sequence have arrived, the messages of this sequence are queried from the database in ascending order of their ord component (see the view place $ch_{p'}$ and its corresponding query). The query result is represented as a list that is forwarded to ch_{out}. Note that, similarly to the Aggregator in Fig. 7.6, the completion condition can be extended by a custom logic in T_3 (e. g., a condition on the number of message to be aggregated).

7.3.5   Control Flow with Transacted Resource and Time: Circuit Breaker

To demonstrate a family of patterns that are based on a control flow with transacted resources and time, we selected as its representative the Circuit Breaker pattern

---

[8] Note that since sid is not bound to variables in the input flow of T_i ($i \in \{1, 2, 3\}$), it can be treated as a fresh variable that, whenever the transition is executed, gets a unique value of a corresponding type assigned to it.

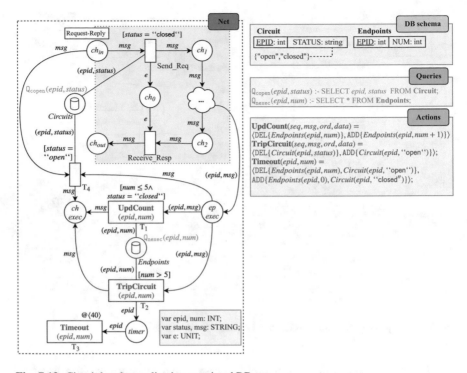

Fig. 7.13 Circuit breaker realization as a timed DB-net

(see Fig. 7.2). It addresses failing or hang up remote communication, which impacts the control flow of the Request-Reply pattern by using transacted access to external resources. Figure 7.13 shows a representation of the request-reply pattern in timed DB-nets, extended by a circuit breaker "wrapper" that protects the remote call. At the beginning, every (endpoint-dedicated) circuit[9] in the circuit breaker is closed (i.e., its status in table *Circuit* is initially set to *closed*), thus allowing for the communication via the Request-Reply pattern part. If the request-reply pattern executes normally, the resulting message is placed in ch_{out}. Otherwise, in the case when an exception has been raised, the information about the failed endpoint is stored both in the *Endpoints* table of the persistent storage and a special place *ch exec*. Such a table contains all endpoints together with the number of failures that happened at them. If the number of failures reaches a certain limit (e. g., $num > 5$), the circuit trips and updates its status in the corresponding entry of the *Circuit* relation to *open*. This in turn immediately blocks the communication process that, however, can be resumed (i. e., the circuit is again set to *open*, and the failure count is set to 0) after 40 time units have been passed. Note that whenever at least one

---

[9] For simplicity, every endpoint is identified with a unique number EPID.

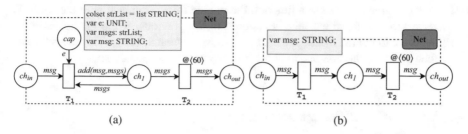

Fig. 7.14 Throttler and delayer realizations as a timed DB-net. (**a**) Throttler. (**b**) Delayer

circuit remains closed, the messages from ch_{in} will be immediately redirected to $ch\,exec$.

7.3.6   Control Flow with Time: Throttler, Delayer

The representative patterns of this group mostly require control flow and time aspects and thus can be represented using timed CPNs. The first pattern is the Throttler. It helps to ensure that a specific receiver does not get overloaded by regulating the number of transferred messages. Figure 7.14a shows the realization of a throttler that emits at most n messages (here n is the number of "simple," black tokens assigned with an initial marking to place cap) per 60 time units to the receiving place ch_{out}.

A slightly different pattern of this category is the Delayer that uses a timer to reduce the frequency of messages sent to the receiving place ch_{out}. As shown in Fig. 7.14b, the sent message is delayed by 60 time units.

7.3.7   Data Flow with Transacted Resources Time: Aggregator

The combination of data, transacted resources, and time aspects in patterns makes them the semantically most complex ones. For example, Fig. 7.6 specifies the semantics of a commonly used stateful Aggregator pattern. The Aggregator persistently collects messages, which can be seen in a dedicated view place ch_p, and aggregates them using the *Aggregate* transition based on a completion condition (i.e., a sequence that the message is related to is complete) or on a sequence completion timeout. For this, an incoming message msg is correlated to an existing sequence based on a sequence label seq attached to it. If the message is first in a sequence, a new sequence is created in the *Sequences* table, and the message, together with a reference to this sequence, is recorded in the persistent storage using the *Messages* table. If a message correlates to an existing sequence seq, which has been aggregated due to a timeout, the update fails. This results in the rollback behavior: the database instance is restored to the previous, while the net uses the rollback arc to put the message back to the message channel ch_{in}. This message can be then added as the first one to another newly created sequence seq.

7.3.8   Notes on Pattern Realizations

The DB-net foundation implicitly covers requirements of complex data, format, and CRUD data access in the form of a relational formalization with database transactions. Together with the realizations of the Content-based Router, Load Balancer, and Aggregator in Fig. 7.6, we showed realizations for all of the requirements from Sect. 7.2.2.1. The expiry of tokens, depending on time information within the message, can be represented using CPNs and DB-nets by modeling it as part of the token's color set and transition guards (similar to [4]). Nevertheless, to model the transition timeouts and delays, one needs to resort to more refined functionality realized in timed transitions provided by the timed extension of DB-nets. Similarly, the message/time ratio (cf. REQ-3(d)) can be represented (see Throttler pattern in Fig. 7.14a).

The categorization of patterns according to their characteristics allows for an *instructive* formalization based on candidates of these categories and shows that even complex patterns can be defined in timed DB-nets. This, in turn, allowed us not to discuss candidates of all the categories from Sect. 7.2.2.1, since they can be seamlessly derived by the introduced patterns from other categories. For example, *control* and *data* with resource patterns do not require transacted resources and can thus be realized similar to their transacted resource cases by substituting view places with normal ones. The building blocks for the realization of *transacted resource* as well as *data flow with time* patterns can be derived from, e. g., the Resequencer or Aggregator patterns. Finally, the *data flow with format* patterns can be represented using CPNs, and thus are not further discussed here.

Thanks to our model-checking result presented in the previous section and those derived from DB-net (e. g., liveness property from [155][Theorem 2] based on the argument on μ-calculus for data-centric dynamic systems [154] that enjoy a liveness property due to proof in [20]), the correctness of the realization of each pattern can be formally verified. However, due to the absence of a model checker for (timed) DB-nets, the formal analysis (cf. [155]) of such cannot currently be automatically performed. Nevertheless, as an alternative to the model checking approach, it is possible to perform the correctness testing using the experimental validation via (repeated) simulation of DB-net models. We discuss this approach in the following section.

7.4 Pattern Composition and Integration Processes

The modeling of composed patterns in languages like BPMN (e. g., Fig. 7.3) allows for a structurally correct composition of patterns in the form of abstracting the low-level pattern logic by high-level graphs, in which each pattern denotes a node in the graph. The pattern contracts are implicitly represented by the edges, which enforce the correct composition of adjacent patterns. While the graph approach conveniently abstracts from the internal pattern logic, and thus from unnecessary complexity from a user perspective, the semantic correctness is not yet covered. As motivated before, for the problem of formalizing pattern compositions, we propose a solution grounded on timed DB-nets. Pattern contracts are represented as what we call *boundaries*. These boundaries encode pattern characteristics for correct compositions in the form of contracts, accounting for the inner pattern semantics.

In the PN domain, *Open Nets* [19, 25] are usually considered for compositional contracts and thus taken up in the workflow (e. g., [63, 117]) and service interaction (e. g., [64]) domains. These approaches focus on the composition of the control flow and correctness, e. g., in the sense of the accordance of private and public views in an interaction [63]. In case of the integration patterns, not only the data flow but also the identified structural and semantic pattern characteristics have to be taken into account, when formalizing compositions and checking their correctness. For that, we selected the work by Sobociński [206] on nets with boundaries—essentially a sufficiently expressive variant of open nets—for our case. Subsequently, we discuss the background on nets with boundaries for better understandability close to our contribution, timed DB-nets with boundaries or open timed DB-nets, which follow immediately afterward.

7.4.1 Nets with Boundaries

The composition of PNs of the same type (e. g., timed DB-nets) can be facilitated by "ports" or "open boundaries" for communicating with each other (e. g., [19, 25]). Thereby PN tokens can progress from one PN to another through these ports, which can have a structural boundary configuration that allows for their correctness checking, called *synchronization* [86, 206]. The subsequently introduced nets are mostly based on [206].

Let $\underline{k}, \underline{l}, \underline{m}, \underline{n}$ range over finite ordinals $n = \{0, 1, \ldots, n - 1\}$. Intuitively, the notion of a left $^\bullet-$ and a right $-^\bullet$ *boundary* is introduced in Definition 7.12 that extends the already known predecessor and successor relations, here made explicit by $^\circ-$, $-^\circ$, respectively. Being explicit about these relations allows for a differentiated visualization of the different conventional control and new boundary places.

Definition 7.12 (Net with Boundaries [206]) Let $m, n \in \mathbb{N}$. A (finite) net with boundaries $N : m \to n$, is a sextuple $(P, T, {}^\circ-, -^\circ, {}^\bullet-, -^\bullet)$ where:

- P is a set of places;
- T is a set of transitions;
- ${}^\circ-, -^\circ : T \to 2^P$ are predecessor and successor functions;
- ${}^\bullet- : T \to 2^{\underline{m}}, -^\bullet : T \to 2^{\underline{n}}$ are boundary functions. □

We say that m and n denote the left and right boundaries of N, respectively. Further, a homomorphism $f : N \to M$ between two nets with equal boundaries $N, M :$ $m \to n$ is a pair of functions $f_T : T_N \to T_M$, $f_P : P_N \to P_M$, s.t. ${}^\circ-_N; 2^{f_P} = f_T;$ ${}^\circ-_M, -^\circ_N; -^\circ_M, {}^\bullet-_N = f_T; -^\bullet_M$ and ${}^\bullet-_N = f_T; -^\bullet_M$. If its two components are bijections, a homomorphism is an isomorphism. We write $N \cong M$, if there is an isomorphism from N to M.

For contract situations, Sobociński [206] introduces an independence of transitions, i.e., transitions t, u are independent, if ${}^\circ t \cap {}^\circ u = \emptyset$. Moreover, for some transition t, a place p can be both in ${}^\circ t$ and t°. We extend the notion of independence of transitions to nets with boundaries by: $t, u \in T$ are *independent*, if:

$$ {}^\circ t \cap {}^\circ u = \emptyset, t^\circ \cap u^\circ = \emptyset, {}^\bullet t \cap {}^\bullet u = \emptyset \text{ and } t^\bullet \cap u^\bullet = \emptyset. $$

To define composition along the boundary of two nets $M : l \to m$ and $N : m \to n$, we introduce the concept of a *synchronization*: a pair (U, V), with $U \subseteq T_M$ and $V \subseteq T_N$ mutually independent sets of transitions $U^\bullet = \{u^\bullet | u \in U\}$ and ${}^\bullet V = \{{}^\bullet v | v \in V\}$, s.t.:

- $U \cup V \neq \emptyset$;
- $U^\bullet = {}^\bullet V$.

A set of synchronisations inherits an ordering from the subset relation, i.e., $(U', V') \subseteq (U, V)$, if $U' \subseteq U$ and $V' \subseteq V$. The synchronization is *minimal*, if it is minimal with respect to this order:

$$ T_{M;N} \stackrel{\text{def}}{=} \{(U, V) | U \subseteq T_M, V \subseteq T_N, (U, V) \text{ a minimal synchronization}\}. $$

Notably, any transition t in M (or N) that is not connected to a shared boundary m denotes a minimal synchronization $(\{t\}, \emptyset)$.

We define ${}^\circ-, -^\circ : T_{M;N} \to 2^{P_M \sqcup P_N}$, with the disjoint union $\sqcup$, by ${}^\circ(U, V) = {}^\circ U \cup {}^\circ V, (U, V)^\circ = U^\circ \cup V^\circ$, as well as ${}^\bullet- : T_{M;N} \to 2^{\underline{l}}$ by ${}^\bullet(U, V) = {}^\bullet U$ and $-^\bullet : T_{M;N} \to 2^{\underline{n}}$ by $(U, V)^\bullet = V^\bullet$. Consequently, the *composition* of M and N is written $M; N : l \to n$ with:

- set of transitions $T_{M;N}$;
- set of places $P_M \sqcup P_N$;
- ${}^\circ-, -^\circ : T_{M;N} \to 2^{P_M \sqcup P_N}, {}^\bullet- : T_{M;N} \to 2^{\underline{l}}$

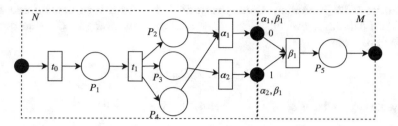

Fig. 7.15 Example net with boundaries

Proposition 7.1

- Let $M, M' : k \rightarrow n$ and $N, N' : n \rightarrow m$ be nets with $M \cong M'$ and $N \cong N'$, then $M; N \cong M'; N'$;
- Let $L : k \rightarrow l, M : l \rightarrow m, N : m \rightarrow n$ be nets, then $(L; M); N \cong L; (M; N)$.

Further we define the *tensor product* as another binary operation on nets with boundaries. For nets $M : k \rightarrow l$ and $N : m \rightarrow n$, the resulting tensor product is the net that results from their parallel composition. More precisely, $M \otimes N : k \sqcup m \rightarrow l \sqcup n$ in the net with:

- set of transitions $T_M \sqcup T_N$;
- set of places $P_M \sqcup P_N$;
- $^\circ-$, $-^\circ$, $^\bullet-$, $-^\bullet$ defined in the obvious way.

Example 7.8 The composition $N; M$ of a nets with boundaries $M : 1 \rightarrow 2$ and $N : 2 \rightarrow 1$ is shown in Fig. 7.15. Thereby, $T_N = \{t_0, t_1, \alpha_1, \alpha_2\}$, $T_M = \{\beta_1\}$ and $P_N = \{P_1, .., P_4\}$, $P_M = \{P_5\}$. The non-empty values of $^\circ-$ and $-^\circ$ are: $t_0^\circ = \{P_1\}$, $^\circ t_1 = \{P_1\}$, $t_1^\circ = \{P_2, P_3, P_4\}$, $^\circ\alpha_1 = \{P_2, P_4\}$, $^\circ\alpha_2 = \{P_3\}$, and $\beta_1^\circ = \{P_5\}$; and the non-empty values of $^\bullet-$, $-^\bullet$: $\alpha_1^\bullet$, $^\bullet\beta_1 = \{0\}$, $\alpha_2^\bullet$, $^\bullet\beta_1 = \{1\}$.   □

7.4.2   Timed DB-Nets with Boundaries

We recall timed DB-nets from Sect. 7.2.2.4 and describe them as nets that are open, in the sense that they have "ports" or "open boundaries" for communicating with the outside world: tokens can be received and sent on these ports [86, 206]. Similar to nets with boundaries [206], we define a boundary configuration that records what we expect from the external world for the net to be functioning. This is not the most general notion of open timed DB-nets, but it is general enough for our purposes.

The boundary configurations so far only concerned the number of "ports" [86, 206] for the synchronization of nets. Hence in Definition 7.13, we define a boundary configuration considering the number of ports but also the data exchanged between nets.

Definition 7.13 (Boundary Configuration) Let $\mathfrak{D}$ be a type domain and $\mathcal{L} = (Q, A)$ a data layer over it. A *boundary configuration* over $(\mathfrak{D}, \mathcal{L})$ is an ordered finite list of colors

$$c \in \{\mathcal{D}_1 \times \ldots \times \mathcal{D}_m \mid D_i \in \mathfrak{D}\}$$

We write such a list as $c_1 \otimes \ldots \otimes c_n$, and I for the empty list.   □

The length of a boundary configuration list gives the number of "open ports" of the boundary [86, 206]. Each color c in the list describes the type of the data to be sent/received on the port. An open timed DB-net has a left and a right boundary, both described by boundary configurations.

The boundary configurations allow for the extension of the timed DB-net definition in Definition 7.10 with boundaries concerning the data exchange to timed DB-nets with boundaries given in Definition 7.14.

Definition 7.14 (Timed db-net with Boundaries) Let $\mathfrak{D}$, $\mathcal{P}$, and $\mathcal{L}$ be a type domain, a persistence layer, and a data layer respectively, and let $\otimes_{i<m} c_i$ and $\otimes_{i<n} c'_i$ be boundaries over $\mathfrak{D}$, $\mathcal{L}$. A control layer with left boundary $\otimes_{i<m} c_i$ and right boundary $\otimes_{i<n} c'_i$ is a tuple

$$(P, T, F_{in}, F_{out}, F_{rb}, \texttt{color}, \texttt{query}, \texttt{guard}, \texttt{action})$$

which is a control layer over $\mathcal{L}$, except that F_{in} is a flow from $P \uplus \{1, \ldots m\}$ to T and F_{out} and F_{rb} are flows from T to $P_c \uplus \{1, \ldots, n\}$, i.e.,

- $P = P_c \uplus P_v$ is a finite set of places partitioned into control places P_c and view places P_v,
- T is a finite set of transitions,
- F_{in} is an input flow from $P \uplus \{1, \ldots m\}$ to T (where we assume $\texttt{color}(i) = c_i$),
- F_{out} and F_{rb} are, respectively, an output and rollback flow from T to $P \uplus \{1, \ldots, n\}$ (where we assume $\texttt{color}(j) = c'_j$),
- $\texttt{color}$ is a color assignment over P (mapping P to a Cartesian product of data types),
- $\texttt{query}$ is a query assignment from P_v to Q (mapping the results of Q as tokens of P_v),
- $\texttt{guard}$ is a transition guard assignment over T (mapping each transition to a formula over its input inscriptions)
- $\texttt{action}$ is an action assignment from T to A (mapping transitions to actions triggering updates over the persistence layer).

We write $(\mathfrak{D}, \mathcal{P}, \mathcal{L}, \mathcal{N}, \tau) : \otimes_{i<m} c_i \to \otimes_{i<n} c'_i$ for timed DB-nets with control layers with the given boundaries and call such a tuple a *timed DB-net with boundaries*.   □

Note that the boundaries are carefully incorporated into the timed DB-net definition by solely concerning the exchanged data elements and thus in particular that a timed DB-net with empty boundaries is by definition a timed DB-net. We can extend the $\otimes$ operation on colors to nets, by defining $N \otimes N' : \vec{c} \otimes \vec{c}' \to \vec{d} \otimes \vec{d}'$ for $N : \vec{c} \to \vec{d}$ and $N : \vec{c}' \to \vec{d}'$ to be the two nets N and N' next to each other—this gives a tensor product or "parallel" composition of nets. The point of being explicit about the boundaries of nets is to enable also a "sequential" composition of nets, whenever the boundaries are compatible. In Definition 7.15, we use the notation $X \uplus Y$ for the disjoint union of X and Y, with injections $\text{in}_X : X \to X \uplus Y$ and $\text{in}_Y : Y \to X \uplus Y$. For $f : X \to Z$ and $g : Y \to Z$, we write $[f, g] : X \uplus Y \to X'$ for the function with $[f, g](\text{in}_X(x)) = f(x)$ and $[f, g](\text{in}_Y(y)) = g(y)$.

Definition 7.15 (Synchronization) Let $(\mathcal{D}, \mathcal{P}, \mathcal{L}, \mathcal{N}, \tau) : \otimes_{i<m} c_i \to \otimes_{i<n} c_i'$ and $(\mathcal{D}', \mathcal{P}', \mathcal{L}', \mathcal{N}', \tau') : \otimes_{i<n} c_i' \to \otimes_{i<k} c_i''$ be two timed DB-nets with boundaries. We define their composition as

$$(\mathcal{D} \cup \mathcal{D}', \mathcal{P} \cup \mathcal{P}', \mathcal{L} \cup \mathcal{L}', \mathcal{N}'', \tau'') : \otimes_{i<m} c_i \to \otimes_{i<k} c_i''$$

(where union of tuples is pointwise) with

$$\mathcal{N}'' = (P'', T'', F_{in}'', F_{out}'', F_{rb}'', \text{color}'', \text{query}'', \text{guard}'', \text{action}'')$$

where

$$P'' = P \uplus P' \uplus \{x_1, \ldots, x_n\}$$

$$T'' = T \uplus T'$$

$$F_{in}''(x, y) = \begin{cases} F_{in}(p, t) & \text{if } (x, y) = (\text{in}_P(p), \text{in}_T(t)) \\ F_{in}'(p', t') & \text{if } (x, y) = (\text{in}_{P'}(p'), \text{in}_{T'}(t')) \\ F_{in}'(j, t') & \text{if } (x, y) = (x_j, \text{in}_{T'}(t')) \\ \emptyset & \text{otherwise} \end{cases}$$

$$F_{out}''(x, y) = \begin{cases} F_{out}(p, t) & \text{if } (x, y) = (\text{in}_P(p), \text{in}_T(t)) \\ F_{out}'(p', t') & \text{if } (x, y) = (\text{in}_{P'}(p'), \text{in}_{T'}(t')) \\ F_{out}(j, t) & \text{if } (x, y) = (x_j, \text{in}_T(t)) \\ \emptyset & \text{otherwise} \end{cases}$$

$$F_{rb}''(x, y) = \begin{cases} F_{rb}(p, t) & \text{if } (x, y) = (\text{in}_P(p), \text{in}_T(t)) \\ F_{rb}'(p', t') & \text{if } (x, y) = (\text{in}_{P'}(p'), \text{in}_{T'}(t')) \\ F_{rb}(j, t) & \text{if } (x, y) = (x_j, \text{in}_T(t)) \\ \emptyset & \text{otherwise} \end{cases}$$

$$\text{color}'' = [\text{color}, \text{color}', x_i \mapsto c_i]$$

$$\text{query}'' = [\text{query}, \text{query}']$$

$$\text{guard}''(\text{in}_T(t)) = \text{guard}(t)$$

$$\text{guard}''(\text{in}_{T'}(t')) = \text{guard}'(t')$$

$$\text{action}'' = [\text{action}, \text{action}']$$

$$\tau'' = [\tau, \tau'].$$

□

The composed net consists of the two constituent nets, as well as n new control places x_i for communicating between the nets. These places take their color from the shared boundary.

Remark We only use nets with boundaries to plug together open nets. In other words, we only consider the execution semantics of nets with no boundary, and since these are literally ordinary timed DB-nets, we inherit their execution semantics from those. Consequently, the resulting nets preserve essential properties like liveness (cf. [155][Theorem 2]) or reachability (cf. [192]).

Composition of nets behaves as expected: it is associative, and there is an "identity" net, which is a unit for composition. All in all, this means that nets with boundaries are the morphisms of a strict monoidal category [204]:

Lemma 7.1 *For any timed DB-nets N, M, and K with compatible boundaries, we have $N \circ (M \circ K) = (N \circ M) \circ K$, and for each boundary configuration $c_1 \otimes \ldots \otimes c_n$, there is an identity net $\text{id}_c : c_1 \otimes \ldots \otimes c_n \to c_1 \otimes \ldots \otimes c_n$ such that $\text{id}_c \circ N = N$ and $\text{id}_c \circ M = M$ for every M and N with compatible boundaries. Furthermore, for every N, M, and K, we have $N \otimes (M \otimes K) = (N \otimes M) \otimes K$.*

Proof Associativity for both $\circ$ and $\otimes$ is obvious. The identity net for $c_1 \otimes \ldots \otimes c_n$ is the net with exactly n places $x_1, \ldots, x_n$, with $\text{color}(x_i) = c_i$.

In particular, the lemma implies that we can use a graphical language (e. g., "string diagrams" [204]) to define nets and their compositions (cf. [118]). Moreover, the composition of two open nets results in an open net again (e. g., [63]).

7.5   Case Studies

So far, we have learned how to formally define the integration logic of single patterns with timed db-nets and how they can be composed to represent integration scenarios using nets with boundaries. In this section, we introduce the a prototypical implementation of timed db-nets with boundaries in the well-known CPN Tools system, with which we study the formalism with respect to its applicability to two scenarios from the analysis: one hybrid on-premise to cloud and one Internet of things (IoT) scenario.

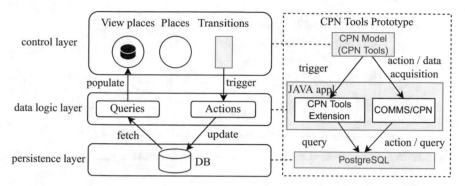

Fig. 7.16 CPN tools prototype

7.5.1 CPN Tools Prototype

We prototypically implemented the formalism in CPN Tools v4.0.1[10] for modeling and simulation. As compared to other PN tools like Renew v2.5,[11] CPN tools support third-party extensions that can address the persistence and data logic layers of our formalism. Moreover, CPN Tools handle sophisticated simulation tasks over models that use the deployed extensions. To support db-nets, our extension[12] adds support for defining view places together with corresponding SQL queries as well as actions and realizes the full execution semantics of db-nets using Java and a PostgreSQL database.

Figure 7.16 shows the mapping of db-net layers to their corresponding realization in CPN Tools. The graphical user interface is that of CPN Tools, extended by view places as well as configuration view for connection details to the database/persistence layer. The data logic layer is realized by a Java application that uses the CPN Tools extension mechanism for populating the view places with data in the corresponding database tables. The COMMS/CPN component of CPN Tools is used to connect to external environments/processes (e. g., service endpoints), which is a database in our case. Through the COMMS/CPN component, CRUD actions/operations are executed (i. e., create, retrieve, update, delete). The persistence layer is modeled in the well-known PostgreSQL database, which is accessed by the JAVA application via JDBC.

---

[10] https://cpnide.org/.

[11] http://www.renew.de/.

[12] CPN Tools extension for timed db-net with boundaries and pattern models is available for download: https://github.com/dritter-hd/db-net-eip-patterns.

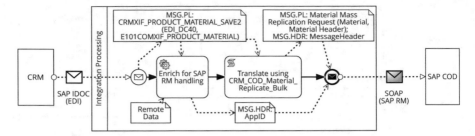

Fig. 7.17 A *hybrid integration* replicate material scenario from SAP Business Suite in BPMN (using SAP Signavio®)

7.5.2   Hybrid Integration: Replicate Material

Many organizations have started to connect their on-premise applications such as Customer Relationship Management (CRM) systems with cloud applications such as SAP Cloud for Customer (COD) using integration processes similar to the one shown in Fig. 7.17. A *CRM Material* is sent from the CRM system via EDI (more precisely SAP IDOC transport protocol) to an integration process running on SAP Cloud Platform Integration (SAP CPI).[13] The pattern compositions in this catalog are represented in a BPMN model (e. g., [196]), and thus we subsequently represent our examples in this way. The integration process enriches the message header (MSG.HDR) with additional information based on a document number for reliable messaging (i. e., AppID), which allows redelivery of the message in an exactly-once service quality (cf. [196]). The IDOC structure is then mapped to the COD service description and sent to the COD receiver.

Formalization For this study, we manually encoded the BPMN scenario into a timed DB-net as shown in Fig. 7.18. While the message translator could be represented as CPN, the Content Enricher (incl. the query on the machine's state) should be represented as timed DB-nets. Hybrid integration usually denotes data movement between on-premise and cloud applications, which do not require complex integration logic. For these less complex hybrid integration scenarios, the timed DB-net representation gives richer insight into the data stored in the database as well as its manipulation (as opposed to, e.g., BPMN), while the models remain still intuitively understandable.

Simulation The replicate material scenario in a timed DB-net (cf. Fig. 7.18) is implemented as a hierarchical net with our CPN Tools extension, which references the pattern implementations of the enricher and translator, annotated with *enricher* and *translator*, respectively. In the hierarchical model representing this scenario, the *MSG* message from the ERP system is enriched with master data. The

---

[13] https://api.sap.com/shell/discover.

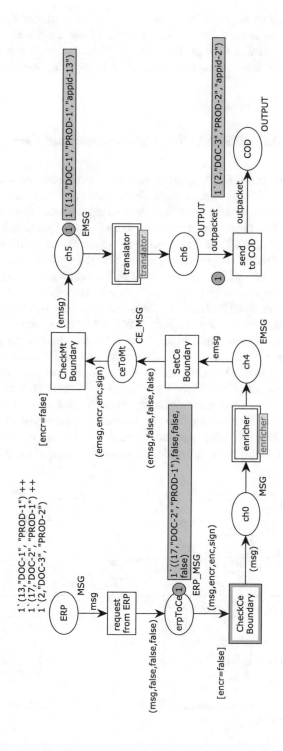

Fig. 7.18 Material replicate scenario simulation

derived enriched message of type $EMSG$ is then sent to the translator that maps the intermediate message format to the one understood by the COD system, thus generating a new message of type $OUTPUT$. Note that in this case, the arc inscriptions abstractly account for messages without revealing their concrete structure.

7.5.3 Internet of Things: Predictive Maintenance and Service

In the context of digital transformation, an automated maintenance of industrial machinery is imperative and requires the communication between the machines, the machine controller and ERP systems that orchestrate maintenance and service tasks. Integrated maintenance is a device integration scenario from IoT, which helps to avoid production outages and track the maintenance progress. Thereby, notifications are usually issued in a Predictive Maintenance and Service (PDMS) solution as shown in Fig. 7.19 from SAP CPI, represented in BPMN according to [196].

Although we simplified the scenario, relevant aspects are preserved. Industrial manufacturing machines, denoted by *Machine*, measure their own states and observe their environment with sensors in a high frequency. When they detect an unexpected situation (e. g., parameter crosses threshold), they send an incident to a local endpoint (e. g., IoT edge system), the *PDMS*, indicating that a follow-on action is required. The PDMS system creates alerts for the different machines and forwards them to a mediator, connecting the PDMS to the ERP system. To throttle the possibly high frequent alerts, several incidents are collected (not shown) and sent as list of alerts. Before the ERP notification can be created, additional data from the machines are queried based on the split and single alerts and then enriched with information that adds the feature type. The information of the single alerts is used to

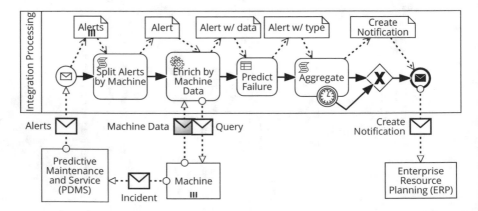

Fig. 7.19 Predictive maintenance—create notification scenario IoT scenario in BPMN as modeled by a user (using SAP Signavio®)

predict the impact by value and machine type and then gets aggregated to be sent to
ERP. In case the notification has been created successfully in ERP, the PDMS gets
notified including the service task identifier and thus stops sending the alert (not
shown).

Formalization   Again, we manually translated the BPMN scenario into a timed
DB-net as shown in Fig. 7.20. Note that alerts in the PDMS system are created
based on query Q_{alert} that returns the device id and the critical value act_val.
The additional feature type $feat\_type$ is provided by query Q_{get}, using the content
enricher from Fig. 7.11b.

Simulation   The predictive maintenance scenario in timed DB-nets (cf. Fig. 7.19)
is implemented as hierarchical net with our CPN Tools extension in Fig. 7.22, which
references the pattern realizations of the enricher and aggregator, annotated with
enricher and *message_aggregator*, respectively. In the original scenario, the PDMS
sends lists of incidents to the integration system to reduce the number of requests as
shown in Fig. 7.21. The incidents have an incident ID, a machine ID, and the actual
critical incident value (e. g., (101, 1, 76)). Unfortunately, due to the fact that CPN
Tools do not support third-party extensions with complex data types like lists, it was
decided to make the *PDMS* component emit single messages. Consequently, the
splitter is not required for separating the single incidents, but the incident messages
of type *REPORT* are immediately enriched by the *enricher*. After master data has
been added to the message, a new one of type *E_REPORT* has been produced. The
net then immediately proceeds with predicting the impact using transition *predict*,
which usually assesses the probability of a timely machine error based on previous
experiences with the particular machine type. The aggregated incident messages are
then sent to the *ERP* system. With the final marking in $m(ERP)$ and $m_{exp}(ERP) =$
{"Assembly Robot", "Engine Robot"|"Engine Robot"|"Engine Robot"},   for   the

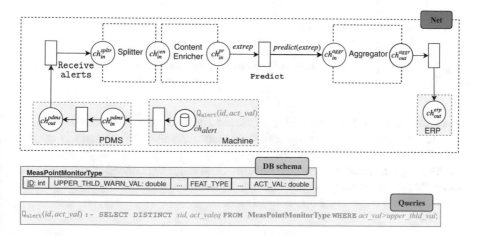

Fig. 7.20   Create notification scenario translated into timed DB-nets (schematic)

view_place : create_notification.IncidentReports: SELECT IncidentReport.id, IncidentReport.mid, IncidentReport.aval
FROM create_notification.IncidentReport, create_notification.Machine WHERE Machine.threshold_wrn<IncidentReport.aval;

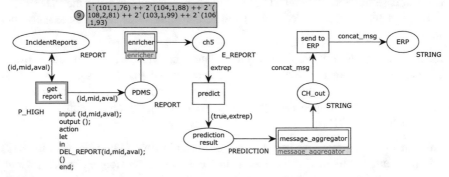

connectDB("Create_Notification_Connection",9001)

disconnectDB("Create_Notification_Connection")

Fig. 7.21 Create notification pattern composition as hierarchical timed DB-net before simulation (in CPN Tools)

view_place : create_notification.IncidentReports: SELECT IncidentReport.id, IncidentReport.mid, IncidentReport.aval
FROM create_notification.IncidentReport, create_notification.Machine WHERE Machine.threshold_wrn<IncidentReport.aval;

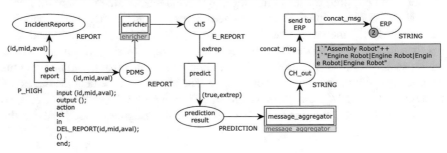

connectDB("Create_Notification_Connection",9001)

disconnectDB("Create_Notification_Connection")

Fig. 7.22 Create notification pattern composition as hierarchical timed DB-net after simulation (in CPN Tools)

three incidents from machine *Engine Robot* and one from *Assembly Robot*, we can see that $m(ERP) \sim m_{exp}$ and thus conjecture that the scenario is correct (Fig. 7.22).

Although the resulting timed DB-net provides so far unmatched insights into the different aspects of integration scenarios, the complexity of the composed patterns increased even when using hierarchical nets.

7.5.4   Conclusion and Lessons Learned

The design of executable integration processes to enable interoperability between various participants (e. g., applications, services, processes) is based on composable integration patterns. The integration patterns cover nontrivial integration logic that includes (iii) managing persistent state; (iv) transactional, exception semantics, and compensation; and (v) time-related aspects, beyond the usual (i) control and (ii) data flow. For a semantically correct behavior of integration processes that are composed of integration patterns, standard Coloured Petri Nets (covering (i), (ii)), are extended to timed DB-nets (covering (iii)–(v)), which allows for simulation and verification regarding execution semantics. For the composition, timed DB-nets are extended to nets with boundaries, which allow for reasoning over compositions of integration patterns (i. e., integration processes). Overall, timed DB-nets with boundaries constitute a powerful formalism to establish semantically correct integration processes and thus trustworthy interoperability between participants.

Subsequently, Chap. 8 lifts integration processes to inter-organizational process choreographies with different business partners connected by message exchange.

Further Reading

1. Hohpe, G., Woolf, B.: Enterprise Integration Patterns: Designing, Building, and Deploying Messaging Solutions. Addison-Wesley Professional, New York (2004)
2. Jensen, K., Kristensen, L.M.: Coloured Petri nets: modelling and validation of concurrent systems. Springer Science and Business Media, New York (2009)
3. Paweł, S.: Representations of Petri net interactions. In: International Conference on Concurrency Theory (2010), pp.554–568
4. Fahland, D., Gierds, C.: Analyzing and Completing Middleware Designs for Enterprise Integration Using Coloured Petri Nets. CAiSE: 400–416 (2013)
5. Zimmermann, O., Pautasso, C., Hohpe, G., Woolf, B.: A decade of enterprise integration patterns: a conversation with the authors. IEEE Softw. **33**(1), 13–19 (2016)
6. Ritter, D., May, N., Rinderle-Ma, S.: Patterns for emerging application integration scenarios: A survey. Inf. Syst. **67**, 36–57 (2017)
7. Marco, M., Rivkin, A.: Db-nets: on the marriage of colored petri nets and relational databases. In: Transactions on Petri Nets and Other Models of Concurrency XII (2017), pp. 91–118
8. Ritter, D., May, N., Forsberg, F.N., Rinderle-Ma, S.: Optimization strategies for integration pattern compositions. ACM DEBS (2018), pp. 88–99
9. Ritter D., Rinderle-Ma, S., Montali, M., Rivkin, A.: Formal foundations for responsible application integration. Inf. Syst. **101**, 101439 (2021)

Chapter 8
Process Choreography

8.1 Motivation and Goals

Process choreographies integrate the process orchestrations (cf. Chaps. 5 and 6) of different business partners via message exchanges. Chapter 8 discusses the top-down and bottom-up design of process choreographies (cf. Fig. 8.1). Moreover, execution mechanisms such as correlation, logging, and monitoring are presented.

Chapters 5 and 6 focus on the model-driven development of process orchestrations that integrate human tasks, applications, systems, and physical devices along a well-defined process logic and hence enable their interoperability. Chapter 7 addresses enterprise application integration, building upon the concepts presented in Chaps. 5, 6, and 7. This chapter furthers the concept of process orchestration "beyond the borders" of process participants, i.e., extends the focus on intra-organizational process orchestration to the inter-organizational choreography of the process orchestrations of different companies or organizations. The goal is that the collaboration of the partners leads to achieving a common business goal. The interaction of their process orchestrations is realized by message exchanges. Consider the following running example:

> **Skateboard Manufacturing**
>
> Imagine that small skateboard manufacturer *WBoards* envisions the production of a new high-end skateboard. The manufacturer is specialized in producing wooden boards and assembling skateboards, but does not produce the wheels. For this *WBoards* contacts wheel manufacturer *ProWheels*. In addition, *WBoards* wants to outsource marketing and sales and hence contacts marketing specialist *SMarkty*. The collaboration between the partners—to be described as process choreography—starts with an order placed at

(continued)

© Springer Nature Switzerland AG 2024
S. Rinderle-Ma et al., *Fundamentals of Information Systems Interoperability*,
https://doi.org/10.1007/978-3-031-48322-6_8

SMarkty and passed on to *WBoards*. *WBoards* plans the production of the wooden boards, starts production, and passes on the request of wheels to *ProWheels* accordingly. *ProWheels* produces the wheels and sends them back to *WBoards*, including the invoice for the wheels. On receiving the wheels, *WBoards* assembles the skateboards, ships them to the customer, and sends the invoice to *SMarkty*.

The use case suggests that three partners aim to achieve a common business goal, i.e., the manufacturing and selling of skateboards, through their collaboration. *"Process technology serves as enabler for process-oriented collaborations between distributed business partners, realized and implemented through so-called process choreographies"* [79]. According to [79], process-oriented collaborations are prevalent across almost any application domain, including blockchain-based processes [144, 146] and logistics [42, 50].

What cannot be seen from the use case is that the partners might already run process orchestrations at their side, e.g., that skateboard manufacturer *WBoards* has already adopted the execution support of its manufacturing process based on a process engine. Figure 8.2 depicts the process orchestration model of partner *WBoards*. After receiving an order, the stock is checked, wheels are ordered if necessary (from any partner), the necessary parts are produced, and the boards are assembled and shipped, and the invoice is sent. As described in the use case,

Levels ... / Tasks ↓	Syntactical	Semantic	Organizational
Exchange	Exchange formats, e.g., XML, relational databases, JSON, BSON, YAML, MessagePack; query languages: XPath, XQuery, SQL; transformation languages, e.g., XSLT	Schema matching and mapping; ontologies;	Message exchange; correlation
Integrate	SQL/XML standard; native XML databases; REST and GraphQL	Edge table, shredding; XML schema and RNG; schema and data integration; service integration	Correlation and choreography
Orchestrate	BPMN, Petri Nets, Workflow Nets, RPST, CPEE Trees, Colored Petri Nets	Verification, task and worklist design; service invocation; correlation; integration patterns and processes	Choreography

Fig. 8.1 Interoperability perspectives I: Chap. 8

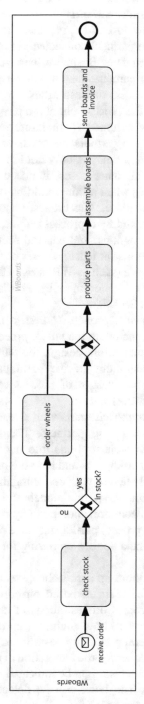

Fig. 8.2 Process orchestration of collaboration partner WBoards (using SAP Signavio®)

WBoards aims to always order wheels from partner *ProWheels* from now on, and to do marketing and sales via partner *SMarkty*.

Now the question arises how to build a process choreography, consisting of the process orchestrations of the partners connected via message exchange, i.e., to establish interoperability between them. Basically, there are two options, depending on the starting situation of the partners, i.e., *top-down* and *bottom-up* [151]. If the partners do not have any process orchestrations already in place, a *top-down* design and implementation of the process choreography can be done. Top-down choreography design is mostly assumed in literature and will be discussed in Sect. 8.2. The assumption that the partners do not have any explicit or implicit process orchestration in place might maybe only hold in the case that the partners start the business together. In all other cases, if one or several of the partners have been already doing business when joining/building up the choreography, they have a process orchestration in place. The orchestration might be implicit, i.e., not (entirely) modeled and executed by a process engine, but implicitly consist of implemented services, device programs, and enacted routines by humans. Hence, the more realistic case might be that at least a subset of the partners already have some process orchestration in place (such as *WBoards* in the use case example) that have to be integrated into the process choreography. This is referred to as *bottom-up* approach and will be targeted in Sect. 8.3.

When following the *top-down approach*, at first, a conceptual choreography model is designed and modeled, including the *public* processes of the choreography participants. Then, in the implementation design, the public processes are refined into the *private* process orchestrations of the participating partners. Different notations for top-down conceptual design of process choreographies exist, and mainly BPMN notation (cf. Sect. 5.2) is used.

By contrast, the *bottom-up approach* starts with already-existing (private) process orchestrations of the participating partners. Then, the partners first have to abstract their private process orchestrations into public ones that capture the interactions with other process participants and hide the private details that they do not want to reveal. This is closely tied in with designing the choreography model in the conceptual design by matching the public models and verification of the result. Moreover, in order to arrive at a common choreography model, often, complex and costly negotiations between the process participants take place [77]. Nonetheless, it might be more realistic to assume a bottom-up setting for all or at least a subset of the process participants.

For both the top-down and bottom-up approaches, execution of the choreography instances during runtime can be realized based on correlation as introduced in Sect. 6.6. For correlating the process orchestrations of choreography participants, the correlator connects different workflow engines, (represented by the services in Fig. 6.24), executing one or several partner orchestrations. It is also vital to monitor the process execution and, consequently, the integration of application/programs and services. Possible execution problems might be indicated by, for example, overlong execution times or data drifts. The latter can be detected early during process monitoring and remedy actions can be taken.

Monitoring, analyzing, and diagnosing process choreography executions can be conducted by applying process mining techniques on process event logs (ex post) or process event streams, i.e., the events produced by and emitted during process execution (online), as shortly explained in Sect. 6.8. As the event logging in a process choreography takes place in a distributed manner, the integration of process event logs and streams might become necessary across the executions of the process orchestrations of the process participants. This can be compared to event stream integration from heterogeneous sources such as different process engines. For the integration of the process event streams, knowledge on the invoked application programs and services can be useful in order to overcome the limitations imposed by label equivalence [180]. In addition to integrating the event stream information, it is necessary that the privacy/confidentiality requirements set out in the private process orchestrations of the partners are preserved during cross-organizational [6, 229] or inter-organizational [73] process mining. Confidentiality requirements of the partners mean that they log the execution information of their (private) process orchestrations at their side, but are not willing to share them with other partners. If we assume a central coordinator in the choreography, then it might be an option that this entity holds the event logs of all partners. However, in a fully decentralized setting, such a central entity does not exist. One solution to this challenge is the application of privacy-preserving techniques on the partner orchestration logs and for the application of process mining techniques by, e.g., employing differential privacy techniques (see, e.g., [73]). Correlation, execution, and logging concepts in process choreographies will be discussed in Sect. 8.4.

8.2 Top-Down Approach

Assume the use case of skateboard manufacturing as described in Sect. 8.1. As can be seen from the description, three partners are participating in the choreography, i.e., WBoards, ProWheels, and SMarkty. Figure 8.3 depicts the *choreography model* describing their interaction in BPMN notation.

In general, a choreography model represents the *global view* of a collaborative process in which several partners interact via *message exchanges* [76]. For the use case, the choreography model starts with a start event representing the receiving of an order. Then *choreography task* forward order (see label in the center) is executed by forwarding the order to choreography participant WBoards by choreography participant SMarkty. This is reflected by denoting SMarkty as *sender* at the top of the corresponding choreography task and WBoards as *receiver* at the bottom. All four choreography tasks are positioned in a sequence reflecting the sequence of message exchanges as described in the use case. Note that a choreography model might also include more structural patterns such as alternative and parallel branchings. A more complex supply chain example choreography model can be found in [79].

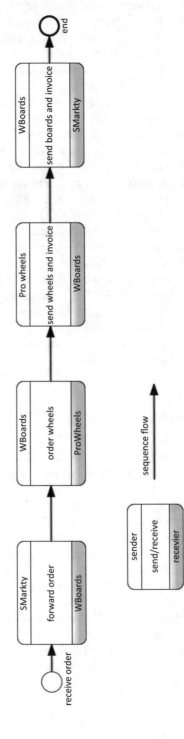

Fig. 8.3 Skateboard manufacturing example: choreography model (using SAP Signavio®)

A choreography model gives an overview of the choreography partners and their interactions, but not on their *public processes* and *private processes*. Public processes contain the *interaction tasks* of the partners plus potentially additional tasks that are visible to the other partners. *Private processes* reflect the internal processes of the partners containing the public tasks plus private tasks that are invisible to the other partners. Overall, a *process choreography* can be defined as follows:

Definition 16 (Process Choreography, Taken and Adapted from [79]) Let $\mathcal{P}$ be the set of all process partners in a given business domain and M be the set of messages that can be sent/received between the process participants. Then a process choreography is defined as a tuple (P, I, CM, L, Π, ψ, γ, θ) where:

1. $P \subseteq \mathcal{P}$ is the set of partners participating in the choreography.
2. $I \subseteq 2^{P \times M \times P}$ is the set of interactions between the choreography participants where $i = (p, m, p\prime)$ means that message $m \in M$ is sent to $p\prime$ by p.
3. CM is the choreography model representing the interactions between partners in P, i.e., CM reflects the the interactions $I \in I$ by choreography tasks and puts them into the control flow logic of the choreography.
4. $L = \{l_p\}_{p \in P}$ is the set of public process models for all choreography participants in P. Public process models l_p are process orchestrations.
5. $\Pi = \{\pi_p\}_{p \in P}$ is the set of private process models for all process participants in P. Private process models pi_p are process orchestrations.
6. $\psi = \{\psi_p : l_p \leftrightarrow \pi_p\}_{p \in P}$ is a partial mapping function between nodes of the public and private models.
7. $\gamma : l \leftrightarrow l\prime$ is a partial mapping function between nodes of different public models.
8. $\theta : CM \leftrightarrow l \times l$ is a partial mapping function between nodes of the choreography model and the public models.

The choreography model PM depicted in Fig. 8.3 contains the set of choreography participants P = {WBoards, ProWheels, SMarkty}, the set of interactions I = { (SMarkty, forward order, WBoards), (WBoards, order wheels, ProWheels), (ProWheels, send wheels and invoice, WBoards), ...} between them, and the overarching control flow. What is missing for defining the entire choreography according to Definition 16 are the public process models and the private process models for the three participants.

The question is whether (i) the public and private processes can be derived and modeled based on the choreography "from scratch" or (ii) there are already private processes present at the partners' sides. Case (i) is followed up as top-down modeling and implementation in this section and Case (ii) as bottom-up development of a process choreography in Sect. 8.3.

Starting from the choreography model presented in Fig. 8.3, the public and private processes of the choreography participants are designed and realized in a top-down manner. We start with the design and modeling of the public processes that capture the behavior of the partner processes which are visible to the other partners, in particular, the sending and receiving of messages.

Figure 8.4 depicts the behavioral interface of partner SMarkty. From the choreography model, we can derive that SMarkty has to be able to send (forward) message order and to receive message invoice later. Both interactions take place with partner WBoards.

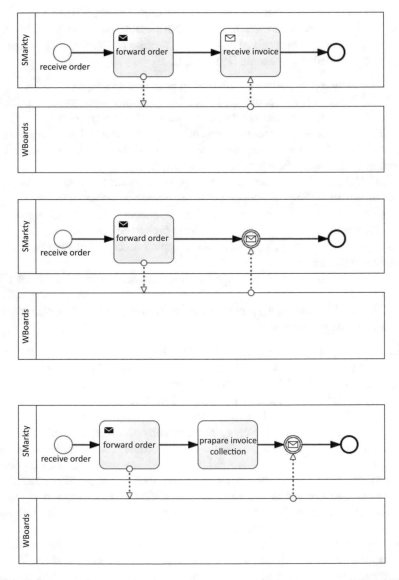

Fig. 8.4 Behavioral interfaces of process choreography participant SMarkty (using SAP Signavio®)

The behavioral model on the top depicts the public process of SMarkty and at the same time its interface, i.e., which messages are sent and which are received. We could say that these are the requirements of SMarkty in participating in the choreography. The behavioral model in the middle only differs that task receive invoice is replaced by the corresponding intermediate message receiving event. The figure on the bottom augments the behavioral model by public task prepare invoice collection that does neither send nor receive a message, but is supposed to by visible to the other partners in the choreography.

Figure 8.5 displays the public process orchestration models of all partners in a *collaboration model* and hence all behavioral interfaces of the process choreography example. Note that partner ProWheels also features a public task that does not send or receive any message (i.e., produce wheels), but is nonetheless visible to the other partners. The choreography model together with the public processes constitutes the *contract* for the collaboration between the partners [12], i.e., each partner assures to send and receive the messages from the defined partners in the given order in order to achieve the common goal of the choreography, e.g., producing skateboards. In this book, we employ BPMN as choreography and hence contract description language because BPMN is the de facto standard in process orchestration and choreography modeling and has been already explained in Sect. 5.2. Note that there have been other proposals for choreography description languages, including declarative languages such as the Dynamic Response Graphs (DRC Graphs) [103].

With the choreography and the public processes, the interactions between the partners are embedded into the public process logic. The private process logic is hidden "behind" the public process logic in the private processes of the process participants, i.e., the public processes constitute views or abstractions on the private processes. In turn, the private processes refine the public ones by private tasks and process logic. Take the private process of process participant WBoards as depicted in Fig. 8.2. The private process contains all public tasks plus private ones such as check stock. We can also see a subsequent XOR decision where parts are produced if they are not in stock. Finally, after receiving the wheels by ProWheels, the boards are assembled.

In a top-down fashion, starting from negotiating and modeling the choreography model, the choreography participants design and model their public processes and based on the public processes the private ones which, in turn, are then translated into executable process orchestrations (cf. Chap. 6). The skateboard example presented before is simple, but real-life choreographies can become much more complex. Hence, in order to finally obtain a choreography that works, i.e., does not get stuck somewhere, requires the sound design of the choreography model and all public and private processes.

In order to achieve a properly working choreography, a set of soundness criteria must hold. To check and illustrate the soundness criteria, we transform the public process orchestrations of the partners first into *Workflow Modules* [142] (see Fig. 8.6). Workflow Modules capture the process logic as Workflow Nets (cf. Sect. 6.2.1) and augment them with places that represent sent messages (output

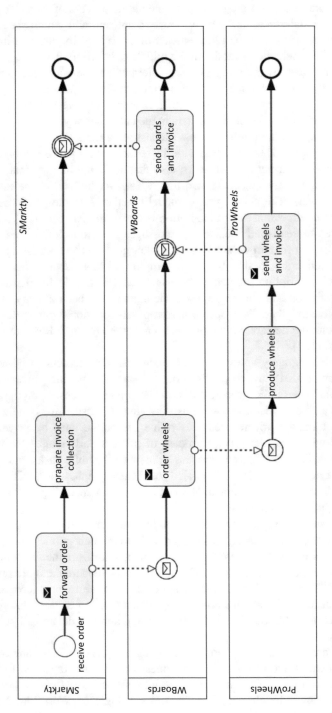

Fig. 8.5 Collaboration model containing public process orchestration models (using SAP Signavio®)

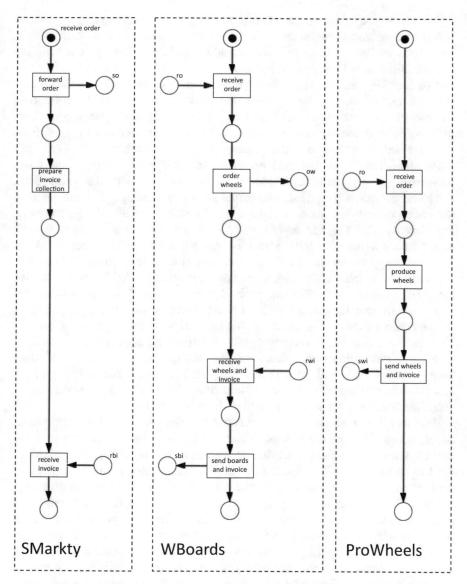

Fig. 8.6 Public processes of SMarkty, WBoards, ProWheels modeled as separated Workflow Modules (using SAP Signavio®)

places) and received messages (input places). For partner SMarkty, for example, the output place so represents the sent message by forward order, and input place rbi represents the message received by task receive invoice. Similar approaches to Workflow Modules exist such as net modules for modeling agents in Heraklit [153] and the fundamental work on compositional service trees in [10].

The choreography model and all participating process orchestrations adhere to structural correctness criteria set out by orchestration/choreography meta models, e.g., Business Process Modeling and Notation (BPMN).[1] Examples include the absence of isolated elements such as tasks.

Compatibility ensures that the participating process orchestrations "play together" as intended by the choreography model, i.e., the interactions between the partners are successful. Problems might arise within the messages *if, for instance, different message formats were used in a collaboration and one participant does not understand the content of a message sent by another participant* [220]. Aside from these more technical problems, the design of the interactions and public process orchestrations might result in problems with the interactions. *Structural compatibility [...] demands that for every message that can be sent, the corresponding interaction partner must be able to receive it. Furthermore, for every message that can be received the corresponding partner must be able to send such a message* [62]. Structural compatibility might be too strict for certain choreography scenarios. Hence, weak structural compatibility criteria exist. We will abstain from discussing them here and refer to [62] for more details. (Strict) structural compatibility can be checked on the Workflow Modules depicted in Fig. 8.6 by matching and merging corresponding input and output places of the separated modules. The resulting Workflow Net for the separated Workflow Modules depicted in Fig. 8.6 is shown in Fig. 8.7. Every input place has been merged with the corresponding output place (and vice versa), i.e., none of the input/output places remains unmerged. This shows the (strict) structural compatibility of the process orchestrations of the participating partners. Note that in order to construct a Workflow Net, one start and one final place have been added.

That way, the execution of the Workflow Net starts with firing transition `tau1`, adding tokens into the three output places. With the token on place `receive order`, transition `forward order` is enabled and, when firing, puts tokens on the two output places. The token in place `order` enables transition `receive order`, i.e., represents the sending and receiving of the corresponding message `order`. Next, transitions `prepare invoice collection` and `receive order` can fire. When `receive order` fires, tokens are put into the output places and with a token in `order`, transition `receive order` becomes enabled.

We can see that by playing the token game, both the control flow of the three partners and the message exchanges are executed. In particular, it can be shown using reachability analysis (cf. Sect. 5.4) that the conditions for behavioral soundness of Workflow Nets as set out in Definition 6.2 are fulfilled, i.e., the final marking with one token in the final place can be reached, no other places carry any tokens, and there are no dead transitions. This means that the merged Workflow Net is also behaviorally sound.

Note that behavioral soundness of the choreography of the public orchestrations as represented by the Workflow Net can be violated even if the participating

---

[1] bpmn.org.

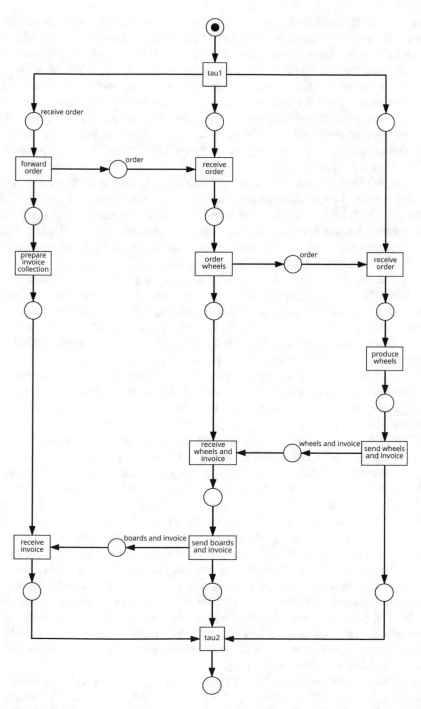

Fig. 8.7 Public processes of SMarkty, WBoards, ProWheels composed into a Workflow Net (using SAP Signavio®)

process orchestrations are behavioral sound and structural compatibility holds. Take the example orchestrations depicted in Fig. 8.8. The (a) partner orchestrations are behavioral sound themselves. Augmenting them with input and output places (b) results in compatible Workflow Modules. However, the merged Workflow Net (c) contains a deadlock. This deadlock is caused by cyclic waiting for input messages. Another reason for a deadlock in a merged Workflow Net is the unsynchronized sending and receiving of messages in the context of alternative branchings. For an example, we refer to [220]. Hence, behavioral soundness must be checked in addition to structural compatibility on the merged Workflow Net and is referred to as *behavioral compatibility* [62].

There are further approaches to merge process orchestrations into one model that can be checked for soundness properties. One example is Typed Jackson Nets [28], which are built by merging the process orchestrations not based on places but on transitions. Merging based on places enables asynchronous communication, i.e., a token representing a message has not been consumed right away. The merging based on transitions realizes synchronous communication.

At this point, we are able to design a choreography model comprising the behavior of the partners, their public process orchestrations, and to check compatibility and behavioral soundness of the choreography model with public process orchestrations. What is still missing are the *private process orchestrations*, i.e., the process orchestrations at the partners' sides that implement the behavioral interfaces described by the public process orchestrations. Intuitively, the private and public process orchestrations of one partner should be consistent, i.e., the private process orchestration should offer the behavior described by the public process orchestration and possibly refine it. Conversely, the behavior described by the public process orchestration abstracts the behavior described by the private one [30].

This *consistency* between public and private process orchestration of one partner is achieved by understanding the extensions of a private process orchestration on the public one based on a set of refinement operations that preserve the inheritance relation defined by [30] between public and private process orchestration, i.e., the public process orchestration is a super-process of the private one, or conversely, the private process orchestration is a sub-process of the public one. Extending the public process orchestration (super-process) into the private one (sub-process) is based on refinement. Reducing the private process orchestration (sub-process) into the public one (super-process) is based on abstraction. The abstraction of the private into the public process orchestration under preserving consistency is achieved by blocking and/or hiding behavior of the private process orchestration [30]. *[B]locking of tasks means that these tasks are not considered for execution. Hiding tasks implies that the tasks are renamed to the silent task τ* [176]. After applying these operations, the super- and sub-process can simulate each other's behavior, i.e., they are related under some bi-simulation relation [30].

Consider Workflow Net PN depicted in Fig. 8.9a. Its behavior consists of executing transition t1 expressed by execution trace $\sigma_{PN} = < t1 >$. Refinement of PN should result in Workflow Nets that refine the behavior and can be abstracted by hiding or blocking tasks in order to preserve inheritance between the nets, as this, in

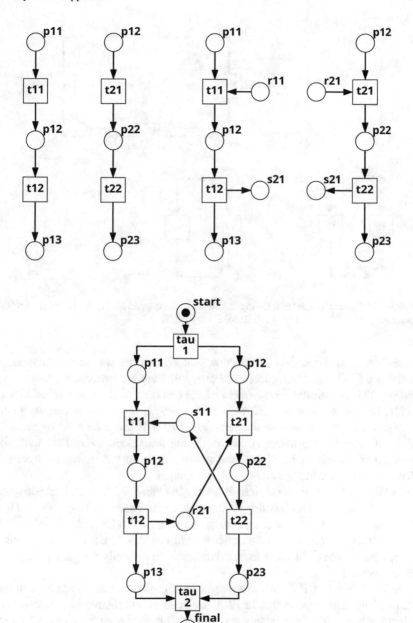

Fig. 8.8 Compatible partner orchestrations resulting in deadlock in the choreography model (using SAP Signavio®)

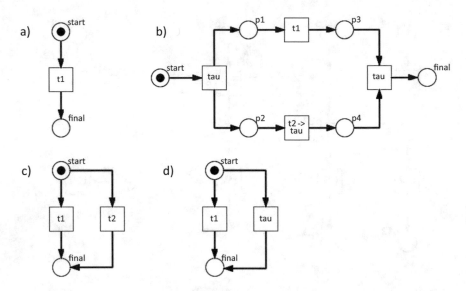

Fig. 8.9 Hiding and blocking of tasks in order to achieve sub-processes under inheritance relations (using SAP Signavio®). (**a**) PN. (**b**) PN1. (**c**) PN2. (**d**) PN3

turn, ensures their consistency. Workflow Net PN1 (b) shows the parallelization of transition t1 with new transition t2. For parallelization, two silent transitions are required. This constitutes a refinement of the behavior of PN into execution traces of PN1, i.e., $\{\sigma1_{PN1} =< t1, t2 >, \sigma2_{PN1} =< t2, t1 >\}$. How can we abstract the behavior of PN1 to achieve the behavior of PN? This can be done by hiding the additional behavior (abstraction), i.e., replacing transitions t2 in PN1 with silent transitions τ. As silent transitions are unobservable in the execution traces, the behavior is abstracted to the one of PN as intended.

For Workflow Net PN2 (c), transition t1 is embedded into an alternative split with transition t2. This results in the execution traces $\{\sigma1_{PN2} =< t1 >,$ $\sigma2_{PN2} =< t2 >\}$. In this case, hiding transition t2 with τ does not yield the right result as an empty execution trace would result, i.e., t1 could be bypassed. Hence, t2 needs to be blocked from execution such that only the path including t1 can be executed.

For Workflow Net PN3 (d), at first glance, the situation seems to be similar to PN2 (c). The difference is that in PN3, we have an alternative branch containing a silent transition τ. The semantics is comparable to the alternative branching in the public process of collaboration partner WBoards in Fig. 8.2, i.e., transition t1 can be executed or the empty branch is chosen, resulting in execution traces $\{\sigma1_{PN3} =< t1 >, \sigma2_{PN3} =<>\}$. As stated in [30], silent transitions are not to be hidden or blocked, as only transitions having a label can be hidden or blocked. Consequently, we cannot abstract the behavior of PN3 into PN, i.e., PN3 is not a sub net of PN.

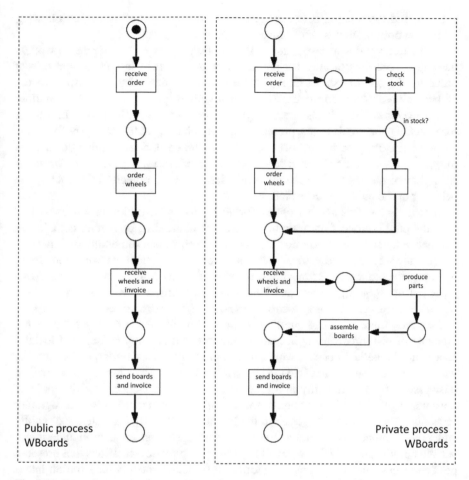

Fig. 8.10 Inconsistency between public and private processes of partner WBoards (using SAP Signavio®)

As a consequence, the private process of WBoards cannot be abstracted into the public process as depicted in Fig. 8.10, i.e., public and private process of WBoards in their current form are not consistent. This is correct as based on its private process WBoards could execute the process without sending the message order wheels. As shown in Fig. 8.6 partner ProWheels relies on receiving this message, and as a consequence, the choreography instance would just block at this point. This means that the violated consistency property affects the compatibility of the partner processes and, in the sequel, the behavioral soundness of the process choreography.

The "trouble" in this case stems from the fact that we assume WBoards to already have a private process, which is not the case for a strict top-down design of process choreographies. Hence, we will comment on how to resolve the consistency problem and the relation between consistency and compatibility in the following section on bottom-up design of process choreographies.

In a strict top-down design stack, the public process of WBoards as well as the public processes of all other partners would be refined into consistent private processes. Figure 8.11 shows three possible options for designing the private process orchestration of WBoards that are consistent with the public process orchestration. In WBoards1, the wheels are always ordered, i.e., the alternative branching for checking the stock is not present anymore. Hence, additional (private) tasks, check stock, produce parts, and assemble boards, are hidden. Then $\sigma_{WBoards1}$ =<receive order, order wheels, receive wheels and invoice, send boards and invoice> reflects (simulates) the behavior of the public process orchestration.

WBoards2 shows another option for a process orchestration that is consistent with the public process orchestration. Here, the alternative branching contains an alternative labelled transition test where WBoards does something alternatively to order the wheels. As this transition is labelled, we can block its execution. Then, by hiding the other private transitions, the execution trace of abstracted WBoards2 turns out as $\sigma_{WBoards2}$ =<receive order, order wheels, receive wheels and invoice, send boards and invoice>.

However, there is a valid question in the context of WBoards2: what does the blocking of task test mean in reality, and how is it actually enforced? Blocking as a more theoretical concept would result, in reality, in a deletion of task test, which is most probably not intended by partner WBoards as usually tasks realize business-related functionality in a process orchestration. Hence, blocking tasks is not a practically feasible operation to ensure consistency in real-world choreography scenarios. Therefore, as suggested in the literature [12, 220], consistency of public and private processes is based on hiding tasks, i.e., on *projection inheritance* between public and private process. [12, 220] also provide operations that preserve projection inheritance and thus transform the (public) process orchestration into a consistent (private) process orchestration, i.e., (i) adding a loop, (ii) adding a detour, and (iii) adding a concurrent branch. (i) adds a loop construct to a place of the public process orchestration. An example for (iii) is PN1 in Fig. 8.9b.

Finally, WBoards3 also contains a labelled alternative transition to order wheels, i.e., send empty order, which has to be regarded as public activity. Then the alternative split would be lifted up to the public process orchestration, resulting in a corresponding alternative branching in the public process orchestration as depicted in Fig. 8.12. This adaptation of the public process of WBoards constitutes an interface adaptation to partner ProWheels, requiring ProWheels to adapt its interface, public process orchestration, and private process orchestration accordingly. As WBoards cannot impose the adaptation on ProWheels, potentially costly and time-consuming negotiations have to take place [76–78, 80].

The top-down approach presented in this section allows the step-wise modeling and refinement of the choreography model over the collaboration model, the public orchestration models, to the private orchestration models. For the different refinement steps, correctness criteria exist that enable the correct transition from one

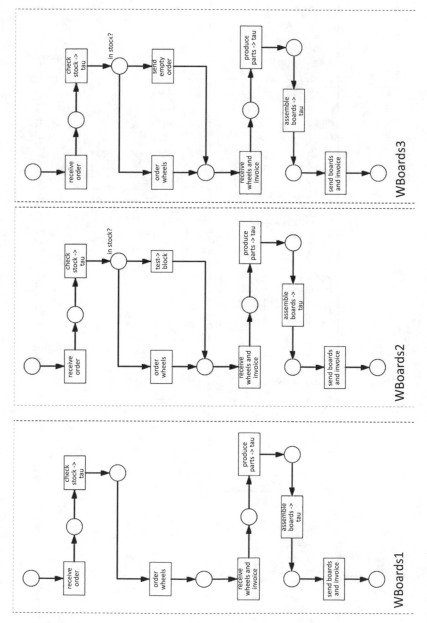

Fig. 8.11 Three private process orchestration models for WBoards (using SAP Signavio®)

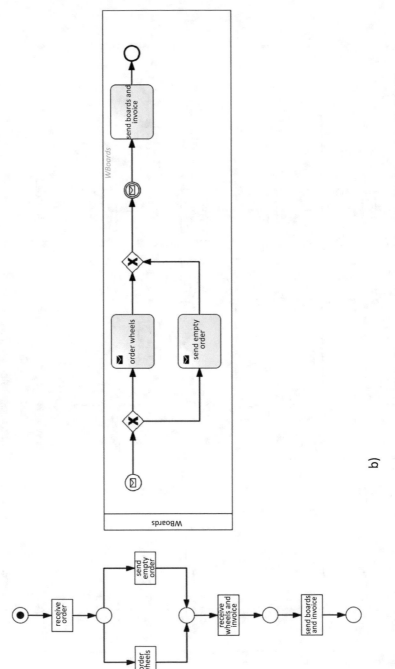

Fig. 8.12 Adapted public process orchestration for WBoards3 (using SAP Signavio®). (a) WBoards3 public (Workflow Net). (b) BPMN

model to the other along the top-down model stack. The question is whether such a strict top-down approach is realistic, i.e., all partners start the choreography design from scratch. Thus, in the following section, the other direction, i.e., the bottom-up approach, starting from the partner processes will be examined.

8.3 Bottom-Up Approach: Model Matching and Verification

A top-down approach starts from a choreography model that serves as a contract between the partners, including their public process orchestrations for which structural and behavioral compatibility must hold. Then, the public process orchestrations can be refined into private process orchestrations by ensuring consistency.

Existing bottom-up approaches span a range of initial situations, i.e., which input does the approach start with: (i) the choreography model exists ↦ *P2P Approach* [12]; (ii) partners provide their public process orchestrations as interfaces; (iii) private process orchestrations of partners exist, and no public orchestrations/interfaces and no choreography model are available. The particular initial situation is tied in with the type and topology of the process choreography. *B2B solutions offered by vendors fall into two broad categories: hub-and-spoke (interaction between partners takes place through a central hub that acts as an intermediary), and peer-to-peer (interaction takes place directly between partners)* [205]. Hub-and-spoke structures occur, for example, for a big OEM and its smaller and dependent suppliers. In this case, it is more likely that the central entity can enforce a contract, i.e., a choreography model with public process orchestrations (i).

(i) P2P Approach In [12], the authors propose the approach to design the choreography, partition it according the the participating partners, and then *make use of its autonomy to create a private workflow*, but the partner *may only choose a private workflow which is a subclass of its public part* under projection inheritance. This corresponds basically to the top-down approach with some degrees of freedom in (a) the partitioning of the choreography process orchestration model w.r.t. partners and (b) the design or choice of the private process orchestrations. In particular, if a partner already has a private process, it can be checked whether or not it is consistent to the public process orchestration model assigned to this partner during partitioning. If yes, the partner can participate in the choreography right away. If not, the partner cannot participate in the choreography.

This is then related to the property of *realizability*, i.e., *checking whether a choreography can be realized or not by a set of peers* [96]. In the example, the choreography model depicted in Fig. 8.3 cannot be realized by partner WBoards. In this case, the partner can adapt its process accordingly (as WBoards has done) or abstain from participating in the choreography. Doing so, the realizability of the choreography is ensured. However, this would not be possible with the private process orchestration of WBoards, which is not related to the public process as set out by the choreography model under any inheritance relation.

Another option is to adapt the private and public process orchestrations of WBoards. Here, the adaptation with the minimal effects on the process choreography is preferable in order to keep ripple effects on the other partners low and to avoid possibly costly negotiations. As investigated in [80], changes and adaptations of private partner orchestrations can have significant impact on the partners that directly interact with this partner and potentially also transitive effects on other partners. As typically the details of the private process orchestrations of other partners are not known, only affected change regions can be determined [79].

At this point, it has to be recalled that the inconsistency between private and public process orchestration for WBoards in their original design poses a red flag for the intended choreography for a good reason, i.e., if a message is sent out of only one branch of an alternative branching, the message might not be sent and subsequently, and the choreography might block at the point where one or several partners wait in receiving the message. The adaptation of the private process and lifting it up to the public process as in WBoards3 (cf. Fig. 8.12) heal this problem as either way a message is sent, either an order message or an empty order. Moreover, as depicted in Fig. 8.13, the public process orchestrations of SMarkty and ProWheels remain unaffected by the adaptation. However, ProWheels is now executing task produce wheels, even if receiving an empty message. This is not sensible from a business point of view. Hence, ProWheels might want to also adapt its process orchestrations by, e.g., mimicking the alternative branching and introducing an empty branch to bypass the production step. This is an interesting example where the soundness is okay, but the semantics is not. Checking the semantics of a process orchestration and choreography is referred to as *validation* and requires domain expertise.

(ii) Public Process Orchestrations Exist and Are Offered by the Partners Here, two situations can be distinguished, i.e., one partner joins an already-existing choreography, and a set of partners forms a choreography. In the first case, the partner has to check whether his public process is compatible with the choreography. Then, it is possible for the partner to participate. This situation occurs, for example, if a partner in an existing choreography is replaced by another one and is related to the service selection and composition problem (cf. Chap. 4 and, e.g., [121]). A possible difference in replacing services in a service composition and replacing a partner process in a choreography might be the different interface descriptions, i.e., in case of the service more in an "input-output" fashion and in a process choreography in terms of an interface defining a sequence of message exchanges with the partner.

The second situation occurs if multiple partners want to form a choreography based on their public processes. This case calls for model matching and is based on compatibility, i.e., *message exchange activities within different processes are connected to enable information sharing and process collaboration* [159].

In literature, process model matching is mostly concerned with finding similarities in process models based on activity labels, structure, and behavior (cf. Chap. 3 and [67, 128]). In [47], several techniques and applications for process

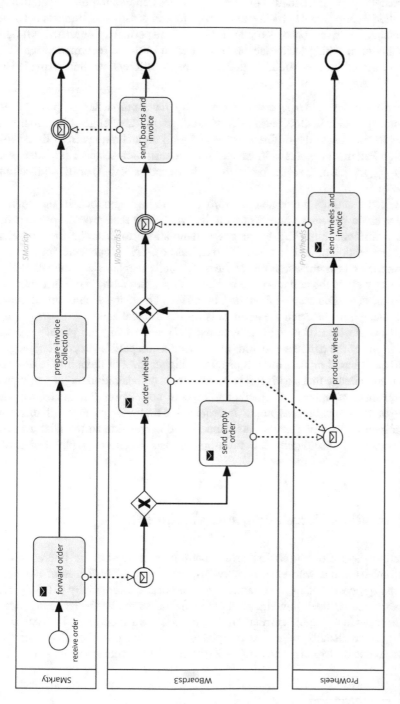

Fig. 8.13   Adapted process orchestration (using SAP Signavio®)

model matching are described. For creating process choreographies, specifically, process model matching can be useful in order to find possible alignments between the public and/or private process orchestrations of the partners. For testing different process model matching techniques as described in [47], we recommend the real-world test set of process orchestration models in different variants provided in [120].[2]

(iii) Private Process Orchestrations Exist Only few approaches propose (clear) bottom-up approaches. One possibility to address the challenge is to employ a *mediator* to coordinate the different partners based on techniques from Enterprise Integration Patterns (see details in Chap. 7) or orchestration services (see details in Chaps. 4–6) [151]. Doing so, the problem can be traced back to (i) or (ii) with central coordinator.

In [27], the authors advocate a bottom-up modeling approach in the context of supply chain processes and focus on the challenge that process participants might use different modeling languages and notations to describe their internal (private) process orchestrations (see Chaps. 5 and 6). [27] propose an approach to transform the process orchestrations of the different partners in a common modeling language as well as the collaborative model (aka choreography model). Doing so, the differences in the usage of modeling languages are addressed but remain open how the interactions between the partners is (correctly) realized.

Based on the idea of process fragments, [97] starts from the private process orchestrations of the partners and aims at deriving a compatible process choreography. Fragment-based process models provide a higher level of flexibility in order to address the challenge that a (private) partner process orchestration might participate in several choreographies. Another challenge is correlation (cf. Sect. 6.6): one instance in a partner process might interact with multiple instances of different choreographies. We will discuss data aspects and correlation in the next section. Moreover, we will discuss how a bottom-up approach to choreography design can be supported by process mining.

8.4   Execution, Correlation, and Monitoring

As stated in Sect. 6.6, correlation is an instrument to realize the interaction of process orchestrations with external services, other process instances of the same or different process models, and partners in a process choreography [61, 97]. The latter is examined in the following: as stated in the literature, the challenge in process choreographies is to realize correlation in a manifold manner, i.e., a task executed for one partner instance might be correlated with messages of multiple partner instances of one or several partners in the same or different choreographies. The goal

---

[2] https://zenodo.org/record/7783492.

is to always assign messages to the right instance, the right partner, and the right choreography. For this, as elaborated in Sect. 6.6, the choreography messages are analyzed by the correlator based on rules w.r.t. their type and the required correlation information in the message, i.e., identifiers, based on which the necessary matching, e.g., between instances, can be done.

There are several options for "multi-correlation": either several correlation ids are aggregated, e.g., the order id in a message, the instance id, and the choreography id or the entire identification information is contained in each message to be extracted by the correlator.

Correlation is tied in with the data flow in a process orchestration and choreography (cf. Sect. 6.3). In [151, 152], several data flow challenges for choreographies are stated, including data heterogeneity referring to possibly heterogeneous data models at the different partners, which have to be mapped to messages that can be understood by the other partner, correlation (see above), and 1:n communication referring to the communication *with a multitude of (external) uniform participants.* [98] define a choreography data model that reflects a data contract between the choreography participants. In any case, a sophisticated correlation mechanism is the prerequisite for the successful realization of any process choreography.

If a choreography has been successfully realized, one or multiple choreography instances are created, initiated, and executed. As for process orchestrations, during runtime, logging and monitoring are important tasks of the process engine(s) managing and executing the choreography instances. In general, logging stores execution data in process event logs, which are then available for different analysis tasks in an ex post way. Logging, in particular for process choreographies, can be integrated into individual pieces of the architecture, i.e., each Web service or each software component logs individually. Monitoring, by contrast, means to observe process/choreography behavior during runtime, based on process event streams. Similar to logging, these streams have to be potentially aggregated from individual pieces of the architecture. The basic element for logging and monitoring is the event. Basically, an event contains a time stamp, an event name, life cycle information, and additional content. Note that each component or process might deliver different events, i.e., in a different granularity, at different velocity, and with a different event content format.

Logs have a specific format, e.g., the NCSA Common Log Format[3] or the IEEE 1849-2016 XES Standard,[4] and a file type, e.g., XML and JSON or CSV and YAML. The choice of the file type can be based on criteria such as computational effort and readability. According to [181], *YAML is as human readable as XML [...] and offers advantages over XML for directly logging events in the XES format since the computational effort is lower because new events, instead of parsing an XML tree for the correct position, can be easily appended to a file, an operation which in many operating systems is optimized.*

---

[3] https://en.wikipedia.org/wiki/Common_Log_Format.
[4] https://xes-standard.org/.

Logs have to be collected, unified, integrated, and enriched. Log collection takes place from different places/sources, e.g., databases and files. Unification means transformation into a common format. Connection is realized through timestamp or better through semantic knowledge of data artefacts such as order id. Setting up this connection is termed "correlation" in the process community [32] and has some relation to the correlator concepts for process execution. In the course of this book, we refer to correlator mechanisms from the engine or system perspective. Finally, enrichment is achieved by using, e.g., order data or customer data.

Security and privacy are crucial challenges in the context of process logs and process mining [73]. Logs have to be securely stored or archived as logs might be subject for economic espionage, data leaks, or falsification, e.g., falsified production logs may lead to voided warranty and financial penalties. Moreover, logs might be subject to privacy requirements as logs might contain sensitive data. Here, the medical domain, for example, might have higher privacy requirements than the manufacturing domain. For ensuring privacy of sensitive data, transformation such as anonymization and pseudonymization can be applied. Moreover, specialized storage techniques can be used, including k-anonymity, which removes identifiers and pre-groups data and differential privacy [140], which adds additional artificial data, such that the data analysis is not skewed, but it becomes hard to identify individual subjects. For process event streams, the same challenges for collection, unification, connection, and enriching as well as regarding security and privacy occur.

In particular, in the context of process choreographies, parts of the logs reflecting the private processes might be hidden/not visible to the other partners due to confidentiality requirements of the partners.

In particular, if we aim at employing process mining in order to create process choreographies in a bottom-up manner starting from the event logs or event streams of the private and/or public partner processes, two challenges arise, i.e., (1) *mining distributed event logs/streams* and (2) *distributed mining of event logs/streams*. Challenge (1) is a data challenge and Challenge (2) an algorithmic one. (1) and (2) might occur together.

In order to tackle Challenge (1), different approaches propose *log integration* or *log merging* techniques. [52] proposes a rule-based merging approach for logs of different partners in a process choreography. The rules are defined by the user based on selected attributes of the log such as order id. [171] offer an approach to merge logs at different granularity levels, e.g., sub- and super-processes. In [223], we merge process event logs based on the case identifier. Applying process mining on merged logs results in process models, but not yet in collaboration models, as the different processes of the partners are not separated from each other using, e.g., swim lanes, and, moreover, the message exchanges are not discovered and displayed. It is even likely that the discovered process models are spaghetti-like [7], i.e., exhibit a certain complexity.

Log merging increases in complexity if the logs stem from different, heterogeneous sources. This is the case for process choreographies where the partners are organizationally separated and—as discussed above—can also occur within organizations if the logs are collected from different systems and services. The challenges comprise different granularity levels [57] and heterogeneous event labels [123]. The latter challenge is caused by the general assumption of *label equivalence* in process mining, i.e., two events are considered as equivalent if they have the same or textually similar labels. However, this assumption is not realistic in heterogeneous settings as in different systems or organizations, the same activity or functionality might be labelled differently, and vice versa, different activities/functionalities might have the same label [180]. Hence, it is more advisable to turn to an attribute-based, semantic equivalence notion [123, 180]. As suggested in [123], different levels of matching for events in a log can be applied, from the case and event ids to the endpoints given in the event.

Challenge (2) comprises also the parallel execution of process mining algorithms for performance reasons (e.g., [75]), which is beyond the scope of this discussion. For the bottom-up creation of process choreographies, distributed process mining means to discover partner process orchestration models in a distributed way and to merge them afterward. In the process mining community, this interpretation of distributed process mining is referred to as *collaboration mining*. The Colliery approach [55], for example, assumes that n partners participate in the choreography, and each of them has an event log. Then using existing process mining techniques (e.g., Inductive Miner, Split Miner, or Heuristic Miner [7]), n process orchestration models in BPMN notation (cf. Sect. 5.2) are discovered. These n process orchestration models are then merged (*model merging*) or integrated (*process model integration*) into a collaboration model based on the analysis of the message exchanges, by assuming unique message identifiers. A similar approach has been suggested in the context of inter-departmental event logs in the healthcare domain by [132]. Zeng et al. [228] extends the consideration of messages by the consideration of shared resources. All of these approaches base the process model integration on *collaboration patterns* or *interaction patterns*. Interaction patterns have been proposed in [29] and include *one-to-many-send* and *one-to-many-receive*. Note that all mentioned approaches (implicitly) assume the existence of a central entity/coordinator, which might not exist in a decentralized setting. A fully decentralized mining approach for the bottom-up design of process choreography is—to the best of our knowledge—currently still missing.

8.5 Case Study: Supply Chain

Overall, real-world case studies for process choreographies are relatively rare, though the importance of such applications is high as more and more companies offer more and more (fine-grained) services and, at the same time, outsource parts of their work to external partners. In particular, in service-dominant industries, companies nowadays do not own physical property anymore but only offer services instead, e.g., Uber, i.e., business models transit from good-dominant to service-dominant [214].

Examples used frequently in literature comprise a distributed booking of a trip [76] and supply chain scenarios, e.g., [51]. In [79], a real-world supply chain scenario between 3 partners is described, which is realized by creating a process choreography in a top-down manner (cf. Fig. 8.14).

Figure 8.15 depicts the collaboration model for the car manufacturing use case based on the choreography model shown in Fig. 8.14. More precisely, the collaboration model contains the public process orchestrations of the 3 partners realizing the interfaces of the choreography diagram. Given that the message formats and contents can be understood by the communicating partners, compatibility is ensured as all messages that are sent are received and vice versa. The first message is sent by the Car manufacturer to place an order at the Injection molding partner. Then Injection molding informs the Car manufacturer on the completion of the order. The Car manufacturer sends a message to the Electro plater, which initiates its process (represented by message receive event). Finally, the Electro plater sends the parts to the Car manufacturer.

In the collaboration model, complex BPMN tasks are used in order to hide private process details of the process participants. For task put parts in stock, for example, a private sub-process is hidden. This corresponds to the criterion of consistency, i.e., the private processes are sub-processes of the public processes by hiding them.

The supply chain choreography was implemented using the Cloud Process Execution Engine (CPEE), cf. Sect. 6.2.3. The correlation was realized based on the message contents. Note that on top of the message exchanges, the partners *specified implicit connections, i.e., dependencies between (private) activities that are not covered by message exchanges and express mostly data dependencies* [79]. For the Car manufacturer, for example, task wait for order completion with its hidden private sub-process implicitly depends on *the data produced by activities prepare for manufacturing, manufacturing of parts, and quality control* [79] as tasks in the Injection molding process with its hidden sub-processes. One reason for these hidden dependencies is proper resource planning, which is part of the contract between the partners, i.e., Injection molding has to react to an order placed by Car manufacturer in a certain contractually specified time.

How to check such hidden dependencies? For this, we apply a technique for checking compliance in process choreographies as follows: in general, process choreography might be subject to compliance requirements that are specified on top of the choreography models. For compliance requirements, we can distinguish between local compliance requirements comprising assertions and local compliance rules that are imposed on the private/public processes of one partner and global compliance rules that span across several partners. Local compliance rules and assertions can be checked by the partners separately. Global compliance rules have to be checked in collaboration. Here, checking is more easy if the global compliance rule refers to public process details of different partners only. If they also refer to private process details of different partners, we have proposed a decomposition algorithm in [79] that deconstructs a global compliance rule into assertions in a

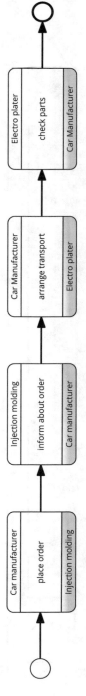

Fig. 8.14   Real-world use case: car manufacturing choreography model, based on [79] (using SAP Signavio®)

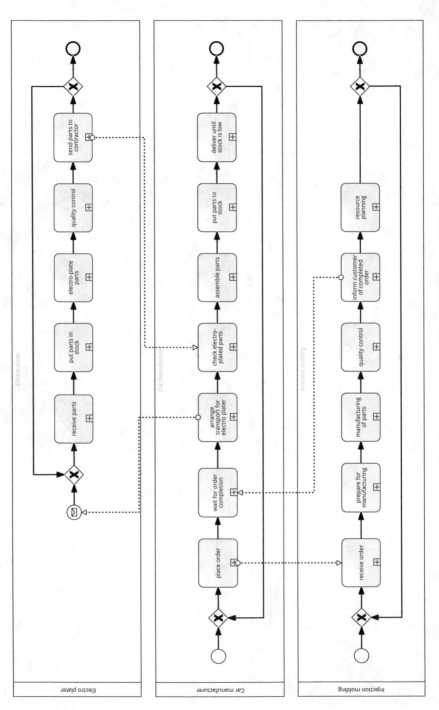

Fig. 8.15 Real world use case: car manufacturing collaboration model, based on [79] (using SAP Signavio®)

lossless way, such that these assertions can be checked by the partners locally and, together, the compliance of the global rule is assured.

Coming back to the implicit data dependencies, using the decomposition algorithm, it was not only possible to check the hidden dependencies but to create explicit message sending and receiving tasks that "lift up" the hidden dependency to an explicit message exchange in the choreography model.

8.6 Conclusion and Lessons Learned

Process choreographies constitute a powerful instrument to create interoperability between business partners and their processes. Application areas are manifold ranging from healthcare scenarios for clinical trials including multiple hospitals and biobanks to supply chain scenarios [79]. Especially with the shift from good-dominant to service-dominant industries [214], the composition, orchestration, and choreography of services and processes become increasingly interesting. The interoperability in process choreographies has been realized through message exchanges so far. For this, the choreography partners offer their interfaces describing sequences of message sending and receiving events, to the other partners. Behind these public interfaces, partners run their secret, private processes. In order to realize a choreography between the partners without running into problems or unwanted effects such as missing messages or blocking choreography instances, a set of correctness criteria must hold on the choreography, ranging from compatibility between the public process orchestrations and the behavioral correctness of the collaboration model to the consistency between public and private processes. When employing a top-down design approach, starting from a choreography model as contract and its refinement into public and private processes, the correctness criteria can be checked in each of the transformation steps. Proceeding in a bottom-up manner, starting from the private partner processes or their event logs is more complex, and comprehensive approaches are still missing. Mostly, a mixed setting with existing private processes and a contract between the partners setting out the choreography is conceivable. Then, possibly, adaptations to the private processes might become necessary, which can be also subject to negotiations with the other partners.

Further Reading
1. Basten, T., van der Aalst, W.M.P.: Inheritance of behavior. J. Log. Algebraic Methods Program. **47**(2), 47–145 (2001)
2. Decker, G., Weske, M.: Behavioral consistency for B2B process integration. CAiSE, 81–95 (2007)
3. Fdhila, W., Knuplesch, D., Rinderle-Ma, S., Reichert, M.: Verifying compliance in process choreographies: foundations, algorithms, and implementation. Inf. Syst. **108**, 101983 (2022)

4. Fdhila, W., Indiono, C., Rinderle-Ma, S., Reichert, M.: Dealing with change in process choreographies: design and implementation of propagation algorithms. Inf. Syst. **49**, 1–24 (2015)
5. Weske, M.: Business Process Management - Concepts, Languages, Architectures, 3rd edn, pp. 1–417. Springer, Berlin (2019). ISBN 978-3-662-59431-5

Chapter 9
Conclusion and Further Interoperability Aspects

9.1 Further Interoperability Perspectives

The book provides a holistic view on interoperability challenges and solutions ranging from the integration and exchange of data, services, and applications to service exchange and process orchestration and choreography. It introduces fundamental concepts, real-world cases, as well as implementation details, including a tool and system view. The challenges and solutions are illustrated based on a selection of case studies from different domains. They can be used as guide for stakeholders when designing and implementing interoperability solutions for their demands.

We set out by motivating three interoperability perspectives, i.e., regarding interoperability levels and tasks (cf. Table 1.1), regarding integration scenarios and methods (cf. Fig. 1.1), and with respect to the interoperability concerns data, services, and processes (cf. Fig. 1.2. In the following, we revisit the perspectives and discuss a selection of further perspectives that are not addressed in this book.

Table 1.1 represents the syntactical, semantic, and organizational interoperability levels with the interoperability tasks exchange, integrate, and orchestrate. According to [217], the fourth interoperability level is **technical interoperability** (cf. Fig. 9.1). *"Technical Interoperability is usually associated with hardware/software components, systems and platforms that enable machine-to-machine communication to take place. This kind of interoperability is often centred on (communication) protocols and the infrastructure needed for those protocols to operate."* [217]. From this definition, we can see that to some extent, technical interoperability is touched upon in this book as well. In Sect. 2.2, for example, protocols to exchange data between client and server in the context of Web services (e.g., SOAP and WSDL) are mentioned. Moreover, for the case study of (smart) manufacturing described in Sect. 1.3.2 and used in Chaps. 5 to 8, machine-to-machine communication is an essential goal to achieve, especially in a process-oriented way. However, this

Levels .../ Tasks ↓	Technical	Syntactical	Semantic	Organizational
Exchange		Exchange formats, e.g., XML, relational databases, JSON, BSON, YAML, MessagePack; query languages: XPath, XQuery, SQL; transformation languages, e.g., XSLT	Schema matching and mapping; ontologies;	Message exchange; correlation
Integrate		SQL/XML standard; native XML databases; REST and GraphQL	Edge table, shredding; XML schema and RNG; schema and data integration; service integration	Correlation and choreography
Orchestrate		BPMN, Petri Nets, Workflow Nets, RPST, CPEE Trees, Colored Petri Nets	Verification; task and worklist design; service invocation; correlation; integration patterns and processes	Choreography

Fig. 9.1 Interoperability perspectives I with missing interoperability perspectives

book does not address direct machine-to-machine communication and the related protocols.

As can also be seen from Fig. 9.1, an aspect that has not been addressed in its entirety is **ontologies**. Ontologies play an important role in order to address semantic interoperability, i.e., to equip concepts in, for example, existing schemas with meaning in order to resolve naming conflicts. This has been mentioned in Sect. 3.5 on schema matching and mapping. An ontology can be understood as a set of ideas/terms/words we want to become understandable, in relationship to each other. Ontologies describe a domain and contain concepts. A domain refers to the topic or area that the words can occur in, e.g., "bank" as used in geography (domain) or finance (domain). A concept describes a single idea and its properties and relationship to other concepts, e.g., a horse is a concept and connected to the concept mammals. It can have a color and name. "Black Beauty" is an instance of horse.

One language for describing ontologies in the context of semantic Web is the Resource Description Framework (RDF),[1] together with the query language SPARQL 1.1 [101]. RDF is used to describe the ontology. In the context of interoperability, we can use the ontologies then to connect the semantics of the concepts of different parties, for example: Company A has an ontology, and company B has an ontology. Company A creates a new ontology to describe how

---

[1] https://www.w3.org/RDF/.

the concepts of company A are related to their own concepts. SPARQL can then be used to identify concepts and to extract data, for example, identify all persons that have sisters and green eyes. Several tools for ontology engineering exist, for example, Protègè.[2]

Standards or **standardization** are connected to ontologies and often discussed in the course of interoperability. In the context of this book, we refer to standards and standardization at the information systems level and not, for example, to standardization for child seats. There are several standardization bodies at national and international level such as the International Organization for Standardization (ISO).[3] The goal of ontologies and standards is similar, i.e., to create a common understanding for several parties in order to facilitate their interoperability. *"Projects such as NIEM (http://niem.gov) in the US [...] have developed a library of common vocabulary for consistent, repeatable exchanges of information between governmental organisations"* [215], and Health Level Seven International (HL7)[4] provides standards for the exchange and sharing of data through electronic health information systems. Standards or standardization can therefore be helpful in interoperability projects but also come with several disadvantages [174]: at first, standardization can be a cumbersome process as typically the interests of several parties have to be considered and integrated into the standard. Moreover, as contrary to ontologies, standards are prescriptive, and as a consequence, a change in a standard requires all parties adhering to the standard to adapt to this change. Further on, in larger interoperability projects with several parties, there is a chance that some partners will not employ the standard that reduces the positive effect of using the standards. Finally, for certain concepts, standardization is not possible, e.g., defining a standard precision for temporal information. Hence, [174] discuss the applicability of **mediation** as interoperability approach as an alternative to standardization.

While several techniques and concepts are discussed in this book, so far, no explicit discussion on **interoperability approaches** has been provided. We will catch up on this in the next section.

9.2 Interoperability Approaches

Let us assume that we run an interoperability project with five parties to interoperate. In [167], four high-level steps for an interoperability approach are outlined, i.e., (i) find and describe interoperability problem, (ii) involve users, (iii) think of changes in the interoperability requirements, and (iv) automate the project/process as much as possible. Answering (i) requires the analysis of the involved parties, i.e., how aligned the formats used by the different parties are. Possible results of

---

[2] https://protege.stanford.edu/.

[3] iso.org.

[4] hl7.org.

this analysis and subsequent interoperability approaches may lead to the following interoperability approaches [48]: The *integrated approach* assumes that all parties follow a common format which can be provided by standards. The *unified approach* assumes a common format at the meta-model level. The *federated approach* does not assume any common format but a shared ontology.

As discussed at the end of the previous section and in [174], common standards, meta models, or ontologies are not always applicable to foster interoperability, and hence **data mediation** as interoperability strategy might become interesting as an alternative. *"A data mediator is a computer program which translates data between two systems with different data schemas"* [174]. We can think of the data mediator as an entity, i.e., a software layer according to [221], between two information systems A and B that aim at exchanging data. Both A and B can send data to the data mediator, which translates the data then into a common format. Mediators can be also used for establishing interoperability in message exchange protocols. Patterns for this are presented in [164], which solely focus on the protocol and not on the message content. A mediation-based approach for Web services interoperability is proposed in [158]. Assume two Web services W1 and W2 where W1 aims at sending a message of a certain structure to W2. Overall, this book offers several of the interoperability technologies and concepts required for mediation, i.e., the transformation techniques for data formats such as XSLT (cf. Sect. 3.3) and the concepts for schema matching and mapping (cf. Sect. 3.5).

As stated in [221], mediators are focused on domains due to maintainability reasons. This leads to an increase of the number of mediators with the number of domains involved in an interoperability projects. Moreover, interoperability projects might concern data, services, and processes and hence require an approach to establish interoperability across these levels.

How can an interoperability approach support interoperability both between multiple parties/concerns and across different interoperability levels? From a method-based point of view, similar to the design of process orchestrations and choreographies (cf. Chaps. 5 to 8), we can establish cross-concern interoperability between multiple parties and concerns through a **model-driven orchestration approach**. This approach uses the process orchestration model together with the task design (cf. Sect. 6.4) in order to define how the invoked services are exchanging data in the process context (cf. Sect. 6.3). More specifically, if service A is invoked by the process orchestration model, the data provided by the service is transferred and translated into process data/context using correlation (cf. Sect. 6.6). Process data/context is then available for other tasks and their invoked services, i.e., can be used as input data. Moreover, human workers can be integrated based on the worklist design as presented in Sect. 6.5. The model-driven orchestration approach can be equipped with interoperability requirements (see Sect. 9.3 for more details) as described in [135]. It can be seen that most of the interoperability requirements are already fulfilled if all process orchestrations models and all services are described and the choreography and collaboration models are specified. Hence, the process orchestrations and choreographies cannot only be subsumed as interoperability concepts but provide interoperability approaches as well.

Hence, at its core, this book features an interoperability approach, i.e., model-driven orchestration, that supports cross-level interoperability between multiple parties/concerns. However, the question is whether it fits all possible interoperability scenarios. This question is followed up in the next section.

9.3 Success Factors of Interoperability Projects

Section 9.2 sketches a selection of interoperability approaches, i.e., mediation and model-driven orchestration. The selection and success of an interoperability approach depend on multiple factors such as number of parties to interoperate; the structure of the collaboration network, e.g., networked vs. process-driven, which can be measured by, e.g., the connectivity index [175]; and *interoperability requirements* [58]. Interoperability requirements can be defined along the interoperability concepts data, service, and processes and the interoperability levels technical/syntactical, semantic, and organizational. The requirements target four properties, i.e., compatibility, which describes how two partners are aligned in their interaction, e.g., sharing an ontology; interoperations, which refers to the strategies of how the partnership is run; autonomy of the partners; and reversibility, which *"means that partners can return to their original state at the end of collaboration with regards to their performance and including positive and/or negative variation accepted prior to any real collaboration"* [135]. For the process concern, for example, at semantic and organizational level, a compatibility requirement is *"The internal processes are modeled,"* and an interoperation requirement is *"The collaborative process is modeled"* [58].

Interoperability requirements provide a first way of evaluating the success of an interoperability project, i.e., based on the number of fulfilled requirements and the degree of fulfillment [175]. Yahia et al. [225] propose a quantification of semantic interoperability between two information systems resulting in an assessment of full/partial/no interoperability. The quantification is based on the number of concepts in on information system for which semantic relations to concepts in the other information system can be established, e.g., by a domain expert or by schema matching.

In summary, for successful interoperability projects, the following recommendations can be made:

- Plan sufficient time and resources for the analysis phase of your interoperability project as a detailed assessment of the initial situation is indispensable for the success of the project. In particular, the analysis should comprise:

  - How many parties are involved? At which interoperability level?
  - What is the targeted interoperability structure, i.e., how to the parties plan to interoperate? Examples comprise bidirectional, networked, and process-oriented interoperation.

- Which formats/notations do the parties use for their data, services, or processes?
- Do standards, meta models, or ontologies exist that can support to establish interoperability?

• Plan sufficient time and resources for the schema and data format preparation, transformation, and integration.
• Specify interoperability requirements at the different interoperability levels.
• Include domain experts in the all phases.
• Document all phases, possibly using tool support.
• Be prepared for change.

9.4 Outlook

In Sects. 9.2 and 9.3, we have shown how interoperability projects can be undertaken, including interoperability approaches and success factors. Moreover, in Sect. 9.1, interoperability perspectives that have not been treated in detail in this book have been examined.

Still, there are open interoperability challenges, especially arising in the light of new trends and technologies. Hence, this section sketches a selection of three current trends in interoperability, i.e., compliance, sensor fusion, and blockchain technology.

Interoperability requirements as described for the assessment of the success of interoperability projects in Sect. 9.3 refer to the technical, syntactical, semantic, and organizational level. For many applications, there can be additional requirements/constraint levels, including the compliance and legal level in, for example, the governmental domain [2]. Also from a semantic and organizational level, i.e., for process orchestrations and process choreographies, compliance plays an important role. Specifically, for process choreographies, **compliability** [122] can be added as an additional soundness criterion on top of existing criteria such as compatibility and consistency (see Sect. 8.2). Compliability means that all process orchestrations and their interactions in a given process choreography must not violate global compliance constraints imposed on the choreography. A global compliance constraint refers to a constraint that spans across two or more partners in the choreography. So even if a choreography and its process orchestration models are compatible and consistent, they might violate a global compliance rule, and hence the interoperability of the process orchestrations as to be established by the choreography is endangered. Compliance is also a challenge for process orchestrations as the orchestrations of services as intended with respect to the interoperability project goals can be in violation with compliance constraints. Although a body of work exists for compliance verification in process orchestrations (see, e.g., surveys in [134, 182]) and a few approaches for process choreography compliance (e.g., [79]), the effects of compliance requirements and constraints on interoperability as well as suitable mitigation strategies still have to be further investigated. In other words: if all effort is spent on an interoperability project and compliance is not considered, this can lead to costly consequences (fines, loss of trust) and endanger or hinder the entire interoperability project.

In the rise of IoT applications, **sensor fusion** has become increasingly important. Sensor fusion aim at fusing the data streams from multiple sensors in such a way that the result reduces uncertainty due to the heterogeneity and varying reliability of the sensor sources [116]. The challenges for sensor data fusion are similar to data fusion, including data quality and conflicting data. Overall, sensor fusion is contributing to interoperability, in particular, in IoT environments, e.g., a smart homes. Recently, a new line of research has been started addressing the combination of process orchestrations and IoT data [113]. Application areas are manufacturing, logistics, and healthcare. In manufacturing, for example, producing a part can be accompanied by more than 80 sensors continuously providing information about the context of the production process. The fusion of the IoT sensor stream data with the process data, i.e., the process event logs or process event streams, seems promising with respect to the advanced analysis of the underlying processes [209]. This lifts up sensor fusion to sensor and process event stream fusion for which a first proposal toward the format SensorStream [137] has been proposed.

Interoperability is currently also researched in the realm of **blockchain** technology. Blockchains are per se promising to realize interoperability applications due to their de-centralized manner. There are two directions, i.e., how to use blockchain to establish interoperability and how to establish interoperability between blockchains. Using blockchains to establish interoperability has been proposed for, for example, the healthcare domain to enable patient-driven interoperability, where the patient can mediate his/her patient data [92]. Interoperability between blockchains necessitates similar interoperability considerations as stated in general for interoperability in the introduction (see, e.g., Table 1.1) regarding technical and semantic interoperability. Interesting concepts to realize cross-blockchain interoperability are Internet-of-blockchains and the blockchain of blockchains. While there are concepts and solutions for the technical cross-blockchain interoperability, semantic interoperability and stakeholder inclusion are still open challenges [92].

Overall, new interoperability challenges arise with the advent of new technologies. As mentioned for blockchains in [92], fast advances in a technology might become an obstacle for interoperability. This problem can occur as interoperability projects might require a substantial amount of time. Moreover, considering all interoperability levels also in their interplay is still an open challenge.

References

1. Information technology—database languages—sql—part 14: Xml-related specifications (sql/xml). Tech. Rep. ISO/IEC 9075-14 (2006)
2. Maturity levels for interoperability in digital government. Gov. Inf. Q. **26**(1), 75–81 (2009). https://doi.org/10.1016/j.giq.2008.03.003
3. van der Aa, H., Leopold, H., Reijers, H.A.: Comparing textual descriptions to process models–the automatic detection of inconsistencies. Inf. Syst. **64**, 447–460 (2017)
4. van der Aalst, W.M.P.: Interval timed coloured Petri nets and their analysis. In: International Conference on Application and Theory of Petri Nets (PN), pp. 453–472 (1993)
5. van der Aalst, W.M.P.: Formalization and verification of event-driven process chains. Inf. Softw. Technol. **41**(10), 639–650 (1999). https://doi.org/10.1016/S0950-5849(99)00016-6
6. van der Aalst, W.M.P.: Configurable services in the cloud: Supporting variability while enabling cross-organizational process mining. In: On the Move to Meaningful Internet Systems, pp. 8–25 (2010). https://doi.org/10.1007/978-3-642-16934-2_5
7. van der Aalst, W.M.P.: Process Mining—Data Science in Action, 2nd edn. Springer, Berlin (2016). https://doi.org/10.1007/978-3-662-49851-4
8. van der Aalst, W.M.P., Bichler, M., Heinzl, A.: Robotic process automation. Bus. Inf. Syst. Eng. **60**(4), 269–272 (2018). https://doi.org/10.1007/s12599-018-0542-4
9. van der Aalst, W.M.P., van Hee, K.M., ter Hofstede, A.H.M., Sidorova, N., Verbeek, H.M.W., Voorhoeve, M., Wynn, M.T.: Soundness of workflow nets: classification, decidability, and analysis. Formal Aspects Comput. **23**(3), 333–363 (2011). https://doi.org/10.1007/s00165-010-0161-4
10. van der Aalst, W.M.P., van Hee, K.M., Massuthe, P., Sidorova, N., van der Werf, J.M.E.M.: In: Applications and Theory of Petri Nets, pp. 283–302 (2009). https://doi.org/10.1007/978-3-642-02424-5_17
11. van der Aalst, W.M.P., Stahl, C.: Modeling Business Processes—A Petri Net-Oriented Approach. In: Cooperative Information Systems series. MIT Press, New York (2011)
12. van der Aalst, W.M.P., Weske, M.: The P2P approach to interorganizational workflows. In: Seminal Contributions to Information Systems Engineering, pp. 289–305 (2013). https://doi.org/10.1007/978-3-642-36926-1_23
13. Albouq, S.S., Sen, A.A.A., Almashfi, N., Yamin, M., Alshanqiti, A.M., Bahbouh, N.M.: A survey of interoperability challenges and solutions for dealing with them in IoT environment. IEEE Access **10**, 36416–36428 (2022). https://doi.org/10.1109/ACCESS.2022.3162219
14. Alonso, G., Casati, F., Kuno, H., Machiraju, V.: Web Services. Springer, Berlin (2004)

© Springer Nature Switzerland AG 2024
S. Rinderle-Ma et al., *Fundamentals of Information Systems Interoperability*,
https://doi.org/10.1007/978-3-031-48322-6

15. Anderson, N.H.: Foundations of Information Integration Theory. No. 1 in Foundations of Information Integration Theory. Academic Press, New York (1981). https://books.google.de/books?id=3XN9AAAAMAAJ

16. Atzeni, P., Bugiotti, F., Cabibbo, L., Torlone, R.: Data modeling in the NoSQL world. Comput. Stand. Interfaces **67**, 103149 (2020). https://doi.org/10.1016/j.csi.2016.10.003

17. Aumüller, D., Thor, A.: Mashup-Werkzeuge zur ad-hoc-Datenintegration im Web. Datenbank-Spektrum **8**(26), 4–10 (2008)

18. Badouel, E., Hélouët, L., Morvan, C.: Petri nets with structured data. In: International Conference on Application and Theory of Petri Nets (PN), pp. 212–233. Springer, Berlin (2015)

19. Baez, J.C., Master, J.: Open Petri Nets. CoRR **abs/1808.05415** (2018). http://arxiv.org/abs/1808.05415

20. Bagheri Hariri, B., Calvanese, D., De Giacomo, G., Deutsch, A., Montali, M.: Verification of relational data-centric dynamic systems with external services. In: International Conference on Management of Data (SIGMOD), pp. 163–174. ACM, New York (2013)

21. Bahta, R., Atay, M.: Translating JSON data into relational data using schema-oblivious approaches. In: Lo, D., Kim, D., Gamess, E. (eds.) ACM Southeast Conference, pp. 233–236. ACM, New York (2019). https://doi.org/10.1145/3299815.3314467

22. Bahtchevanova, L.: What is Interoperability in Financial Services? (2021). https://interop.io/what-is-interoperability-in-financial-services/

23. Bakhouyi, A., Dehbi, R., Talea, M., Hajoui, O.: Evolution of standardization and interoperability on e-learning systems: an overview. In: Information Technology Based Higher Education and Training, pp. 1–8 (2017). https://doi.org/10.1109/ITHET.2017.8067789

24. Balbo, G.: Introduction to stochastic Petri nets. In: School Organized by the European Educational Forum, vol. 2090, pp. 84–155. Springer, Berlin (2001)

25. Baldan, P., Bonchi, F., Gadducci, F., Monreale, G.V.: Modular encoding of synchronous and asynchronous interactions using open Petri nets. Sci. Comput. Program. **109**, 96–124 (2015)

26. Banavar, G., Chandra, T., Strom, R., Sturman, D.: A case for message oriented middleware. In: International Symposium on Distributed Computing, pp. 1–17. Springer, Berlin (1999)

27. Barcelona, M.A., García-Borgoñón, L., Cuaresma, M.J.E., Ramos, I.M.: Cbg-framework: a bottom-up model-based approach for collaborative business process management. Comput. Ind. **102**, 1–13 (2018). https://doi.org/10.1016/j.compind.2018.06.002

28. Barenholz, D., Montali, M., Polyvyanyy, A., Reijers, H.A., Rivkin, A., van der Werf, J.M.E.M.: There and back again—on the reconstructability and rediscoverability of typed Jackson nets. In: Application and Theory of Petri Nets and Concurrency, pp. 37–58 (2023). https://doi.org/10.1007/978-3-031-33620-1_3

29. Barros, A., Dumas, M., ter Hofstede, A.H.M.: Service interaction patterns. In: Business Process Management, vol. 3649, pp. 302–318 (2005). https://doi.org/10.1007/11538394_20

30. Basten, T., van der Aalst, W.M.P.: Inheritance of behavior. J. Log. Algebraic Methods Program. **47**(2), 47–145 (2001). https://doi.org/10.1016/S1567-8326(00)00004-7

31. Batini, C., Lenzerini, M., Navathe, S.B.: A comparative analysis of methodologies for database schema integration. ACM Comput. Surv. **18**(4), 323–364 (1986). https://doi.org/10.1145/27633.27634

32. Bayomie, D., Ciccio, C.D., Mendling, J.: Event-case correlation for process mining using probabilistic optimization. Inf. Syst. **114**, 102167 (2023). https://doi.org/10.1016/j.is.2023.102167

33. Bernstein, P.A., Madhavan, J., Rahm, E.: Generic schema matching, ten years later. Proc. VLDB Endow. **4**(11), 695–701 (2011). http://www.vldb.org/pvldb/vol4/p695-bernstein_madhavan_rahm.pdf

34. Berthomieu, B., Peres, F., Vernadat, F.: Bridging the gap between timed automata and bounded time petri nets. In: Formal Modeling and Analysis of Timed Systems, pp. 82–97 (2006). https://doi.org/10.1007/11867340_7

35. Bertino, E., Catania, B.: Integrating XML and databases. IEEE Internet Comput. **5**(4), 84–88 (2001). https://doi.org/10.1109/4236.939454

36. Bettenhausen, K.D., Kowalewski, S.: Cyber-Physical Systems: Chancen und Nutzen aus Sicht der Automation (2013). https://www.vdi.de/ueber-uns/presse/publikationen/details/cyber-physical-systems-chancen-und-nutzen-aus-sicht-der-automation

37. Binder, M., Dorda, W., Duftschmid, G., Dunkl, R., Fröschl, K.A., Gall, W., Grossmann, W., Harmankaya, K., Hronsky, M., Rinderle-Ma, S., Rinner, C., Weber, S.: On analyzing process compliance in skin cancer treatment: an experience report from the evidence-based medical compliance cluster (EBMC2). In: Advanced Information Systems Engineering, pp. 398–413 (2012). https://doi.org/10.1007/978-3-642-31095-9_26

38. Birman, K., Joseph, T.: Exploiting virtual synchrony in distributed systems. SIGOPS: Operating Systems Review **21**(5), 123–138 (1987)

39. Bleiholder, J., Naumann, F.: Data fusion. ACM Comput. Surv. **41**(1), 1:1–1:41 (2008)

40. Böhm, M.: Cost-based optimization of integration flows. Ph.D. thesis, Dresden University of Technology (2011). https://nbn-resolving.org/urn:nbn:de:bsz:14-qucosa-67936

41. Bolognesi, T.: From timed Petri nets to timed LOTOS. In: International Workshop on Protocol Specification, Testing and Verification, IFIP WG6. 1, pp. 377–406 (1990)

42. Borkowski, M., Fdhila, W., Nardelli, M., Rinderle-Ma, S., Schulte, S.: Event-based failure prediction in distributed business processes. Inf. Syst. **81**, 220–235 (2019). https://doi.org/10.1016/j.is.2017.12.005

43. Bourreet, R.: Xml and Databases (2005). http://www.rpbourret.com/xml/XMLAndDatabases.htm

44. Bunke, H., Shearer, K.: A graph distance metric based on the maximal common subgraph. Pattern Recognit. Lett. **19**(3-4), 255–259 (1998). https://doi.org/10.1016/S0167-8655(97)00179-7

45. Buschmann, F., Meunier, R., Rohnert, H., Sommerlad, P., Stal, M.: Pattern-Oriented Software Architecture—Volume 1: A System of Patterns. Wiley Publishing, New York (1996)

46. Casanova, C.: AIOps Needs A Superstructure of Interoperability (2022). https://www.forrester.com/blogs/aiops-needs-a-superstructure-of-interoperability/

47. Çayoglu, U., Dijkman, R.M., Dumas, M., Fettke, P., García-Bañuelos, L., Hake, P., Klinkmüller, C., Leopold, H., Ludwig, A., Loos, P., Mendling, J., Oberweis, A., Schoknecht, A., Sheetrit, E., Thaler, T., Ullrich, M., Weber, I., Weidlich, M.: Report: the process model matching contest 2013. In: Business Process Management Workshops, vol. 171, pp. 442–463. Springer, Berlin (2013). https://doi.org/10.1007/978-3-319-06257-0_35

48. Chen, D.: Enterprise interoperability framework. In: Open Interop Workshop on Enterprise Modelling and Ontologies for Interoperability, *CEUR Workshop Proceedings*, vol. 200 (2006). https://ceur-ws.org/Vol-200/19.pdf

49. Ciardo, G.: Reachability set generation for petri nets: can brute force be smart? In: Cortadella, J., Reisig, W. (eds.) Applications and Theory of Petri Nets, vol. 3099, pp. 17–34. Springer, Berlin (2004). https://doi.org/10.1007/978-3-540-27793-4_2

50. Ciccio, C.D., van der Aa, H., Cabanillas, C., Mendling, J., Prescher, J.: Detecting flight trajectory anomalies and predicting diversions in freight transportation. Decis. Support Syst. **88**, 1–17 (2016). https://doi.org/10.1016/j.dss.2016.05.004

51. Ciccio, C.D., Cecconi, A., Dumas, M., García-Bañuelos, L., López-Pintado, O., Lu, Q., Mendling, J., Ponomarev, A., Tran, A.B., Weber, I.: Blockchain support for collaborative business processes. Inform. Spektrum **42**(3), 182–190 (2019). https://doi.org/10.1007/s00287-019-01178-x

52. Claes, J., Poels, G.: Merging event logs for process mining: A rule based merging method and rule suggestion algorithm. Expert Syst. Appl. **41**(16), 7291–7306 (2014). https://doi.org/10.1016/j.eswa.2014.06.012

53. Corporation, I.: Business process execution language for web services BPEL4WS (version 1.1) (2002)

54. Corradini, F., Muzi, C., Re, B., Rossi, L., Tiezzi, F.: BPMN 2.0 or-join semantics: Global and local characterisation. Inf. Syst. **105**, 101934 (2022). https://doi.org/10.1016/j.is.2021.101934

55. Corradini, F., Re, B., Rossi, L., Tiezzi, F.: A technique for collaboration discovery. In: Enterprise, Business-Process and Information Systems Modeling, pp. 63–78 (2022). https://doi.org/10.1007/978-3-031-07475-2_5

56. Curry, E.: Message-oriented middleware. Middleware for Communications, pp. 1–28 (2004)

57. Cuzzocrea, A., Diamantini, C., Genga, L., Potena, D., Storti, E.: A composite methodology for supporting collaboration pattern discovery via semantic enrichment and multidimensional analysis. In: Soft Computing and Pattern Recognition, pp. 459–464 (2014). https://doi.org/10.1109/SOCPAR.2014.7008050

58. Daclin, N., Daclin, S.M., Chapurlat, V., Vallespir, B.: Writing and verifying interoperability requirements: application to collaborative processes. Comput. Ind. **82**, 1–18 (2016). https://doi.org/10.1016/j.compind.2016.04.001

59. Dalamagas, T., Cheng, T., Winkel, K., Sellis, T.K.: A methodology for clustering XML documents by structure. Inf. Syst. **31**(3), 187–228 (2006). https://doi.org/10.1016/j.is.2004.11.009

60. Davoudian, A., Chen, L., Liu, M.: A survey on NoSQL stores. ACM Comput. Surv. **51**(2), 40:1–40:43 (2018). https://doi.org/10.1145/3158661

61. Decker, G., Kopp, O., Leymann, F., Weske, M.: Interacting services: from specification to execution. Data Knowl. Eng. **68**(10), 946–972 (2009). https://doi.org/10.1016/j.datak.2009.04.003

62. Decker, G., Weske, M.: Behavioral consistency for B2B process integration. In: Advanced Information Systems Engineering, pp. 81–95 (2007). https://doi.org/10.1007/978-3-540-72988-4_7

63. van der Aalst, W.M.P.: Making work flow: on the application of Petri nets to business process management. In: International Conference on Application and Theory of Petri Nets (PN), pp. 1–22. Springer, Berlin (2002)

64. van der Aalst, W.M.P., Lohmann, N., Massuthe, P., Stahl, C., Wolf, K.: Multiparty contracts: agreeing and implementing interorganizational processes. Comput. J. **53**(1), 90–106 (2010)

65. Derntl, M., Mangler, J.: Web services for blended learning patterns. In: Advanced Learning Technologies (2004). https://doi.org/10.1109/ICALT.2004.1357488

66. Dias, C.: Corporate portals: a literature review of a new concept in information management. Int. J. Inf. Manag. **21**(4), 269–287 (2001)

67. Dijkman, R.M., Dumas, M., van Dongen, B.F., Käärik, R., Mendling, J.: Similarity of business process models: metrics and evaluation. Inf. Syst. **36**(2), 498–516 (2011). https://doi.org/10.1016/j.is.2010.09.006

68. Dijkman, R.M., Dumas, M., Ouyang, C.: Semantics and analysis of business process models in BPMN. Inf. Softw. Technol. **50**(12), 1281–1294 (2008). https://doi.org/10.1016/j.infsof.2008.02.006

69. Doan, A., Halevy, A., Ives, Z.: Principles of Data Integration. Elsevier, Amsterdam (2012)

70. Dumas, M., La Rosa, M., Mendling, J., Reijers, H.A.: Fundamentals of Business Process Management. Springer, Berlin (2013). https://doi.org/10.1007/978-3-642-33143-5

71. Ehrendorfer, M., Mangler, J., Rinderle-Ma, S.: Assessing the impact of context data on process outcomes during runtime. In: Service-Oriented Computing, pp. 3–18 (2021). https://doi.org/10.1007/978-3-030-91431-8_1

72. El-Halwagi, M.M.: Process Integration, vol. 7. Elsevier, Amsterdam (2006)

73. Elkoumy, G., Fahrenkrog-Petersen, S.A., Sani, M.F., Koschmider, A., Mannhardt, F., von Voigt, S.N., Rafiei, M., von Waldthausen, L.: Privacy and confidentiality in process mining: threats and research challenges. ACM Trans. Manag. Inf. Syst. **13**(1), 11:1–11:17 (2022). https://doi.org/10.1145/3468877

74. Eugster, P.T., Felber, P.A., Guerraoui, R., Kermarrec, A.M.: The many faces of publish/subscribe. ACM Comput. Surv. (CSUR) **35**(2), 114–131 (2003)

75. Evermann, J., Assadipour, G.: Big data meets process mining: implementing the alpha algorithm with map-reduce. In: Symposium on Applied Computing, pp. 1414–1416 (2014). https://doi.org/10.1145/2554850.2555076

76. Fdhila, W., Indiono, C., Rinderle-Ma, S., Reichert, M.: Dealing with change in process choreographies: design and implementation of propagation algorithms. Inf. Syst. **49**, 1–24 (2015)

77. Fdhila, W., Indiono, C., Rinderle-Ma, S., Vetschera, R.: Finding collective decisions: change negotiation in collaborative business processes. In: On the Move to Meaningful Internet Systems, pp. 90–108 (2015). https://doi.org/10.1007/978-3-319-26148-5_6

78. Fdhila, W., Indiono, C., Rinderle-Ma, S., Vetschera, R.: Multi-criteria decision analysis for change negotiation in process collaborations. In: Enterprise Distributed Object Computing, pp. 175–183 (2017). https://doi.org/10.1109/EDOC.2017.31

79. Fdhila, W., Knuplesch, D., Rinderle-Ma, S., Reichert, M.: Verifying compliance in process choreographies: foundations, algorithms, and implementation. Inf. Syst. **108**, 101983 (2022). https://doi.org/10.1016/j.is.2022.101983

80. Fdhila, W., Rinderle-Ma, S., Indiono, C.: Change propagation analysis and prediction in process choreographies. Int. J. Cooperative Inf. Syst. **24**(3), 1541003:1–1541003:33 (2015). https://doi.org/10.1142/S0218843015410038

81. Fehling, C., Leymann, F., Retter, R., Schupeck, W., Arbitter, P.: Cloud Computing Patterns—Fundamentals to Design, Build, and Manage Cloud Applications. Springer, Berlin (2014)

82. Fielding, R.T.: Architectural styles and the design of network-based software architectures. Ph.D. thesis, University of California, California (2000)

83. Finkel, A.: The minimal coverability graph for petri nets. In: Rozenberg, G. (ed.) Advances in Petri Nets 1993, Papers from the 12th International Conference on Applications and Theory of Petri Nets, Gjern, Denmark, June 1991. Lecture Notes in Computer Science, vol. 674, pp. 210–243. Springer, Berlin (1991). https://doi.org/10.1007/3-540-56689-9_45

84. Firestone, J.M.: Enterprise information portals and knowledge management. Routledge, UK (2007)

85. Florescu, D., Kossmann, D.: Storing and querying XML data using an RDMBS. IEEE Data Eng. Bull. **22**(3), 27–34 (1999)

86. Fong, B.: The algebra of open and interconnected systems. Ph.D. thesis, University of Oxford, Oxford (2016)

87. Forresi, C., Gallinucci, E., Golfarelli, M., Hamadou, H.B.: A dataspace-based framework for OLAP analyses in a high-variety multistore. VLDB J. **30**(6), 1017–1040 (2021). https://doi.org/10.1007/s00778-021-00682-5

88. Ganly, D., Kyte, A., Rayner, N., Hardcastle, C.: Predicts 2014: the rise of the postmodern ERP and enterprise applications world (2013)

89. Gartner: Information Technology (IT) Glossary—Essential Information Technology (IT) Terms & Definitions (2023). https://www.gartner.com/en/information-technology/glossary

90. Georgakopoulos, D., Hornick, M., Sheth, A.: An overview of workflow management: from process modeling to workflow automation infrastructure. Distrib. Parallel Databases **3**(2), 119–153 (1995)

91. Gillis, A.: What is IoT (Internet of Things) and How Does it Work? | Definition from TechTarget (2023). https://www.techtarget.com/iotagenda/definition/Internet-of-Things-IoT

92. Gordon, W.J., Catalini, C.: Blockchain technology for healthcare: facilitating the transition to patient-driven interoperability. Comput. Struct. Biotechnol. J. **16**, 224–230 (2018). https://doi.org/10.1016/j.csbj.2018.06.003

93. Grinberg, A.: Shredding XML, pp. 101–134. Apress, Berkeley (2018). https://doi.org/10.1007/978-1-4842-3117-3_4

94. Grossmann, W., Rinderle-Ma, S.: Fundamentals of business intelligence. In: Data-Centric Systems and Applications. Springer, Belin (2015)

95. Group, O.M.: Business process model and notation (BPMN). Object Management Group, Needham (2010)

96. Güdemann, M., Poizat, P., Salaün, G., Ye, L.: Verchor: a framework for the design and verification of choreographies. IEEE Trans. Serv. Comput. **9**(4), 647–660 (2016). https://doi.org/10.1109/TSC.2015.2413401

97. Haarmann, S., Lichtenstein, T., Weske, M.: Fragment-based service choreographies. In: Services Computing, pp. 164–173 (2022). https://doi.org/10.1109/SCC55611.2022.00035

98. Hahn, M., Breitenbücher, U., Kopp, O., Leymann, F.: Modeling and execution of data-aware choreographies: an overview. Comput. Sci. Res. Dev. **33**(3-4), 329–340 (2018). https://doi.org/10.1007/s00450-017-0387-y

99. Halevy, A.Y., Ashish, N., Bitton, D., Carey, M.J., Draper, D., Pollock, J., Rosenthal, A., Sikka, V.: Enterprise information integration: successes, challenges and controversies. In: ACM SIGMOD (2005)

100. Hanisch, H.M.: Analysis of place/transition nets with timed arcs and its application to batch process control. In: International Conference on Application and Theory of Petri Nets (PN), pp. 282–299. Springer, Berlin (1993)

101. Harris, S., Seaborne, A., Prud'hommeaux, E.: SPARQL 1.1 Query Language (2013). https://www.w3.org/TR/sparql11-query/

102. Hidders, J., et al.: DFL: a dataflow language based on Petri nets and nested relational calculus. Inf. Syst. **33**(3), 261–284 (2008)

103. Hildebrandt, T.T., Mukkamala, R.R., Slaats, T., Zanitti, F.: Contracts for cross-organizational workflows as timed dynamic condition response graphs. J. Log. Algebraic Methods Program. **82**(5–7), 164–185 (2013). https://doi.org/10.1016/j.jlap.2013.05.005

104. Hinz, S., Schmidt, K., Stahl, C.: Transforming BPEL to Petri nets. In: van der Aalst, W.M.P., Benatallah, B., Casati, F., Curbera, F. (eds.) Business Process Management, vol. 3649, pp. 220–235 (2005). https://doi.org/10.1007/11538394_15

105. Hohpe, G.: Enterprise integration patterns. In: Conference on Pattern Language of Programs (PLoP). Citeseer, New York (2002)

106. Hohpe, G.: Conversation patterns. In: The Role of Business Processes in Service Oriented Architectures, no. 06291 in Dagstuhl Seminar Proceedings, p. 7 (2006)

107. Hohpe, G., Woolf, B.: Enterprise integration patterns: designing, building, and deploying messaging solutions. Addison-Wesley Professional, New York (2004)

108. Holupirek, A., Scholl, M.H.: Implementing filesystems by tree-aware DBMSS. Proc. VLDB Endow. **1**(2), 1623–1630 (2008)

109. Hu, Y., Sundara, S., Srinivasan, J.: Supporting time-constrained SQL queries in Oracle. In: International Conference on Very Large Data Bases (VLDB), pp. 1207–1218 (2007)

110. Hütter, T., Augsten, N., Kirsch, C.M., Carey, M.J., Li, C.: JEDI: these aren't the JSON documents you're looking for? In: Ives Z.G., Bonifati, A., Abbadi, A.E. (eds.) Management of Data, pp. 1584–1597. ACM, New York (2022). https://doi.org/10.1145/3514221.3517850

111. {IBM Corporation}: IBM Business Process Manager overview (2021). https://www.ibm.com/docs/en/bpm/8.6.0?topic=manager-business-process-overview

112. Jacobsen, L., Jacobsen, M., Møller, M.H., Srba, J.: Verification of timed-arc Petri nets. In: SOFSEM, pp. 46–72. Springer, Berlin (2011)

113. Janiesch, C., Koschmider, A., Mecella, M., Weber, B., Burattin, A., Di Ciccio, C., Fortino, G., Gal, A., Kannengiesser, U., Leotta, F., Mannhardt, F., Marrella, A., Mendling, J., Oberweis, A., Reichert, M., Rinderle-Ma, S., Serral, E., Song, W., Su, J., Torres, V., Weidlich, M., Weske, M., Zhang, L.: The Internet of Things meets business process management: a manifesto. IEEE Syst. Man Cybern. Mag. **6**(4), 34–44 (2020). https://doi.org/10.1109/MSMC.2020.3003135

114. Javaid, S.: Data Interoperability & Machine Learning in 2023 & Beyond (2023). https://research.aimultiple.com/data-interoperability/

115. Jensen, K., Kristensen, L.M.: Coloured Petri Nets—Modelling and Validation of Concurrent Systems. Springer, Berlin (2009). https://doi.org/10.1007/b95112

116. Khaleghi, B., Khamis, A.M., Karray, F., Razavi, S.N.: Multisensor data fusion: a review of the state-of-the-art. Inf. Fusion **14**(1), 28–44 (2013). https://doi.org/10.1016/j.inffus.2011.08.001

117. Kindler, E., Martens, A., Reisig, W.: Inter-operability of workflow applications: local criteria for global soundness. In: International Conference on Business Process Management (BPM), pp. 235–253. Springer, Berlin (2000)

118. Kissinger, A., Merry, A., Soloviev, M.: Pattern graph rewrite systems. In: Developments in Computational Models (DCM), pp. 54–66 (2012)

119. Klemes, J.J.: Handbook of process integration (PI): minimisation of energy and water use, waste and emissions. Elsevier, Amsterdam (2013)

120. Klievtsova, N., Benzin, J.V., Kampik, T., Mangler, J., Rinderle-Ma, S.: Conversational process modelling: state of the art, applications, and implications in practice. arxiv (2023). https://doi.org/10.48550/arXiv.2304.11065

121. Klusch, M., Kapahnke, P., Schulte, S., Lécué, F., Bernstein, A.: Semantic web service search: a brief survey. Künstliche Intell. **30**(2), 139–147 (2016). https://doi.org/10.1007/s13218-015-0415-7

122. Knuplesch, D., Reichert, M., Fdhila, W., Rinderle-Ma, S.: On enabling compliance of cross-organizational business processes. In: Business Process Management, pp. 146–154 (2013). https://doi.org/10.1007/978-3-642-40176-3_12

123. Koenig, P., Mangler, J., Rinderle-Ma, S.: Compliance monitoring on process event streams from multiple sources. In: Process Mining, pp. 113–120 (2019). https://doi.org/10.1109/ICPM.2019.00026

124. Kriglstein, S., Mangler, J., Rinderle-Ma, S.: Who is who: On visualizing organizational models in collaborative systems. In: Collaborative Computing: Networking, Applications and Worksharing, pp. 279–288 (2012). https://doi.org/10.4108/icst.collaboratecom.2012.250404

125. Lasota, S.: Decidability border for Petri nets with data: WQO dichotomy conjecture. In: International Conference on Application and Theory of Petri Nets (PN), pp. 20–36. Springer, Berlin (2016)

126. Leitner, M., Rinderle-Ma, S., Mangler, J.: AW-RBAC: access control in adaptive workflow systems. In: Availability, Reliability and Security, pp. 27–34 (2011). https://doi.org/10.1109/ARES.2011.15

127. Lenzerini, M.: Data integration: a theoretical perspective. In: Principles of Database Systems, pp. 233–246. ACM, New York (2002). https://doi.org/10.1145/543613.543644

128. Leopold, H.: Business process model matching. In: Sakr, S., Zomaya, A.Y. (eds.) Encyclopedia of Big Data Technologies. Springer (2019). https://doi.org/10.1007/978-3-319-63962-8_107-1

129. Leser, U., Naumann, F.: Informationsintegration—Architekturen und Methoden zur Integration verteilter und heterogener Datenquellen. dpunkt.verlag (2007)

130. Lewis, S.: What is interoperability? | Definition from TechTarget (2019). https://www.techtarget.com/searchapparchitecture/definition/interoperability

131. Li, C., Lalani, F.: The COVID-19 pandemic has changed education forever. This is how (2020). https://www.weforum.org/agenda/2020/04/coronavirus-education-global-covid19-online-digital-learning/

132. Liu, C., Li, H., Zhang, S., Cheng, L., Zeng, Q.: Cross-department collaborative healthcare process model discovery from event logs. IEEE Trans. Autom. Sci. Eng. **20**(3), 2115–2125 (2023). https://doi.org/10.1109/TASE.2022.3194312

133. Ly, L.T., Indiono, C., Mangler, J., Rinderle-Ma, S.: Data transformation and semantic log purging for process mining. In: Advanced Information Systems Engineering, pp. 238–253 (2012). https://doi.org/10.1007/978-3-642-31095-9_16

134. Ly, L.T., Maggi, F.M., Montali, M., Rinderle-Ma, S., van der Aalst, W.M.P.: Compliance monitoring in business processes: Functionalities, application, and tool-support. Inf. Syst. **54**, 209–234 (2015)

135. Mallek, S., Daclin, N., Chapurlat, V.: The application of interoperability requirement specification and verification to collaborative processes in industry. Comput. Ind. **63**(7), 643–658 (2012). https://doi.org/10.1016/j.compind.2012.03.002

136. Mangat, A.S., Mangler, J., Rinderle-Ma, S.: Interactive process automation based on lightweight object detection in manufacturing processes. Comput. Ind. **130**, 103482 (2021). https://doi.org/10.1016/j.compind.2021.103482

137. Mangler, J., Grüger, J., Malburg, L., Ehrendorfer, M., Bertrand, Y., Benzin, J., Rinderle-Ma, S., Asensio, E.S., Bergmann, R.: Datastream XES extension: embedding IoT sensor data

into extensible event stream logs. Future Internet **15**(3), 109 (2023). https://doi.org/10.3390/fi15030109

138. Mangler, J., Rinderle-Ma, S.: Cloud process execution engine: architecture and interfaces. CoRR **abs/2208.12214** (2022). https://doi.org/10.48550/arXiv.2208.12214

139. Mangler, J., Stuermer, G., Schikuta, E.: Cloud process execution engine—evaluation of the core concepts. CoRR **abs/1003.3330** (2010). http://arxiv.org/abs/1003.3330

140. Mannhardt, F., Koschmider, A., Baracaldo, N., Weidlich, M., Michael, J.: Privacy-preserving process mining—differential privacy for event logs. Bus. Inf. Syst. Eng. **61**(5), 595–614 (2019). https://doi.org/10.1007/s12599-019-00613-3

141. MarketScreener: Smile Digital Health—Solving Interoperability Challenges with Managed Services (2023). https://www.marketscreener.com/quote/stock/FORRESTER-RESEARCH-INC-9348/news/Smile-Digital-Health-Solving-Interoperability-Challenges-with-Managed-Services-43855569/

142. Martens, A.: Usability of web services. In: Web Information Systems Engineering Workshops, pp. 182–190 (2003). https://doi.org/10.1109/WISEW.2003.1286801

143. Meike Klettke, H.M.: XML & Datenbanken Konzepte, Sprachen und Systeme. dpunkt.verlag (2003)

144. Meironke, A., Seyffarth, T., Damarowsky, J.: Business process compliance and blockchain: how does the ethereum blockchain address challenges of business process compliance? In: Wirtschaftsinformatik, pp. 1880–1891 (2019)

145. Mendling, J., Moser, M., Neumann, G., Verbeek, H.M.W., van Dongen, B.F., van der Aalst, W.M.P.: Faulty EPCs in the SAP reference model. In: Dustdar, S., Fiadeiro, J.L., Sheth, A.P. (eds.) Business Process Management, vol. 4102, pp. 451–457. Springer, Berlin (2006). https://doi.org/10.1007/11841760_38

146. Mendling, J., Weber, I., van der Aalst, W.M.P., vom Brocke, J., Cabanillas, C., Daniel, F., Debois, S., Ciccio, C.D., Dumas, M., Dustdar, S., Gal, A., García-Bañuelos, L., Governatori, G., Hull, R., La Rosa, M., Leopold, H., Leymann, F., Recker, J., Reichert, M., Reijers, H.A., Rinderle-Ma, S., Solti, A., Rosemann, M., Schulte, S., Singh, M.P., Slaats, T., Staples, M., Weber, B., Weidlich, M., Weske, M., Xu, X., Zhu, L.: Blockchains for business process management—challenges and opportunities. ACM Trans. Manag. Inf. Syst. **9**(1), 4:1–4:16 (2018). https://doi.org/10.1145/3183367

147. Mens, T.: A state-of-the-art survey on software merging. IEEE Trans. Software Eng. **28**(5), 449–462 (2002). https://doi.org/10.1109/TSE.2002.1000449

148. Merlin, P.: A study of the recoverability of computer systems. Ph.D. thesis, University of California, California (1974)

149. Merlin, P., Farber, D.: Recoverability of communication protocols–implications of a theoretical study. IEEE Trans. Commun. **24**(9), 1036–1043 (1976)

150. Meunier, R.: The pipes and filters architecture. In: Pattern Languages of Program Design, pp. 427–440. ACM Press/Addison-Wesley Publishing Co., New York (1995)

151. Meyer, A., Pufahl, L., Batoulis, K., Fahland, D., Weske, M.: Automating data exchange in process choreographies. Inf. Syst. **53**, 296–329 (2015). https://doi.org/10.1016/j.is.2015.03.008

152. Meyer, A., Pufahl, L., Batoulis, K., Kruse, S., Lindhauer, T., Stoff, T., Fahland, D., Weske, M.: Automating data exchange in process choreographies. In: Advanced Information Systems Engineering, pp. 316–331 (2014). https://doi.org/10.1007/978-3-319-07881-6_22

153. Moldt, D., Hansson, M., Seifert, L., Ihlenfeldt, K., Clasen, L., Ehlers, K., Feldmann, M.: Enriching heraklit modules by agent interaction diagrams. In: Application and Theory of Petri Nets and Concurrency. Springer, Berlin (2023). https://doi.org/10.1007/978-3-031-33620-1_23

154. Montali, M., Rivkin, A.: Model checking Petri nets with names using data-centric dynamic systems. Form. Asp. Comput. **28**(4), 615–641 (2016)

155. Montali, M., Rivkin, A.: Db-nets: on the marriage of colored petri nets and relational databases. T. Petri Nets and Other Models of Concurrency **12**, 91–118 (2017)

156. Moos, A.: XQuery und SQL/XML in DB2-Datenbanken. Vieweg+Teubner, Berlin (2008)

157. Murata, T.: Petri nets: properties, analysis and applications. Proc. IEEE **77**(4), 541–580 (1989)
158. Nagarajan, M., Verma, K., Sheth, A.P., Miller, J.A., Lathem, J.: Semantic interoperability of web services—challenges and experiences. In: Web Services, pp. 373–382 (2006). https://doi.org/10.1109/ICWS.2006.116
159. Nie, H., Lu, X., Duan, H.: Supporting BPMN choreography with system integration artefacts for enterprise process collaboration. Enterp. Inf. Syst. **8**(4), 512–529 (2014). https://doi.org/10.1080/17517575.2014.880131
160. Noura, M., Atiquzzaman, M., Gaedke, M.: Interoperability in internet of things: taxonomies and open challenges. Mob. Networks Appl. **24**(3), 796–809 (2019). https://doi.org/10.1007/s11036-018-1089-9
161. Pauker, F., Mangler, J., Rinderle-Ma, S., Ehrendorfer, M.: Industry 4.0 integration assessment and evolution at EVVA GMBH: process-driven automation through *centurio.work*. In: Business Process Management Cases Vol. 2, Digital Transformation—Strategy, Processes and Execution, pp. 81–91. Springer, Berlin (2021). https://doi.org/10.1007/978-3-662-63047-1_7
162. Perry, D.E., Wolf, A.L.: Foundations for the study of software architecture. SIGSOFT Softw. Eng. Notes **17**(4), 40–52 (1992). http://doi.acm.org/10.1145/141874.141884
163. Petcu, D.: Portability and interoperability between clouds: Challenges and case study—(invited paper). In: Towards a Service-Based Internet, pp. 62–74 (2011). https://doi.org/10.1007/978-3-642-24755-2_6
164. Pokraev, S., Reichert, M.: Mediation patterns for message exchange protocols. In: Open Interop Workshop on Enterprise Modelling and Ontologies for Interoperability. CEUR Workshop Proceedings, vol. 200 (2006). https://ceur-ws.org/Vol-200/12.pdf
165. Polaris: E-learning Market Size Global Report, 2022–2030. Tech. Rep. PM2295, Polaris (2022). https://www.polarismarketresearch.com/index.php/industry-analysis/e-learning-market
166. Proulx, M.: Interoperability Will Be Key To Meta's Threads Success (2023). https://www.forrester.com/blogs/interoperability-will-be-key-to-metas-threads-success/
167. Quartel, D.A.C., Pokraev, S., Pessoa, R.M., van Sinderen, M.: Model-driven development of a mediation service. In: Enterprise Distributed Object Computing, pp. 117–126 (2008). https://doi.org/10.1109/EDOC.2008.39
168. Rädler, S., Rupp, M., Rigger, E., Rinderle-Ma, S.: Code generation for machine learning using model-driven engineering and SysML. CoRR **abs/2307.05584** (2023). https://doi.org/10.48550/arXiv.2307.05584
169. Rahm, E., Peukert, E.: Holistic schema matching. In: Encyclopedia of Big Data Technologies. Springer, Berlin (2019). https://doi.org/10.1007/978-3-319-63962-8_12-1
170. Rahm, E., Peukert, E.: Large-scale schema matching. In: Encyclopedia of Big Data Technologies. Springer, Berlin (2019). https://doi.org/10.1007/978-3-319-63962-8_330-1
171. Raichelson, L., Soffer, P., Verbeek, E.: Merging event logs: combining granularity levels for process flow analysis. Inf. Syst. **71**, 211–227 (2017). https://doi.org/10.1016/j.is.2017.08.010
172. Ramchandani, C.: Analysis of asynchronous concurrent systems by timed Petri nets. Ph.D. thesis, Massachusetts Institute of Technology, Cambridge (1973)
173. Reisman, M.: EHRs: The Challenge of Making Electronic Data Usable and Interoperable. Pharmacy and Therapeutics **42**(9). https://www.ncbi.nlm.nih.gov/pmc/articles/PMC5565131/
174. Renner, S., Rosenthal, A., Scarano, J.G.: Data interoperability: standardization or mediation. In: Metadata Conference (1996). http://www.computer.org/conferen/meta96/renner/data-interop.html
175. Rezaei, R., Chiew, T.K., Lee, S.P., Aliee, Z.S.: Interoperability evaluation models: a systematic review. Comput. Ind. **65**(1), 1–23 (2014). https://doi.org/10.1016/j.compind.2013.09.001
176. Rinderle, S., Reichert, M., Dadam, P.: Correctness criteria for dynamic changes in workflow systems—a survey. Data Knowl. Eng. **50**(1), 9–34 (2004). https://doi.org/10.1016/j.datak.2004.01.002

177. Rinderle, S., Reichert, M., Dadam, P.: Flexible support of team processes by adaptive workflow systems. Distrib. Parallel Databases **16**(1), 91–116 (2004). https://doi.org/10.1023/B:DAPD.0000026270.78463.77

178. Rinderle-Ma, S., Benzin, J., Mangler, J.: From process-agnostic to process-aware automation, mining, and prediction. In: Application and Theory of Petri Nets and Concurrency, vol. 13929, pp. 3–15 (2023). https://doi.org/10.1007/978-3-031-33620-1_1

179. Rinderle-Ma, S., Mangler, J.: Process automation and process mining in manufacturing. In: Business Process Management. Lecture Notes in Computer Science, vol. 12875, pp. 3–14 (2021). https://doi.org/10.1007/978-3-030-85469-0_1

180. Rinderle-Ma, S., Reichert, M., Jurisch, M.: On utilizing web service equivalence for supporting the composition life cycle. Int. J. Web Serv. Res. **8**(1), 41–67 (2011). https://doi.org/10.4018/jwsr.2011010103

181. Rinderle-Ma, S., Stertz, F., Mangler, J., Pauker, F.: Process mining—discovery, conformance, and enhancement of manufacturing processes. In: Vogel-Heuser, B., Wimmer, M. (eds.) Digital Transformation—Core Technologies and Emerging Topics from a Computer Science Perspective, pp. 363–383 (2022). https://doi.org/10.1007/978-3-662-65004-2_15

182. Rinderle-Ma, S., Winter, K., Benzin, J.: Predictive compliance monitoring in process-aware information systems: state of the art, functionalities, research directions. Inf. Syst. **115**, 102210 (2023). https://doi.org/10.1016/j.is.2023.102210

183. Ristad, E.S., Yianilos, P.N.: Learning string-edit distance. IEEE Trans. Pattern Anal. Mach. Intell. **20**(5), 522–532 (1998). https://doi.org/10.1109/34.682181

184. Ritter, D.: Experiences with business process model and notation for modeling integration patterns. In: European Conference on Modelling Foundations and Applications, pp. 254–266 (2014)

185. Ritter, D.: Using the business process model and notation for modeling enterprise integration patterns. CoRR **abs/1403.4053** (2014). http://arxiv.org/abs/1403.4053

186. Ritter, D.: Database processes for application integration. In: British International Conference on Databases (BICOD), pp. 49–61. Springer, Berlin (2017)

187. Ritter, D., Holzleitner, M.: Integration adapter modeling. In: Conference on Advanced Information Systems Engineering, pp. 468–482 (2015)

188. Ritter, D., May, N., Rinderle-Ma, S.: Patterns for emerging application integration scenarios: a survey. Inf. Syst. **67**, 36–57 (2017)

189. Ritter, D., May, N., Sachs, K., Rinderle-Ma, S.: Benchmarking integration pattern implementations. In: International Conference on Distributed and Event-Based Systems, pp. 125–136 (2016a)

190. Ritter, D., May, N., Sachs, K., Rinderle-Ma, S.: Benchmarking integration pattern implementations. In: International Conference on Distributed and Event-Based Systems, pp. 125–136 (2016b)

191. Ritter, D., Rinderle-Ma, S.: Toward a collection of cloud integration patterns. arXiv preprint arXiv:1511.09250 (2015)

192. Ritter, D., Rinderle-Ma, S., Montali, M., Rivkin, A.: Formal foundations for responsible application integration. Inf. Syst. **101**, 101439 (2021). https://doi.org/10.1016/j.is.2019.101439

193. Ritter, D., Sosulski, J.: Modeling exception flows in integration systems. In: Enterprise Distributed Object Computing Conference, pp. 12–21 (2014)

194. Ritter, D., Sosulski, J.: Modeling exception flows in integration systems. In: IEEE International Enterprise Distributed Object Computing Conference (EDOC), pp. 12–21. IEEE, New York (2014)

195. Ritter, D., Sosulski, J.: Exception handling in message-based integration systems and modeling using BPMN. Int. J. Cooperative Inf. Syst. **25**(2), 1–38 (2016)

196. Ritter, D., Sosulski, J.: Exception handling in message-based integration systems and modeling using BPMN. Int. J. Cooperative Inf. Syst. **25**(2), 1–38 (2016)

197. Rosa-Velardo, F., de Frutos-Escrig, D.: Decidability and complexity of Petri nets with unordered data. Theor. Comput. Sci. **412**(34), 4439–4451 (2011)

198. Ruh, W.A., Maginnis, F.X., Brown, W.J.: Enterprise application integration: a Wiley tech brief. Wiley, New York (2002)
199. Sadiq, W., Orlowska, M.E.: Analyzing process models using graph reduction techniques. Inf. Syst. **25**(2), 117–134 (2000). https://doi.org/10.1016/S0306-4379(00)00012-0
200. Scheibler, T., Roller, D., Leymann, F.: From pipes-and-filters to workflows. In: Enterprise Interoperability IV, pp. 255–264. Springer, Berlin (2010)
201. Schibell, N.: Invest Now: Your Interoperability Strategy Will Drive Patient Outcomes (2021). https://www.forrester.com/blogs/invest-now-your-interoperability-strategy-will-drive-patient-outcomes/
202. Schöning, H.: XML und Datenbanken. Carl Hanser Verlag, München Wien (2003)
203. Schweinsberg, K., Wegner, L.M.: Advantages of complex SQL types in storing XML documents. Future Gener. Comput. Syst. **68**, 500–507 (2017). https://doi.org/10.1016/j.future.2016.02.013
204. Selinger, P.: A survey of graphical languages for monoidal categories. In: Coecke, B. (ed.) New Structures for Physics. Lecture Notes in Physics, vol. 813, pp. 289–355. Springer, Berlin (2011). https://doi.org/10.1007/978-3-642-12821-9_4
205. Shrivastava, S.K., Little, M.C.: Designing atomic business functions with distributed control. In: Conference on Business Informatics, pp. 51–59. IEEE Computer Society, New York (2015). https://doi.org/10.1109/CBI.2015.17
206. Sobociński, P.: Representations of Petri net interactions. In: International Conference on Concurrency Theory, pp. 554–568. Springer, New York (2010)
207. Srivastava, U., Munagala, K., Widom, J., Motwani, R.: Query optimization over web services. In: International Conference on Very Large Data Bases (VLDB), pp. 355–366. VLDB Endowment, New York (2006)
208. Stertz, F., Mangler, J., Scheibel, B., Rinderle-Ma, S.: Expectations vs. experiences—process mining in small and medium sized manufacturing companies. In: Business Process Management Forum, pp. 195–211 (2021). https://doi.org/10.1007/978-3-030-85440-9_12
209. Stertz, F., Rinderle-Ma, S., Mangler, J.: Analyzing process concept drifts based on sensor event streams during runtime. In: Business Process Management, pp. 202–219 (2020). https://doi.org/10.1007/978-3-030-58666-9_12
210. Stonebraker, M.: Too much middleware. Int. Conf. Manag. Data (SIGMOD) **31**(1), 97–106 (2002). https://doi.org/10.1145/507338.507362. http://doi.acm.org/10.1145/507338.507362
211. Team, S.: The Importance of Interoperability in 3D Software Applications (2022). https://blog.spatial.com/interoperability-importance
212. Teubner, T., Flath, C., Weinhardt, C.: Welcome to the era of chatgpt. In: Business Information Systems Engineering (2023). https://doi.org/10.1007/s12599-023-00795-x
213. Triebel, M., Sürmeli, J.: Homogeneous equations of algebraic Petri nets. arXiv preprint arXiv:1606.05490 (2016)
214. Türetken, O., Grefen, P., Gilsing, R., Adali, O.E.: Service-dominant business model design for digital innovation in smart mobility. Bus. Inf. Syst. Eng. **61**(1), 9–29 (2019). https://doi.org/10.1007/s12599-018-0565-x
215. {United Nations}: Interoperability (2012). https://tfig.unece.org/contents/interoperability.htm
216. van der Aalst, W.M.P., Van Hee, K.M., van Hee, K.: Workflow management: models, methods, and systems. MIT Press, New York (2004)
217. van der Veer, H., Wiles, A.: Achieving technical interoperability. In: European Telecommunications Standards Institute (2008)
218. Vanhatalo, J., Völzer, H., Koehler, J.: The refined process structure tree. Data Knowl. Eng. **68**(9), 793–818 (2009). https://doi.org/10.1016/j.datak.2009.02.015
219. Kazakos, W., Schmidt, A., Tomczyk, P.: Datenbanken und XML. Springer, Berlin (2002)
220. Weske, M.: Business Process Management—Concepts, Languages, Architectures, 3rd edn. Springer, Berlin (2019)
221. Wiederhold, G.: Mediation in information systems. ACM Comput. Surv. **27**(2), 265–267 (1995)

222. Winter, K., Rinderle-Ma, S.: Deriving and combining mixed graphs from regulatory documents based on constraint relations. In: Advanced Information System Engineering, pp. 1–16 (2019). https://doi.org/10.1007/978-3-030-21290-2_27

223. Winter, K., Stertz, F., Rinderle-Ma, S.: Discovering instance and process spanning constraints from process execution logs. Inf. Syst. **89**, 101484 (2020). https://doi.org/10.1016/j.is.2019.101484

224. Woolf, B., Brown, K.: Patterns of system integration with enterprise messaging. In: Conference on Pattern Language of Programs (PLoP). Citeseer, New York (2002)

225. Yahia, E., Aubry, A., Panetto, H.: Formal measures for semantic interoperability assessment in cooperative enterprise information systems. Comput. Ind. **63**(5), 443–457 (2012). https://doi.org/10.1016/j.compind.2012.01.010

226. Zacharewicz, G., Daclin, N., Doumeingts, G., Haidar, H.: Model driven interoperability for system engineering. Modelling **1**(2), 94–121 (2020). https://doi.org/10.3390/modelling1020007

227. Zdun, U.: Systematic pattern selection using pattern language grammars and design space analysis. Softw. Pract. Experience **37**(9), 983–1016 (2007)

228. Zeng, Q., Sun, S., Duan, H., Liu, C., Wang, H.: Cross-organizational collaborative workflow mining from a multi-source log. Decis. Support. Syst. **54**, 1280–1301 (2013). https://doi.org/10.1016/j.dss.2012.12.001

229. Zeng, Q., Sun, S.X., Duan, H., Liu, C., Wang, H.: Cross-organizational collaborative workflow mining from a multi-source log. Decis. Support Syst. **54**(3), 1280–1301 (2013). https://doi.org/10.1016/j.dss.2012.12.001

230. Zenie, A.: Colored stochastic Petri nets. In: International Workshop on Timed Petri Nets, pp. 262–271 (1985)

231. Zimmermann, O., Pautasso, C., Hohpe, G., Woolf, B.: A decade of enterprise integration patterns: a conversation with the authors. IEEE Softw. **33**(1), 13–19 (2016)

232. Zuberek, W.M.: D-timed Petri nets and modeling of timeouts and protocols. Trans. Soc. Comput. Simul. **4**(4), 331–357 (1987)

Index

A
Abstract Syntax Trees (AST), 156
Aggregator (AGG), 189, 192, 199, 203, 205, 209, 211, 212
Attribute-based matching, 99

B
Binary JSON (BSON), 46
Block structure, 130, 157
Boundedness, 147
Business Process Execution Language (BPEL), 20
Business Process Modeling and Notation (BPMN), 20, 127

C
Canonical data model, 190
Chatbot, 134
ChatGPT, 134
Claim check, 190
Cloud computing, 189
Cloud Process Execution Engine, 127
Collaboration mining, 253
Collaboration model, 235
Collaboration patterns, 253
Colored Petri Nets (CPN), 141
Common Object Request Broker Architecture (CORBA), 108
Command message, 189
Compliability, 264
Composed message processor, 191
Content enricher (CE), 190, 208, 220

Content-based router (CBR), 189, 193, 207, 212
Content filter, 190
Contract, 235
Control bus, 190
Conversational process modeling, 134
Correlation, 250
Correlation identifier, 189
CPEE Tree, 158
CPN Tools, 156

D
Data cleaning, 105
Dataflow architecture, 187
Data fusion, 105
Data normalization, 105
Data scrubbing, 105
Datatype channel, 189
Dead letter channel, 189
Deadlock, 143
Detour, 190
DOCTYPE definitions (DTD), 21
Document message, 189
Duplicate, 105

E
electronic business XML (ebXML), 19
Enterprise application integration (EAI), 5, 7, 187–189, 191
Enterprise integration patterns (EIPs), 187, 192, 213
Envelope wrapper, 190

Printed in the United States
by Baker & Taylor Publisher Services